Chicken Soup for the Soul®

Teens Talk

HIGH SCHOOL

Chicken Soup for the Soul:
Teens Talk High School; 101 Stories of Life, Love, and Learning for Older Teens
by Jack Canfield, Mark Victor Hansen, Amy Newmark, Madeline Clapps
Published by Chicken Soup for the Soul Publishing, LLC   www.chickensoup.com

The publisher gratefully acknowledges the many publishers and individuals who
granted Chicken Soup for the Soul permission to reprint the cited material.

Cover photos courtesy of iStockphoto.com/tmacphoto (©Todd McLean), and PunchStock/
Digital Vision. Back cover photos courtesy of PunchStock/Blend Images, and Photos.com.
Interior photo courtesy of PunchStock/Blend Images.

Cover and Interior Design & Layout by Pneuma Books, LLC
For more info on Pneuma Books, visit www.pneumabooks.com

Distributed to the booktrade by Simon & Schuster. SAN: 200-2442

Publisher's Cataloging-in-Publication Data
(Prepared by The Donohue Group)

Chicken soup for the soul : teens talk high school : 101 stories of life,
   love, and learning for older teens / [compiled by] Jack Canfield ... [et al.].

   p. ; cm.

ISBN-13: 978-1-935096-25-2
ISBN-10: 1-935096-25-7

1. High school students--Literary collections. 2. High schools--Literary collections.
3. Teenagers--Literary collections. 4. Teenagers' writings. 5. Teenagers--Conduct of
life--Anecdotes. 6. High schools--Anecdotes. I. Canfield, Jack, 1944- II. Title. III.
Title: Teens talk high school

PN6071.Y68 C45 2008
810.8/02/09283   2008935976

PRINTED IN THE UNITED STATES OF AMERICA
on acid∞free paper
16 15 14 13 12 11 10   02 03 04 05 06 07 08

Chicken Soup for the Soul

Teens Talk

HIGH SCHOOL

101 Stories of Life,
Love, and Learning
for Older Teens

Jack Canfield
Mark Victor Hansen
Amy Newmark
Madeline Clapps

CSS

Chicken Soup for the Soul Publishing, LLC
Cos Cob, CT

Chicken Soup for the Soul

Contents

❸
~Doing the Right Thing~

❹
~Love Gone Bad~

❺
~Fitting In... or Not~

❻

~That Was Embarrassing~

❼

~Consequences~

❽

~Going for It~

❾

~Tough Stuff~

❿

~Family Ups and Downs~

⑪
~Overcoming Challenges~

⑫
~Moving On~

Chicken Soup for the Soul

Foreword

"These are the best days of your life!"

Has anyone ever said that to you that about high school? They said it to us.

We grew up watching movies and TV shows and reading books that made high school out to be such a fantasy. Great-looking prom dates! Football games with friends! Cars! Freedom!

No one every mentioned that we might wake up the morning of the prom with a pimple the size of Mount Everest protruding from the tip of our nose, or that we would have to study like crazy, or that our parents would still tell us what to do. They also failed to tell us that the football team might continuously lose, or that the driver's license doesn't get placed in your hand until you pass the dreaded driver's test. But even though high school has its blemishes, it's guaranteed to be a special time.

That's why we made this book for you. If you're having a tough time adjusting, fitting in, or finding friends, there are stories from teens with similar troubles. If your prom wasn't perfect or your driver's test didn't go so smoothly, never fear—you're not the first or last person to experience these problems. If you have a friend or sibling in trouble, you will find stories from other kids who tell you how they helped someone deal with the same problems. If your life is going great, this book will help you understand that kid who sits alone in the cafeteria, or that boy who keeps staring at you... who maybe isn't as sketchy as you think.

These 101 stories are like having a big group of new friends, sharing their own stories with you of embarrassing moments, painful crushes, mistakes, good and bad times... Think of this book as a high school support group you can carry in your backpack!

Whether you learn logarithms or lacrosse or life lessons, high school isn't worth anything if you don't walk away a different person. So find that person, love that person, and have a great four years. And keep in mind you're still a work in progress. The best is yet to come.

~Amy and Madeline

Teens Talk

HIGH SCHOOL

Happy to Be Me

Beauty to me is being comfortable in your own skin.

~Gwyneth Paltrow

Not Perfect

Nobody can make you feel inferior without your consent.
~Eleanor Roosevelt

No one is perfect,
Yet so many still try.
To tell you the truth,
I really don't see why.

My smile is imperfect,
But I love it anyway.
Neither is my face,
But I like it every day.

I love how I look.
Why can't you?
I know I'm not perfect
Neither are you.

No one is perfect,
Much to your dismay.
I know I'm not perfect.
I like it that way.

~Shiori Miko

Being a Band Babe

We are more than a bunch of nerds.
We can kick butts, too.
~Ryan Jacobson

This story is for all the marching band geeks out there who aren't really geeks. We have friends and lives. We wear make-up and blow-dry our hair. We can hold a conversation without using the words "drill sheets" or "fermata." But we may just happen to play the tuba or the trumpet and start a story or two with "At band camp..." We are regrettably—but proudly—band geeks.

I joined the marching band my sophomore year of high school because I had to. I was no longer doing a fall sport, and my band teacher had made marching band mandatory if you wanted to be in concert band class. I had played the alto saxophone since elementary school.

"Ugh, band camp," I bemoaned to my best friend Natalie, when we both signed up and realized we were going to be joining the nerd brigade at the end of the summer. We looked at each other and made disgusted faces, deciding we would work to keep each other sane.

As we had expected, band camp sucked. From 8 A.M. to 8 P.M. we were outside in the sweltering sun or the rain for an entire week. We were forced to do push-ups when a trumpet gave some attitude. We had to run laps when the tuba forgot his music. I got a very unflattering tan on my chest from my saxophone neck strap and was sweaty, dirty, and exhausted. I'd come home, collapse on the couch, and pray the next day would be better.

It was a love-hate relationship between the Westhill High School Viking Marching Band and me. Because I played the saxophone, a heavily male-dominated instrument, I was the only girl in my section when I started. The boys were obnoxious and obscene and many of their conversations shouldn't be repeated.

"Yo, that girl what's-her-name in color guard has a nice rack," our section leader would say, literally over my head to his friend.

"Yeah," his friend would laugh. "You know what I'd like to do with her..."

I'd stare at them, trying to remind them with my burning gaze that I was present and not at all amused. Of course, our section leader disregarded this completely and continued.

But I found that, by the time I was a junior, I was friends with the whole band. I also not-so-secretly enjoyed the attention I got from my geeky but loveable male bandmates. Natalie and I would wear make-up to band practice and put ribbons on our instruments. I wore my pink pea coat when it got cold out and I fought vainly to feel feminine in the boxy, ugly uniform, waiting as long as I could to put everything on, including the hideous pants with suspenders and drillmaster shoes.

"You look so cute!" my mom would say after she watched a competition. "Just like a little man out there!" I'd then look at her pictures and realize she had taken photographs of someone else, someone who actually was a boy. It was hard to distinguish who was who when we all had on our tall, cylindrical hats with plumes.

I hate to admit it, but marching band was fun. I remember long drives to competitions, on the school bus, with music blasting from a stereo. "We Are the Champions," by Queen, playing and everyone singing along, the bus almost swaying back and forth from our intense jamming.

Competitions would run late and we would sit, fingers crossed, on dark bleachers huddled under blankets, waiting to hear if our name would be called in fourth, third, second, or perhaps even first place. We would scream and hug if the outcome was good, or mope all the way back to the school bus if it was bad. But at least we moped together.

I remember, and sometimes even fondly, the smell of the bus after we'd compete. I'd climb the stairs and be smacked in the face by the vulgar odor of boys' sweat, dirty clothes, and cologne that they thought would make the smell better, but in fact made it almost unbearable. I'd quickly strip down and change — we were all close at this point, and keeping my sweaty band uniform on was way worse than allowing a few teenage boys a glimpse of my bra — and run off the bus, my nose plugged, trying not to gag.

Natalie and I marched our way through three years of band, and by the time we were seniors, we were experts. We showed the freshmen how it was done and proudly put "Section Leader" on our academic resumes. We loved the band, and the band loved us back. Now that I'm in college, I find I have a special bond with people who did marching band in high school. We speak the same language and understand the band lingo that no one else really does. And, sure, we get looks from people as we start to go off on the subject of drum majors and basics practice. But the people I met in marching band and the things I learned from it greatly outweigh the geek factor — by a lot.

~Madeline Clapps

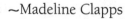

Dancing Queen, Only Seventeen

There is just one life for each of us:
our own.
~Euripides

Storming through my closet, I was trying to piece together the perfect costume for the night. A pair of chinos matched my striped Oxford shirt. Along with my father's vintage pretentious blazer, accented with an obnoxious chain necklace, and paired with some Ray-Ban aviators, my uniform was disco savvy for tonight's 70s themed Homecoming Dance. I was ready to depart for my date with the dance floor. Entering the chauffeur's room, I found her in front of the television watching a movie.

"Mom," I droned, "let's go."

At that moment, I recognized the film she was watching. There was Julia Roberts sitting at a white, linen-covered table talking on her cell phone to her gay best friend.

"Maybe there won't be marriage... maybe there won't be sex... but, by God, there'll be dancing!" Rupert Everett says as he swoops her onto the dance floor and closes the ever-popular film, *My Best Friend's Wedding*.

With her own perfect timing, my mother turned around to find her son decked out in "Dancing Queen" dress. As she eyed me up and down, her expression showed she was finally processing reality. She smiled and shook her head.

Lucky for me, I was not someone whose friends, family, and strangers all knew he was gay before he even uttered the word. I knew first, thanks to Leonardo DiCaprio. (I confess, those baby blues of his made me swoon.) As a child, I actually managed to come out of the closet, go back in, come out again, and, subsequently go back again. This joking-Jekyll and homo-Hyde routine tired quickly, and as the sharp sting of the word "fag" hit my prepubescent ears, I decided I was better off staying in.

Middle school was torture for me. Not necessarily because I liked boys, although that certainly didn't help. As a refuge, I did what many boys like me did and adopted new identities. The theater allowed me to escape insecurity and take control of my surroundings, as well as integrate myself into an accepting group of my peers. Yet, however open they may have been, I still wasn't comfortable with openly embracing that part of me. But, come sophomore year of high school, I was ready.

The joke is that I never actually "came out" of the closet; rather I sort of just "fell out." I'd be with a friend of mine and accidentally catch the eye of a cute guy, pointing him out to her. Often, she would look back at me with an inquisitive grin and then agree. Likewise, I never formally told my parents, but I knew they perceived it.

However, let me say that being gay is not all it's cracked up to be. There is one unfortunate detail that comes with the territory of liking boys—you have to actually deal with them too. My close friend came out to me this past summer. He has had a far rougher time than I, but I stuck by his side, always ready to listen and care for him. Sometimes I cared too much, but he didn't mind.

It's been good getting to know myself more. These experiences have taught me to love life and have given me a sense of humanity. With the greatest humility, I can only say thank you. Thank you to the friends who taught me to love myself. I think of them, how they treated me, and then I think of this quote by Carrie Bradshaw from *Sex and the City*: "...the most exciting, challenging and significant relationship of all is the one you have with yourself. And if you can find someone to love the "you" you love, well, that's just fabulous."

~Kyle Kochersperger

Change the Way You Look at Things

If you change the way you look at things,
the things you look at change.
~Dr. Wayne Dyer

"Hey, Molly, c'mon to the girls' room with me before class! I have to fix my hair." Every day, my friend, Rosie, would haul me off to the bathroom before I'd barely closed my locker.

Freshman year is often traumatic. For me, the change was enormous: bigger classes, lockers, a revolving schedule, riding a bus instead of walking, lots of new people and activities, a much larger, maze-like building, and more competition. Also, as you can imagine, the 225 freshmen at my school had to adjust to a new social pecking order.

Our daily trip to the bathroom allowed Rosie and me to saunter past the corner where cool junior guys hung out. Once around the bend and out of sight, our maturity would vanish, and we'd scurry down the hallway dissolving into giggles.

Our destination was the quiet lavatory outside the band room. There we could fix our hair and make-up, and exchange gossip, minus the intimidating presence of upperclassmen.

Rosie and I had clicked from the first day of school. Students were arranged in homerooms alphabetically, and since she was an

"H" and I was a "G," we had adjacent seats. When schedules were compared, we discovered that we were in every class together.

Back in those unenlightened times, when no one worried about self-esteem, students were placed in academic groups based on entrance exam scores. Rosie and I were placed in "Group A," which contained forty of the overall top scorers.

Social placement took a little longer, but by the end of October it was well established which girls made up the popular crowd. A discouraging number of them had older sisters who were cheerleaders. Worse still, many of them were also in Group A, so Rosie and I didn't even have an academic advantage!

It seems every high school has that one perfect girl, the poster model of all-American good looks and charm. Our representative in the beauty contest of life was Linda, who seemed to have it all. Linda was a petite girl with perfect hair, a winning smile, sparkling personality, and straight As. She could have any guy in the school, but she never flaunted her popularity.

Rosie and I were clearly outside the "in-crowd." Socially, we were second string. Although we had our fair share of talents, we were ordinary compared to the glittering upper tier. I was moderately happy with our comfortable spot in Trinity's ranking system, but Rosie aspired to the heights of cheerleader and in-crowd member, and she was trying to drag me with her.

"Rosie, I can't believe you," I said. "Why aren't you ever happy? You have gorgeous blue eyes, natural blond hair, you're tall and slim, and have a great personality. Be thankful for what you have."

"I'm too tall, that's one problem," she responded. "If you haven't noticed, I tower over most of the freshman boys, including the center on the basketball team! And I don't have freckles or a cute little nose like Linda Carr."

In the beginning, I listened patiently to Rosie's long rants about not having the long brown hair and sprinkling of freckles that Linda had. I tried to help Rosie appreciate her own assets. In the spirit of friendship, I went with her to cheerleader signups and struggled through three weeks of splits, jumps, and routines.

The day of try-outs was the first time I lost patience with my new friend. After being cut in the third round, Rosie was crying and wishing herself shorter, prettier, and more popular. At first I was able to commiserate with her; after all I'd only made it to the second round. Then I tried to soothe her, but nothing worked. Handing Rosie a pile of tissues, I decided to get tough.

"Listen, stop wishing your life away! Not making cheerleader isn't the end of the world. You have a lot going for you, and there are plenty of girls who'd like to trade places with you the way you'd like to trade places with Linda."

"Yeah, right." Rosie looked down at me through tear-reddened eyes.

"I wasn't going to say anything, but I know something about Linda that might change your opinion. This is just between us, okay?"

Rosie nodded.

"My mom grew up with Linda's mother, and they ran into each other a few weeks ago. Mrs. Carr told Mom that Linda has to give herself injections every day. She has to watch her diet and exercise carefully because she has diabetes."

"Wow. That's serious."

"Mrs. Carr says Linda never goes to sleepovers or on overnight field trips because she's embarrassed about her condition. She doesn't go to certain activities because her insulin has to be refrigerated. If she exercises too much, her blood sugar runs low. She can never eat candy and drink soda the way the rest of us do."

"I thought she always drank diet soda just to stay thin."

"Yeah, once you know the truth, it changes the way you see things, doesn't it?" I asked, hoping Rosie had gotten something out of our conversation.

After absorbing the news, Rosie hugged and thanked me. We freshened up and spread some strawberry gloss on our lips before exiting the bathroom to cheer for a friend who was still in the competition.

Of course, at the end of the day, Linda was one of the ten girls who made the squad, but Rosie and I were among the crowd clapping for the lucky winners. Rosie turned to me smiling and said, "Hey, the majorettes and drill team are having sign-ups next week."

In junior year, Rosie and I were still best buddies and the newly elected captain and co-captain of the drill team. Rosie was dating the 6'7" center of the basketball team, whom she later married. She'd finally come to terms with her own gifts and accomplishments.

Four years later, on a beautiful afternoon during our junior year in college, a friend from home came to my dorm with shocking news. Linda had died unexpectedly from an infection. Before Tom finished telling me, the phone rang. It was Rosie.

"As soon as I heard about Linda, I thought of you, Molly. I remembered that day at try-outs when I was so down about life."

During my thirty-year teaching career, I've repeated the story of my classmates, Rosie and Linda. Its theme, "Be happy with yourself, and make the most of what you have," is ageless.

Sometimes students ask, "Why did God take Linda who was so sweet and talented when she was still young?" One teen, wise beyond her years, said, "Maybe it's the other way around; Maybe God was compensating for Linda's short life by giving her all those gifts."

~Molly Roe

Looking Back at Me

If I am not for myself, who will be?
~Pirke Avoth

When I look into the mirror,
I see all my faults and imperfections,
I see how awkward my stance is,
How small my ears are,
How wide my body is.

When I look into the mirror,
I see a girl looking back at me,
She's the only one who really understands me,
She watches me when I laugh,
She watches me when I cry,
She watches me when I lose my temper,
She sees how beautiful I am inside.

When I look into the mirror,
I see everything you make fun of,
I see everything that identifies me,
I see everything I am.
When I look into the mirror,
I am proud of what I see,
I am an individual and I define me.

~Crystal Burgess

Take Back Your Life

If nature had intended our skeletons to be visible
it would have put them on the outside of our bodies.
~Elmer Rice

As I watch the Girls Softball League warm up for their game, Jane, the beautiful seventeen-year-old daughter of a good friend of mine, waves and heads my way. Seeing Jane today, it is hard to believe that three years ago she was knocking on death's door and we didn't even know it.

This is Jane's story as she told it to me that day. If you are one of the million young people in America suffering from an eating disorder, Jane's story could be yours:

I was just starting high school when I decided I needed to knock off a few pounds, so I decided to cut out the in-between meal snacking. It worked. First one pound, then another, then five. It was great, the exhilaration of feeling "thin," and the intoxicating sense of control whenever I stepped on the scale.

I didn't realize it then, but that intoxicating feeling was the beginning of a frightening obsession, a mindset taking over my body and soul, voices in my head telling me, "Okay, you lost ten pounds. Now lose ten more." It was the start of my descent into hell — the world of anorexia nervosa.

Looking in the mirror, all I saw was "fat." Food became the enemy, yet food was all I thought about. I knew the calorie count of everything I put into my mouth. Eleven stalks of broccoli, sixty calories. One half can of green beans, forty-one calories. I could take half an hour to eat half a sandwich. I'd skip meals by telling my mom I'd already eaten. I cut my food into tiny pieces and ate them bit-by-bit, all the time priding myself on my "self-control."

Hunger pangs became constant companions, but if I gave in and ate, the guilt hit hard, and I exercised like a marathoner to burn off those extra calories. My weight slid from 120 pounds to 110, then to 100, but the voices said it wasn't good enough. So my goal became 95 pounds, then 90. Yet when I looked in the mirror, I wasn't thin enough.

Schoolwork suffered because I couldn't concentrate on anything but the pain in my stomach. When friends told me I should eat more, I'd snap, "I do eat," then couldn't believe I had lashed out at them like that. My friends drifted away, and I retreated further into my shell of isolation.

Things came to a head one day while doing my daily workout on the treadmill. My heart started pounding so hard I couldn't breathe. I thought I was having a heart attack and was going to die right there. For the first time, I realized I was in deep trouble, but even then I wouldn't admit to anyone that I had a problem.

Unknown to me, one of my teachers had contacted my mother and told her I was much too thin, that I needed help. When Mom told me she had scheduled a doctor's appointment, I could tell she expected a real explosion from me, but I was actually relieved that the nightmare had finally been taken out of my hands. I was so tired of being cold, hungry, and crabby all the time. I couldn't stand it any longer, but I couldn't stop. So I agreed to an Eating Disorders Assessment.

"Not me," I said when the report came back indicating severe anorexia nervosa. The doctor pointed to the Lanugo (fine hair) all over my stomach and back, indicating blood pressure so low my body could not maintain a normal temperature, a body that had been numb and cold for so long even two pairs of long underwear under my jeans could not keep me warm. When the doctor showed me the chart of anorexia warning signs, reality hit hard. I had every one of the symptoms.

The doctor gave me a high protein, high carbohydrate diet to follow as an outpatient.

"I'll eat," I insisted. "I can do it."

But I couldn't. The food stuck in my throat. I couldn't swallow. The voices in my head kept saying, "you're too fat." But the stubborn determination that made me refuse food finally came to my rescue, and I forced down everything on the list. When I checked back with the doctor, I was shocked into reality. I was still losing weight at an alarming rate. My body could no longer assimilate the food. I was fourteen years old and starving to death in the land of plenty.

I spent the next two weeks in the hospital under constant surveillance, with someone following me around twenty-four hours a day, even into the bathroom, to make sure I didn't throw up or commit suicide. I was put on a 4,000-calorie-a-day diet. If I couldn't eat or retain it, I was fed intravenously. For the next year and a half, I was an outpatient three times a week for physical checkups and behavior management counseling.

Going to treatment was the best thing that could have happened to me. It was there I learned how to fight back, how to eat, how to battle the voices in my head. Most important—I learned I was not alone in this battle. I joined a support group of girls

*(and boys) just like me who had heard the voices, struggled with
the same demons, lived with the same fears. We learned from
each other.*

*I love sports. Before the anorexia took over my body and soul, I
had played right field on a girls' softball team. The coach told
me I would have to maintain a certain weight in order to get
back on the team, so I forced down three solid meals a day, following a diet and exercise program prescribed and monitored by
my doctor. I made the team.*

*That was three years ago. Today, I think I am winning the battle.
But it hasn't been easy. Eating is still a struggle. I still hear the
voices. I may live with those voices for the rest of my life, but I
am determined that the mindset that sent me into the hell of
anorexia will not take control again. I have taken back my life. I
am determined not to look like a concentration camp victim.*

The game is about to start. As I watch Jane run back to the playing
field, I thank God for the concerned teacher who had alerted Jane's
mother to her problem.

If you or someone you know shows any of the warning signs
listed below, tell somebody: your parents, a school counselor, a doctor. As Jane would tell you, "Take back your life. It is too precious a
gift to waste."

Anorexia Warning Signs:
- Intense fear of gaining weight
- Severe food restriction even though not overweight
- Withdrawal from friends and activities
- Moody, irritable
- Obsessive counting of calories
- Extreme weight loss
- Hunger denial
- Compulsive exercising

- Cold chills
- Hair growth on body (Lanugo)

~Jacklyn Lee Lindstrom

My Gay Red Shorts

Fashion can be bought.
Style one must possess.
~Edna Woolman Chase

My least favorite part of being on my school track team was participating in meets. I loved running every day, but I was always timid about running against fellow athletes. In one meet, I was sitting on the bleachers overlooking the high school football field and the 400-meter track encircling it. It was our school's last track and field meet of the season with rivalry hanging heavy in the air. Our school was competing against another nearby school from the area, and I knew a lot of kids who went there. In every meet for the past three years, I was always one of the select long distance runners of the boys' long distance team.

The first heat for the 400-meter event was underway, meaning that I would be running soon. I drank some water; my teammates were dropping like flies from the heat and humidity. It was no different from any other meet that I participated in, so nervousness overtook as it normally did. First, my stomach filled with the butterflies, and then the sudden urge to run to the nearest bathroom.

I breathed deeply and tried to ignore my worries. I had been in countless meets, so what was so different about this one? I had a couple of friends on the other team who I was looking forward to saying hello to. I walked over to some of my friends on my team who ran the 800-meter with me and started to stretch with them.

We were loosening up and getting ready when a girl from the other team came up to us. She was shorter than me and looked like she was in sixth or seventh grade. She had long blond hair and an arrogant, overbearing expression on her face. She walked right up to me and asked curiously, "What grade are you in?"

"Eighth," I answered hesitantly, wondering what concern she had with me.

"What event do you run?" she persisted.

"800-meter."

Then, flat out, with no expression, she asked, "Are you gay?" The question caught me off guard, making me wonder if I had heard her correctly.

"What?" I asked.

"Look at your shorts!" she laughed. "Guys aren't supposed to wear shorts that high. You must be a homosexual or something!"

Then I spied one of my friends from the other school, Rick. The way he treated me sometimes made me feel a little uncomfortable. Rick was approaching with a group of smirking guys, who I guessed were entertained by the situation.

"Mike, for God's sake, put something over those shorts of yours, homo," he laughed.

The word "homo" knocked me straight to the ground as I froze in shock. I didn't know Rick that well, but we had known each other for a long time and I wasn't expecting his taunts. My face red with embarrassment, I looked down at my shorts and finally understood. I had on my red Nike runner's shorts. They were really short, but they were supposed to be — they were running shorts. I never worried about how I looked when I ran; I just ran! I quickly sagged them as much as I could and did the only thing I could: I walked away. I headed for the starting line area and hid behind a group of runners preparing for the 400-meter. As I walked, I noticed that I turned a couple heads, not helping the situation.

It wasn't long before I stepped up to the line for my event. My attitude totally changed as I realized that the 800-meter was my event, and I was going to do my best. Some stupid kid and his friends weren't going to stop me now.

The official raised his cap gun and fired, as about twenty-five runners took off around the first curve. I had run this event in all kinds of weather and I knew exactly what to do. I sprinted up to the lead group, running in front of anyone who got in my way. Once I made it to the top runners, I pushed myself to keep up with athletes twice my size. I may be small, but I have great endurance.

I picked up the runner in seventh place and based my pace on him, making it a little bit harder and a little bit faster. One by one, I made it to the top four, bursting around the track. My anger fueled my energy while my determination stimulated my aggression.

I didn't even hear the official ringing the bell, preparing me for my final lap. Before I knew it, I was on the last curve before the final straightaway. I breathed deeply and lengthened my stride, picking up my soaring speed with each step. I caught up to the runner in third place and we sprinted side-by-side down the last 100 meters—he beat me by a hair at the finish line. I had crushed my original time by at least twelve seconds. My coach gave me a high five as I headed back to the bleachers to see my mom, sitting and waiting for me with a big smile on her face.

I was feeling great until I spotted Rick and his group once again approaching. Negative feelings started to erupt from the pit of my stomach, taking away all the good feelings I just felt. Just then I noticed one of Rick's friends who I ran against. Short-shorts or not, he knew that I had beaten him badly.

Rick was just about to open his mouth but I shut it for him when I said, "Rick, I don't like being called a homosexual for the shorts that I wear and it wouldn't make a difference if I was gay anyway. All that matters is that I run, and I would gladly whoop your butt in the 800-meter any day." I smiled as I started to walk away, and turned around to add, "with or without my gay red shorts."

~Mike Polanski

Chapter 2

Teens Talk

HIGH SCHOOL

Dating, Crushes, and Just Friends

Love is the flower you've got to let grow.

~John Lennon

Not Like in the Movies

Many a true word is spoken in jest.
~English Proverb

He was so cute, standing on my front doorstep in his suit and his grin—the boy taking me to my first formal dinner dance.

For months, I knew I had to bring someone to this special party for the Confirmation class graduates of our Reform Jewish synagogue. But I felt like an old maid at age fourteen—no date and no prospects. I was doomed to die of humiliation, sitting by myself at a table of matched couples.

I called a girlfriend who had a boyfriend to help me out. He called one of his friends, and hallelujah! Here he stood. From our phone call a few days earlier, I knew that his name was Bart, he was almost fifteen, he was on the baseball team at his school, and he was not Jewish.

I was not about to be picky. "Shut up!" I yelled at one of my younger sisters who immediately dubbed my fantasy date, "Bart the Fart."

I answered the door with my family gathered behind me. My sister snickered, "Bart the Fart!" one more time and ran out of the room. Bart and I pretended to ignore her, while my mother got her keys to drop us off at the dance.

At the banquet, Bart and I exuded "sophistication" as we maneuvered around the fancy food and made small talk. Bart mostly talked about baseball and I mostly nodded and listened since I didn't know anything about sports.

After much bragging and head nodding, the band started playing and everyone was invited to the dance floor. I looked hopefully at Bart.

"I don't dance," he said.

"Oh," I countered, trying not to look entirely devastated.

"Let's go for a walk," he said.

"Okay," I replied. At least we wouldn't be sitting alone at the table.

It was a beautiful, balmy spring night. Bart took my hand as we walked, and then put his arm around my shoulders. It was so romantic, I could hardly breathe. We stopped beneath a beautiful flowering tree and Bart stopped talking about baseball (finally!) as he turned to pull me towards him.

Yikes! What do I do? I closed my eyes and felt his face approach mine. As our lips met, suddenly there was this absolutely horrible noise! Was it supposed to sound like that? Didn't he know what to do? I giggled. He pulled back, offended "What's the matter?"

"Nothing."

He leaned in to kiss me again and our mouths made the same horrible noise... again. In the movies, two people kissing evoked the sounds of violins, not flatulence! In my mind, my sister's cruel but prophetic words played over and over again. Bart the Fart, Bart the Fart, Bart the....

I hate it when she's right.

~Lynn Grasberg

A Love Remembered

Why does it take a minute to say hello
and forever to say goodbye?
~Author Unknown

January has always been one of my favorite months. My parents take me skiing, and the second semester begins, meaning new classes and the opportunity to meet new people. Track season is at its peak in January, and my birthday is the 31st.

My love for this month only grew after I started dating Logan during January of my freshman year. We had met the first day of school when I couldn't find my geometry class. Mistaking room 213 for 231, I walked in and sat down at an empty desk. Two seconds later, Logan came and sat beside me. He was no taller than I was, and he didn't really look like your average high school junior. He had a mouth full of braces, a baby face and a head full of uncombed thick, black hair. Naturally, I assumed he was just a freshman from the other middle school that fed into the high school.

"Are you new this year?" he asked.

"Well yeah, aren't you?" I replied. For some reason, I felt nervous and my knees went weak under the desk. I thought he was beautiful.

"This is my second year here. I'm Logan. Are you a sophomore? You look a little young to be taking Calculus A."

I looked around and saw a bunch of kids who were definitely a lot older than I was. I left, completely embarrassed.

During cross-country practice, I told my two friends, Jessie and Maren, about what had happened, and about the cute boy named Logan.

"A junior?!" they both exclaimed.

"Check out all the boys from the other middle school, please," said Maren. "A junior is going way out on a limb, Tash."

Conveniently, Logan was a runner too. After cross-country, he came up to me. "So did you ever find the class where you belonged?"

After that it became routine. He would run the warm-ups with me, then we'd split up into boy and girl drills and meet up after.

We soon started spending every moment together, even getting each other Christmas gifts that made no sense to anyone but ourselves. We had become best friends fast, but I didn't even consider that I had a chance to be anything more.

It wasn't until New Year's, when he screamed "Happy New Year, Tasha!" and gave me a huge hug, that I realized I was falling in love with this boy. I had to tell him how I felt.

But I didn't have to tell him. In January, on his birthday, he got his license. A warm feeling came over me when I heard a minivan pull up that night. I went out to hug him, congratulate him, and wish him a happy seventeenth birthday. The second I stopped hugging him, he kissed me. The kiss was everything I had thought it would be, and more. It was almost like I was dreaming, floating in his touch.

We became an item and dated throughout the rest of the school year. He was my first love, he was all I needed, and I was happy.

That summer, however, I was so caught up in how I felt about him that I didn't notice how distant he was becoming. Finally, right before school started up again, he drove over and sat with me in the humid air on my front porch. We were never the fighting kind of couple, so I guess at this point we had a lot inside that we never let out.

He started explaining how he just didn't feel the same about me anymore. How now if he said, "I love you," it wouldn't mean as much. I held my breath for what was coming. I knew it would eventually come, but I wasn't expecting it this soon. I thought he would take me to his senior prom and we'd smile big smiles and laugh and kiss until he went to college.

"It's just not working, Tasha. We shouldn't see each other anymore."

With that, instead of understanding and reaching over to hug him goodbye, I got angry. I exclaimed how he shouldn't have led me on. I yelled at him for abandoning me. In the middle of my rant, he got up and left.

I spent the rest of the summer whining to my friends about how much I missed him and how much I still loved him. I would wait up some nights for him to appear and reclaim me. I continued like this for months, taking most of my anger and misery out in my schoolwork and running. I matched the county record three times over the fall season and even broke it during the playoffs.

To make things worse, Logan acted as if I didn't exist. He was a senior now, he'd pass me in the halls without even saying hi, and it just made me more miserable. For the whole first semester I cried on and off, and rejected any boys who asked me out, saying I wasn't ready for anything new.

The more time went on, the more it felt as if I had meant nothing to Logan. I finally decided that I had to tell him how I felt. Coincidently, it was January again, one year from when we had started dating.

I wrote a full, thorough letter about everything, including how I wanted him back in my life. I wrote about how angry I was that he was ignoring me, but that I was willing to forgive him. I left the note on his windshield after school one afternoon.

A week later, I heard a familiar car engine outside my window. I thought my heart would beat its way out of my chest. I ran downstairs to find him holding the letter in his hand.

"I love you, Tasha. I'm sorry," is all he could say. He didn't have to say anything else. I moved closer to him and started to close my eyes. This is it! What I've been awaiting for the past five months!

Instead, when his lips met mine, it wasn't what I had expected at all. I had thought that if we ever kissed again, it would be magical and I'd feel the same way I felt the first time I kissed him a year ago. But it didn't feel like that at all. It was just... ordinary. When it was over, and we pulled away to make eye contact, it was written on his face, too. Our love just wasn't there anymore.

He smiled at me and gave me a big hug goodbye. With tears in my eyes, I knew that it was time to let go.

I watched his car leave, and instead of crying, I smiled to myself. It was the first time in months that I could handle the thought of moving on. The next morning when I woke up, my heart didn't hurt anymore.

Logan graduated and went to college across the country. I'll always remember him as my first love, a first love that couldn't be rekindled. It's January again, and my birthday is four days away. I'll be seventeen. I sit in my car, remembering him and smiling, while I wait for Maren to come outside so we can get lunch. I learned so much from Logan. Occasionally we talk online and I called him a couple weeks ago to wish him a happy birthday.

I've started seeing someone new and I'm happy with myself. No matter what, I'll never forget Logan or the times I spent with him. I loved him deeply, and it showed when I finally let him go.

~Tasha Vemulkonda

"ALL I WANT TO BE WHEN I GROW UP IS SOMEONE'S OLD HIGH SCHOOL GIRLFRIEND."

Summer Dreaming

*Real elation is when you feel you could
touch a star without standing on tiptoe.*
~Doug Larson

It was the summer before I went off to college in Chicago. I was happy to finally be free of my horrible high school, and I was ready for the fresh start that college would provide. Yet my thoughts still lingered on one girl, the one who I had been off and on with during my last two years at school. She was none other than Brittany McMannon. She was the only thing that anchored me to St. Louis, the only tie that prevented me from total flight to Chicago.

She really affected me that summer. I couldn't get her off my mind. She was stuck fast and there was no removing her.

I tried several times to contact her over the summer, through e-mail and by phone, but she did not respond. This made me feel so heavy, the kind of weight that only girls can make you feel. I hated it; I couldn't enjoy my summer. I couldn't enjoy hanging out with my good friends, because there was Brittany, always in the back of my mind. It was that nagging depression, the kind that prevents you from having a great day because your thoughts inevitably drift back to what really matters.

June passed and became July. Still, there was no word from her. I couldn't understand it. I became paranoid (as I usually do with girls) that she disliked me, and didn't want to talk with me. However, she had never shown signs of distaste or negligence before, so I couldn't buy the idea that she would just completely abandon me. I had to hold onto some hope, if only for my own sake.

Then, one sweltering summer day, when July was almost at an end, I remember vividly getting a phone call.

It was her.

Her voice was so jubilant and excited. It felt as if she were breathing air directly into my lungs. Her cute mannerisms instantly sparked my heart back to life. She said she had been on vacation — that was why she didn't get back to me sooner. When she said she would come over the next day, I could scarcely believe my ears. I don't even remember responding. I barely slept that night, my head contorted with all of the wild scenarios it could muster.

The early afternoon of the next day arrived. I quickly took a shower, brushed my teeth, combed my hair, and got dressed. I was excited and nervous about seeing her, but then again I had never felt so much for her until this particular summer.

The doorbell rang. I had to stop myself from bounding upstairs. I took careful steps over to the front door, and opened it.

There she stood, her slim frame outlined by the shady glimmer of a partly sunny day. My eyes were drawn to her hair. She had grown it long over vacation. The curly, dark blond locks swayed near her rosy cheeks. Her high-set cheekbones almost pinched the shape of her luminous blue eyes, which sat behind square-framed glasses.

She was grinning. She smiled like it was the first time she had seen me in a million years. I had to make sure to keep my own smile under control. Otherwise, it would have crept upward and ripped through my cheeks, breaking away from my face, out of control.

After some timid pleasantries, we made our way down to my room.

We sat in the two doughy blue chairs I had in the middle of my room. We talked about the summer, about me going to school, about nothing important. We talked about watching a movie. However, I felt like if I didn't say anything before the movie, it would mean the guillotine for everything that had built up to this moment. I distinctly remember shaking uncontrollably. My hands convulsed, everything seemed to become a lot colder. The bottom of my stomach was nowhere to be found.

Then, like a fifth grader, I uttered, "Brittany, I, uh, like you. I mean, I've liked you a lot for a while now, you know?"

She turned towards me gracefully, and a very pleasant smile crept across her face. It took her a moment to process the information, but when she did, it was like the words had turned something on inside her.

"Really? I mean... really?" she asked.

I nodded about seventeen million times. I found it hard to make direct eye contact with her.

I took her bewildered expression as a cue to start the movie. We watched it for a good hour. She didn't say anything. I didn't say anything. I didn't dare look over at her.

Then the mood changed completely. We began to joke around, laughing and smiling sheepishly at each other. She ran her fingers through my hair, complimenting me on how full and soft it was. Her fingers felt like warm water pouring across my head.

Not to be outdone, I too ran my fingers through her hair and commented on exactly the same thing. It was silky and tender. Electricity surged through my fingers as they met the warmth of her scalp.

Brittany crawled over the two chair arms and nestled herself on top of me. She reminded me very much of a cat, crawling so carefully over thin surfaces. She straddled herself over me, raising her torso as she looked down at me.

I looked up at her as she did this, but I didn't have much time to comprehend anything, because almost immediately she moved her face towards mine.

The first kiss was a particularly long one. She took her time once she set her lips on mine. I could feel her smile as she connected this first kiss.

The massive energy between our mouths felt simultaneously like the following: hearing the best song you have ever heard, seeing the greatest part of the greatest movie you have ever seen, feeling infinitely refreshed, covering yourself in a warm blanket, getting caught in a megaton explosion, and being carried off into a beautiful sunset, never to be seen again. And that is really only an inkling of it all.

I could vividly remember feeling her stomach rising, pressing against mine, and when it compressed, mine would exchange the gesture. This simple action made me forget my life, the world, the universe, everything, if only for a moment. Her stomach rising and falling was the most wonderful thing I had ever experienced. It was all I ever needed forever, forever, forever.

After that day, I wouldn't see Brittany again. She had to prepare for her next year of high school and I had to prepare for my first year of college. That's how it works out sometimes, though. Sometimes you do things or don't do things that don't necessarily make sense in the general scheme of it all. It felt right for us, though. We had experienced our moment together, and now it was time to move on. We couldn't have asked for more than that.

~Michael Tenzer

A Little Love

Love — a wildly misunderstood although highly desirable malfunction of the heart which weakens the brain, causes eyes to sparkle, cheeks to glow, blood pressure to rise and the lips to pucker.
~Author Unknown

"**I**s the ground wet? My flip flops feel funny."

"I don't know, go over there and check it out."

"Are you kidding? There are sprinklers! I'm not getting wet!"

"Look, it's our lucky day.... They turned off."

I knew it would be one of the best days of my life. I had a date with a guy who I seemed to have liked forever. It was really only about a year, but with our schedules and separate set of friends, things never seemed to work out. He was so perfect! He was nice, cute, and overwhelmingly sweet. Every time I saw him, my stomach filled up with butterflies. I had a special feeling deep in my heart — tonight was the night! Tonight would be the night that he asked me to be his girlfriend. And I would say YES!

We went to Baskin Elementary, past the school, past the basketball court, right next to the playground. There was an empty field with a nice number of hidden trees a few yards away. And although I didn't know what he was planning until that night, it was perfect. He made me walk in circles for what seemed to be the longest time. He said that he needed to find the "perfect spot."

A few minutes later he stopped, and I knew that this was the spot that he was looking for. Although I could have sworn that I had seen greener patches in the field, I knew that it didn't matter what I sat on as long as I sat next to him. Right when I was about to sit down he said, "STOP." I looked at him with a confused look as he placed his backpack on the ground.

He smiled as he unzipped his backpack, not his normal smile but a silly smile that he would always make when he laughed or was excited about something. All I was thinking was, "Oh God, what is in that bag?" When he popped out a square-shaped object, I smiled although I hadn't quite figured out what it was yet. Then I realized it was a blanket; it was as if he had read my mind. No one had ever done anything like this for me. It was like my own personal fairytale, but it was real!

We sat next to one another on the blanket for a while. I tried to look at the stars, but I couldn't keep my eyes off him. I would look at him, and then turn back to the sky before he could see me. I did this for a few minutes until he caught me. He would just laugh at me; I would have been embarrassed except I would see him doing the same thing out of the corner of my eye. He was not one of those guys who made me blabber to try and keep his attention. We didn't have to talk at all; I could just stare at him and not feel weird.

As we were lying there looking at the formations of stars above our heads, he leaned over and whispered a question in my ear. It was the question that, at the time, I thought would complete my life. He said, "I'm sorry that this has taken me so long, but I was wondering if you would like to be my girlfriend?" I was so happy, I swear that I could hear an orchestra playing Handel's "Hallelujah." I grabbed his face and gave him a huge kiss! He smiled at me, and we both began to laugh.

I couldn't wait until school started again that following Monday. I felt like a thirteen-year-old girl with her first boyfriend. After only a few days, writing "I love Brandon" became like a second signature to me, and no paper within arm's reach was safe from being branded.

The following Saturday was his sixteenth birthday. I reminded him frequently that I was a month and three days older than him just to see the annoyed expression on his face. The Thursday night before his birthday, I went to the pet store and bought him a goldfish. No one understood why, and most people thought that it was a stupid gift, but he liked it and that's all that mattered to me. It was a joke between the two of us from before we got together. One of the things he had said to me was, "I need you like a fish needs water," and ever since then we had an obsession with getting a fish and naming it Herbert. When I was around him, I was happy, and when I wasn't around him all I could think about was being around him.

This was the first time in my life that I actually felt like Cinderella. I'd always seen those cute movies where two people fall in love and are together forever—that's what I felt like. Yes, I am young, and there will most likely be a handful of guys that make me feel that way in the future, but he was the first one, and that makes him so special to me. Although I shared many happy memories with him, it is hard to smile now because we are no longer together. Luckily for me, although it was a heartbreaking experience, we are still good friends. There are so many things that I wish he knew—I wish he knew how much I still love him, I wish he knew that even though we're back to calling each other best friends, I will never see him that way again. I wish he knew how hard it is for me to keep from crying every time I see him with another girl. And although it is hard for me to admit, I want him to find happiness, even if it's not with me anymore.

~Nicole Lee

Just Friends?

There is a bit of insanity in dancing
that does everybody a great deal of good.
~Edwin Denby

He doesn't care too much about clothes. His pants are short and his shirts are small. He wears the same sneakers all the time, with dirty white laces that drag on the ground.

But he is nice and smart. So I like him, just not in that way, you know. He asks me to Prom. He doesn't like me that way either. We are just friends... at least I think we're just friends.

Nothing seems to go right. I stand on my tiptoes in front of the bathroom mirror, holding mascara and blush. It just makes things worse. I just did my nail polish and already it is chipped. I am running late, must dress fast. A thousand hairpins are jabbing into my head. I slip into my sparkly dress, into my silky shoes. Fasten the straps and clip-clop, clip-clop down the stairs. I stand still for a few flashes at the bottom. I'm the star of the show. I'm the clown dressed up for laughs, the human pincushion, the tall man on stilts.

He's standing there, flowers in hand. All dressed up (for me?). I quickly glance at his feet, as if expecting to see the sneakers with laces dragging, but they aren't there. He looks pale and he hardly says a word, awkwardly handing me my corsage. It is purple and white. It matches my dress perfectly. He must have asked one of my friends what color it was. I almost draw blood when I stab his boutonniere into his coat.

He doesn't offer his arm to walk into the hall. Instead we walk side-by-side, arms swinging. He fills up his plate. I can't eat a bite. I am too nervous to eat, to know how to act. And we say hardly anything at all. I wish that we could just go back to study hall this morning. This is awkward. I ask myself, Does this mean anything? Does he want to be my boyfriend? Does he want to kiss me? Or are we really just friends? We make small talk. In the study hall this morning, we could talk about anything. I feel so stupid. I am making a complete fool of myself.

I slip my shoes off, and slide them under my chair. Then we dance, old songs, new songs, fast songs, slow songs. I put my arms around his neck and his arms encircle my waist. He is sweating through his collar and his hands are sweaty on my back. Another person could fit between us. Then he says softly, "You look beautiful tonight." And finally everything just seems right. Even if we are never more than friends.

~Sara E. Rowe

Dealing with the Truth

He that respects himself is safe from others;
he wears a coat of mail that none can pierce.
~Henry Wadsworth Longfellow

I t was spring of my junior year, and I'd just found out my barely-ex-boyfriend was taking someone else to the prom. In fact, let's face it—until this moment, I guess I didn't totally realize he was my ex. I'd thought we were just having one of those fights we'd been having more and more often lately. I'd lost count of how many times he'd been a jerk and I'd dumped him. A day or two after, he'd always come crawling back and apologize sweetly until I took him back.

We had started as friends, soon after I came to the district in middle school. Actually, we soon became best friends. I always said I liked boys better as friends—they were more straightforward than girls. They told you exactly what they thought. They got mad and then they get over it. Girls had stabbed me in the back. They'd talk behind my back; they'd gang up with other girls and not speak to me or eat lunch with me. But not boys like Lucas.

I'd really loved Lucas as a friend—we laughed at the same stuff, but I could also tell him just about anything. One day, he took me to explore a cave on a steep hillside near our houses. He climbed like the amazing monkey boy, but afterward, I couldn't make it back up to the field. It started raining, and the hillside turned to slick mud. I was half-crying, trying to hold on to little twigs and stuff, but my feet kept sliding. I seriously thought I was going to die.

We were already past the time we were supposed to be back, and both my brother and the other boy who'd come along took off for home. But Lucas stayed behind until he got me back up to safety. I could count on him like that.

Well, things got weird at the end of eighth grade, when he started asking me to go out. For a long time, I told him no; I was afraid it would ruin everything. I said, "If we break up, I'll have lost my best friend."

But he kept acting so sad, I felt sorry for him. He was so down on himself and always asking if I thought he was ugly. I tried to fix him up with other girls, but never had any luck. They thought he was too goofy, too skinny, too weird. I couldn't understand why they didn't see him the way I did. He was such a cool person, and he had the world's best smile.

Finally, freshman year, he asked me to go to Homecoming. I said okay—just as friends. But after that, it all changed pretty quickly. Maybe it was being all dressed up, having him give me flowers, going dancing. But when he asked me again to go out, I said I would, and we were boyfriend and girlfriend from then on.

I wasn't allowed to single-date until I was sixteen, but we were always going to movies or to eat with a bunch of friends. We talked on the phone every night. We talked about where we'd go to college together, somewhere with programs for both of us. He wanted to get married someday and live in the woods, and we talked about names for our kids.

Things weren't perfect. In fact, he sometimes drove me flat-out crazy. Time and again, we'd make plans and I'd turn down my other friends, only to find that at the last minute he would cancel because he was grounded, or had to go to his grandparents' house, or get his hair cut—whatever.

By the time we were sophomores, it seemed without fail he'd call the night before I had a big music audition and start a fight, accusing me of flirting with another guy or something. I'd cry till I made myself sick because he wouldn't believe me, and we'd be on the phone much too late. After a while, I noticed a pattern, and began to wonder if he didn't want me going away to music festivals—or maybe just outshining him. He could still be so sweet, but more and more I was seeing a not-so-nice side of him.

By junior year, we were broken up at least as much as we were together. I'd always looked forward to prom, but that spring he said he didn't want to spend the money on it. Then we got into another fight over my not making a big enough deal out of his birthday, and we broke up. Again.

I told one of my friends, "I guess I can't go to prom at all now. It would hurt Lucas too much." But next thing I knew, he was taking a girl he worked with. And once that came out, guys I knew told me he'd been seeing her while I'd been away at festivals, "and they seemed really into each other." They hadn't told me because they had thought it would hurt me too much.

Those were probably the hardest few months of my life. I had to go to school with him and all of our mutual friends every day. Worst of all, everybody still seemed to see him the way I once did—a nice, funny guy who had simply made a "mistake." Some tried to get us back together. Others listened to him and bought his side of the story—that I'd been controlling and mean, and that I'd been cheating on him! My reputation was in shreds. Still, I had to walk the same halls, sit in the same classrooms, and eat lunch in the same cafeteria.

Somehow, I limped through each day. I found a prom date, and I went and held my head up, even though I thought I'd die when Lucas walked in with his date.

After that, the shy Lucas I used to know disappeared. Suddenly, he seemed to have dozens of girl friends—a lot of them coworkers from other schools. When they saw me, they called me names, wrote things on my car, or gave me the finger. Nobody seemed to believe me—or care, even if they did.

I'd like to say he eventually apologized and we became friends, but it never happened. Surprisingly, years later when I was in college, I was still meeting girls he'd been going out with at the same time as me! What happened as a result was I became a lot stronger. I knew the truth, even if nobody else did, and I had learned a lot about which of my friends were truly my friends. I also realized high school doesn't last forever.

Going away to college was a great new beginning for me—I made so many new friends, had exciting experiences, and accomplished a lot. Finally, I did start dating again. But I've become quick at weeding out guys who disrespect me or just aren't good for me. I'd never want to go through that year of high school again, but in the end I think I'm a better person because of it.

~Marcella Dario Fuentes

Reprinted by permission of Off the Mark and Mark Parisi. ©1994 Mark Parisi.

First Kiss

It was brief, swift, and then it was done.
It was a professional job.
I needed to be kissed, and I was kissed.
~Uma Thurman

When Mrs. Collins, my gym teacher, blew her whistle for us to line up in front of the scales, I shrank behind everyone else. I already knew the results. As the smallest and lightest girl in my junior class, I barely tipped the scale at ninety pounds.

Unfortunately for me, my girlfriends were all developing figures that year. Guys had noticed and soon the girls I'd shared pajama parties and shopping trips with were paired off with boyfriends, leaving me to search for friends who were more interested in studying than dating.

Halfway through my school year, I scheduled a semester of Biology. Twin boys, a year younger than me, took the class as well. Before I knew it, the older of the two, (by a couple of minutes), began to talk with me while we studied together. "I work as a clerk at the store near your house," he told me with a wink. With no expertise in the fine art of flirting, I blushed and studied the dead frog on my lab table. "How about stopping by to say hi this weekend?" he asked.

My heart flew to my throat as I choked out a squeaky "Okay." Should I consider his request a date? I hurried to tell my best friend.

"You have to meet him," she ordered. "Who knows if he'll ever ask again?"

That night, I called another friend who lived around the corner from my house. "Do you want to have a sleepover this weekend?" I asked. I explained the circumstances and she immediately agreed. We would put a tent up in her yard so I could sneak out without my parents or two sisters knowing.

At around four P.M., I brushed my hair and changed into my nicest pair of jeans. Since it was almost May, I slipped on a lightweight top and practiced holding back my shoulders—hoping a better posture might improve my endowments. I strolled into the corner store, stopping first at the counter where candy sat in open boxes.

"Hey, come here." Jim whistled from one aisle away. I lifted one hand in a light wave, then searched the store to see if anyone had overheard him. Ducking down the narrow row, I found him waiting with a broom in the dish detergent section. He swooped me up in his arms and twirled me around like a rag doll. Breathless, I tried to think of a clever comment, but the words stuck to the roof of my mouth.

"Meet me later? I'll walk down when I get done and we can talk on your street." His eyebrows raised in a question. I smoothed my shirt, took a step backward and smiled.

"Sure, meet me around the corner at ten when you close. I'll be there." At nine forty-five, I thought I'd throw up the bag of chocolates I'd just consumed. Linda sat back on one sleeping bag. "You'll be fine. But when he comes in for the kiss, don't forget to close your eyes!"

I'd never kissed a boy before. I'd practiced on the mirror hundreds of times and usually left smears for my mother to clean. Again, my stomach twisted like a ride at a carnival.

At ten o'clock, I waited in the cool evening sky under the streetlight at the corner of my road. At five after, Jimmy arrived with a slight saunter. Even in the milky shadows, I saw even teeth glowing against his smooth skin. He was the cutest boy I knew and he wanted me.

"Can I kiss you?" he leaned closer.

I'm still not sure whether I said yes or nodded or just froze on the spot but I know one thing for sure—I forgot my friend's well-meaning advice. I kept my eyes wide open.

"This is my first kiss," I thought. "Make it good." Expecting the cool rush of mirror glass, I was unprepared for the soft touch of skin pressing against my own. Suddenly it didn't matter if I weighed ninety pounds or one hundred and ninety—I was kissing a boy.

We never dated again—I'm not sure if it was my inexperienced kiss, or my lack of coolness, but Jimmy moved on to newer conquests leaving me to eventually date other guys. My kissing improved with time, as did my shyness, but I still can't pass my old streetlight without remembering that special night when I walked into my next stage of life with my eyes wide open.

~Terri Tiffany

That Special Someone

*Nothing takes the taste out of peanut butter quite like
unrequited love.*
~Charlie Brown

From the first moment I met Evan, I knew that he was that special someone. Even if I knew I wouldn't be spending the rest of my life with him, I knew that I absolutely adored him before I even knew his name.

I met him in Drama Club, and I took an immediate liking to him. He wasn't all that handsome, but what I fell in love with was his personality.

I know that you probably think fourteen years old is much too young to claim to be in love, and I agree. However, I could tell when I met him that I would spend a long time mooning over him. As it turned out, I did.

Mine was the type of crush that would stop me in my tracks when I saw him in the hallways. He would sometimes smile at me, sometimes he wouldn't, but I would still let out a breath that I had been holding in after passing him, and once he was gone I could feel my body stop shaking. It was sickening how completely crazy I was about him, especially since I was a freshman and he was a senior.

As I stated before, I met him in Drama Club. It was my first year, and his last, which made things even harder. The first day of Drama Club, I hardly noticed him. It was our first meeting after auditions, and I was nervous, even with my normal friends around me. I saw seniors, and I was extremely afraid of upperclassmen.

One of our first exercises was to get into groups. I wasn't in a group with any of my friends. Instead, I was stuck with a sophomore and two seniors—one of them was Evan.

I smiled faintly, and we went on with the exercise in which we had to say our character name and walk around in a diamond as everyone repeated the name coupled with a dance move. My two-syllable name was perfect for the exercise, and at the end, Evan smiled at me, telling me I had great rhythm. I smiled back, my voice high: "Th-thanks!"

I knew that there was definitely something about him that I liked. Perhaps it was his constant happiness. Whenever he was with me, he would accompany his "hello" with a smile and a cheerful wave.

Maybe I liked how he brightened the room. He could dance and sing, make anyone laugh, and pull off any joke or stunt or outfit... I absolutely adored him through and through.

In our play, he was the antagonistic character, the Devil. He played the part perfectly, and I would sometimes stand backstage to watch his dancing skills as he practiced.

I was fortunate enough that year to find my own skill in dancing, something that caught Evan's eye. The entire Drama Club applauded me with a standing ovation—twice—for my skill, but I would have given it all away just to have him look at me and smile, even faintly. I could tell that he liked me as a friend, at least. Evan would smile, I would melt. He would laugh, I would sigh. The list went on and on.

I suppose that, at this point, I should move on with my life. All that I have left are memories and a few weeks until the end of the school year. I have a few pictures of him—a friend from Drama Club took a picture of Evan with his arm around me, wearing my favorite costume of his from the play. I haven't gotten it from her yet, but once I do I will be framing it and putting it next to my bed.

I adore Evan. I really do. It's too bad I'm a freshman and he's a senior. It's too bad he's graduating this year. It's too bad I won't be able to see him again for a very long time.

And it's too bad he's gay.

~Roxanne Hawthorne

My First "Non" Date

Mistakes are part of the dues one pays for a full life.
~Sophia Loren

The first time a guy asked me out, I panicked and said yes, only to tell him no a few days later. To this day I believe that might have been one of the biggest mistakes of my life.

We were the same age and sat next to each other in Biology. Almost half of the romances that blossomed in our school started in Biology, which just goes to show that kids will do basically anything to avoid drawing membranes and petunias.

He approached me in the library. I have to give him credit for that — it was well thought out. Being the bookish type, he probably decided I would be most comfortable there. I said okay to his request. He said his mother would drive us. "Great," I said, and he disappeared with what looked suspiciously like a blush creeping over his face.

Of course, I immediately told my friends — and this is where doubt raised its little head. "Him!" One friend said in disgust. "But he's so... you know."

"Yes," another agreed. "He really is so... you know." No, I didn't. So... what? I wanted to know.

"Go out with the guy, see how you like it," my mother advised. "I don't know," I told her. "Since when do you care what other people say?" my mother demanded. "Never mind," I grumbled, and slinked off.

For the next few days, I stayed as far away as possible from him. I even bunked Biology, something a nerdy kid like me would never have done in the past. I got caught and one of the teachers sent me home, thinking that I was seriously ill. One of the few advantages of being a nerdy kid is that when you behave like a normal teen, your teachers believe that something must be seriously wrong.

So I ended up alone at home, lying in bed and obsessing about the whole thing. I made up my mind. The following day I told him I couldn't go through with it. He walked away and changed seats so he didn't have to sit next to me in Biology anymore.

"It's better this way," my friends said.

"You idiot," my mother said.

I didn't say anything. I just gazed longingly at him for the rest of the semester.

~Nicola Booyse

The Double Date I Ditched

Popularity? It is glory's small change.

~Victor Hugo

In my sophomore year of high school, I learned that being popular isn't what's most important in life. A friend of mine, Lissa, was dating Aaron, one of the most popular guys in school, and they decided to fix me up with one of Aaron's good friends, Ray. Aaron and Ray were both jocks, big stars on our school's varsity basketball team, and Lissa was quite taken with them both. Needless to say, most of the girls were, and I was no exception.

Ray had the reputation, though, of breaking girls' hearts, which made me a little uncomfortable. He dated many girls and often, so that was why, when Lissa asked me if I wanted to go out with him, I felt puzzled. Why would he be interested in a date with me? I was a nerdy brainiac and budding drama geek. Unlike Lissa, who had curves galore, beautiful dark hair and eyes, and the clearest of complexions, I was considered plain. Most of the boys at school thought of me as a friend but not quite date material. So it was hard to believe that Ray could be any different.

Still, I was flattered to be asked out by such a popular boy, and Lissa's excitement over our future double date was outdone only by mine. We proceeded to make our plans — who would pick up whom, who would drive, where we would go. Drive-in movie theaters were the big rage, and that was where the guys decided to take us. At this decision, my initial discomfort returned. This wasn't my first date—I had gone to both freshman and sophomore homecoming dances—but it was my first date outside a school function, outside a group setting, and it was my first date with Ray. I wasn't exactly loving the idea of the four of us in a parked car in the dark, an obvious make-out scene.

I also didn't tell my parents where we were going because I knew they wouldn't approve. I'd just turned sixteen that summer, and they were pretty strict. It was the magic dating age in our family, sixteen, as if sudden maturity came at the flip of a calendar page. So I told my parents we were going to a movie, minus the drive-in part, and as Saturday night loomed, I grew more nervous.

When Ray picked me up that night, he was the perfect gentleman, chatting with my parents, holding open the passenger door for me. As we drove to pick up Lissa, and then Aaron, I was beginning to feel that maybe this date would turn out okay. Maybe Ray would genuinely like me, and maybe I'd be the one to break the cycle of his endless parade of girls.

Once all four of us were in the car together, we headed directly to the drive-in and settled into our space. It was one of those last mild nights of autumn, the air crisp with wood smoke. With the front window rolled down a little, you could smell that wonderful woodsy smell. It reminded me of my grandfather's fireplace, and I started to relax.

Until a few minutes into the movie, that is. That's when Aaron and Lissa decided to grab a blanket and go outside.

Fear welled within me. I tried telling myself that I was being silly. Ray had been nothing but a gentleman all evening, but with Lissa and Aaron gone, it left just the two of us. The car was very dark by then, with only the reflected light from the movie screen shining in, and Ray didn't waste any time making his move. Seemingly before I knew it, he had me wedged up against the passenger door, his hands everywhere, his mouth everywhere, his kisses far from gentle. After a few moments, I finally succeeded in fending him off. "Okay, I get it," he said. "Guess we need to slow this down." There was no apology, no attempt to hide his intentions. "Don't worry, all the girls do it with me. All the girls love it."

I realized in that moment that I represented just one more conquest for Ray, and I wondered how many other girls he had coaxed into this same situation. How many girls had complied, and how many, like me, had tried to tell him no? I decided right then that if this was what it took to be popular, I wasn't having any of it.

Soon, Ray tried again, and after a bit of struggle, I threw open my car door and stumbled out. "Hey," he called after me, "Stop. Where you going? Wait!"

But I didn't stop and I didn't wait. I rounded the car, found Lissa and Aaron spread out on their blanket, heavy into their own routine. I told them I wanted to leave and I'm sure they could see how distraught I was. We were all whispering, not wanting to attract the attention of other movie watchers—a moot point, since the place was pretty empty. Lissa pulled herself together, sat up, and glared at me.

It was Aaron who made a lame attempt to smooth things over. "Hey, look," he said to me, "Ray can be kinda... fast. Why not stay a little longer, and if you still want to leave, we'll take you home."

By this time Ray was also out of the car. He tried to hold my hand, but I pulled back. "That's okay," I told Aaron, my voice deceptively calm. "I'll call for a ride."

I bade them all goodnight, I made my way to the concession area, found a pay phone, and called my dad. When my dad arrived, he didn't scold me, as I thought he would, for being at the drive-in. Nor did he try to pry as to what specifically had happened. I suspected he knew.

I never spoke to Ray or Aaron again after that night, and hard as it was, when we passed in the halls at school, I held my head high. Lissa and I became distant, which did really hurt, but I suppose I found out that she wasn't the friend I'd once thought.

As for my dad, he never brought up that night again. I'm sure he knew how hard it had been for me to call him. It had been embarrassing and I'd felt like a dork. I worried for the longest time about gossip at school, about what the boys were saying in the locker room, what the girls were saying behind my back. It sure hadn't been the most popular thing to do, calling my dad. But at least I hadn't allowed myself to be pressured into something I'd later regret. At least I hadn't compromised myself for the sake of popularity. I'd stood up for myself and I'd kept myself safe.

~Theresa Sanders

Chapter
3

Teens Talk

HIGH SCHOOL

Doing the Right Thing

The time is always right to do what is right.

~Martin Luther King, Jr.

The Help I Could Give

Dare to reach out your hand into the darkness,
to pull another hand into the light.
~Norman B. Rice

One morning, my best friend comes to me before homeroom and says she needs to tell me something — and show me something. She starts explaining before she even tells me what happened, saying she doesn't know why and doesn't know what to do and she needs my help. She pulls up her shirtsleeve and peels back a Band-Aid. I don't understand at first, but as the world around me slows, all I can focus on is the fact that my best friend, who has always been so strong, is hurting herself. She asks me not to tell anyone, just to help her. She asks me to promise I won't tell and promise I'll help her. I think I can fix her.

We go to her house after school that day and come up with a plan. We will spend as much time together as possible, and anytime she feels the need to cut she will call me. Everything will be okay. Everything will be all right.

A day or two later, she admits to doing it again. She says she really wants to stop but she doesn't know how. She doesn't know what is wrong with her. I tell her we need to tell someone else, find someone to help, even though all I really want to do is fix her by myself. She tells me no, don't tell anyone yet, and that she doesn't want her parents to know. She doesn't want to let them or her sisters down. I tell her we can wait, and if it happens again, we will tell someone. She agrees, promises we'll stick to the plan this time, and everything will be okay.

It happens again, and then again. I can't concentrate on work. I can't concentrate on school. I can't even begin to think about anything but finding a way to help her. It finally hits me one day in first period. I cannot do this myself. As much as it hurts me to not be able to help her myself, I realize that she needs help I can't give. I find a teacher I trust, my health teacher, and tell her about what is going on. I don't tell her my friend's name yet because I am scared about what will happen next. The morning is a blur of tears and explanations as I am brought to the guidance counselor to figure out the next step. We decide that I will go find my friend and try to convince her to come with me and talk.

I know my friend is in study hall during third period. I stand outside her class and get her attention—she gets the hall pass and comes out to meet me. I begin to break down. I tell her I can't help her. I can't do it, and I know she needs help that I can't give. I can support her, I can stand by her, but I can't do everything. Finally, she agrees with me. We walk to the guidance office and sit with our guidance counselor, discussing what to do next. We take a walk to the nurse's office to make sure nothing is infected, and for the nurse's guidance, since she has seen wounds like this before. In a strange way, it is comforting to know we are not the only ones to have dealt with this, to know that there are people that can help.

That was the day the slow healing process began. Months after, we were still working towards being okay and learning how to deal. But the beginning was the hardest part. I had to admit that I couldn't just fix my friend and she needed to admit that she needed help helping herself. This problem is something that will keep us close forever. And I realized that day that even though I didn't fix her myself, I was helping her by getting the outside help she needed. We learned how to face what came at us, and now we both know that we are strong. We know that we can get through anything, and that during times when we need it, it is more than okay to ask for help.

~Aimee McCarron

Slam Book

Whenever anyone has offended me,
I try to raise my soul so high that the offence cannot reach it.
~René Descartes

"I'll never forgive them!" I shouted as I threw my books on my bedroom floor and hurled myself onto my bed. "Never!" My anger boiled with increasing intensity. How could people be so cruel?

It had all started innocently enough—as a game, in fact. I'd read about slam books in a teen magazine and decided to do one with my friends. "After all, what harm could there be in a spiral notebook filled with names?" I reasoned.

So the next time my mom went to the store I asked her to buy a notebook for me. "Do you need an extra one for school?" she asked.

"Kind of," I replied. I didn't want to tell her that the notebook would be used to write good and bad things about people and that it would be open for everyone to read. She'd tell me that it was wrong to gossip, and that someone's feelings could be hurt if the wrong things were written.

To me, the idea of the slam book wasn't so bad. Everyone who wanted to be in it signed his or her name at the top of a page. Then others used the rest of the page to anonymously write whatever they wanted about whomever's name appeared at the top. If you didn't want to participate, you didn't sign your name.

"It'll be fun," I told my best friend, Jenny, as she wrote her name on the page after mine. "We'll pass this around during school, and soon we'll know what the other kids think about us and everyone else."

By the end of the first day, I had over twenty signatures in my slam book. By the second day, the pages began to fill with comments. Soon other kids started their own slam books. You couldn't walk through the hallways without seeing someone handing out a notebook.

Each day I hurried home to read the slam book in the privacy of my room. At first, the comments were all favorable. It was as though everyone was waiting for someone else to break the ice.

But as the days went on, the messages in the book took on a new tone. People become more critical in their comments about others. Names of unpopular kids turned up in my book, and I knew that someone else had written them in. "Oh well," I said. "They'll probably never see what's been written about them anyway."

I would have gone on thinking like that if I hadn't seen Sandy's book. She handed it to me in homeroom and asked if I'd sign something on her page and pass it on to someone else. "Sure," I agreed. Sandy was one of the most popular girls in our class. I was pleased she wanted me to write in her book.

I wrote my comments about Sandy and then started flipping the pages. There were glowing testimonies about all the popular kids. About halfway through the notebook, I stopped. My name was at the top of a page, and I hadn't written it there. I read the comments, first with a smile, then dismay, and finally with increasing anger:

- *So stuck up she'll never get a date!*

- *Thinks she's too good for the rest of us. Should work more on making friends instead of making honor roll.*

- *Brown-noser. Teacher's pet.*

I shut the notebook and glanced up to see Sandy looking at me. I felt my face flame with embarrassment. Did she write any of those comments? I wondered. Did she give me the book on purpose, so I'd see what had been written about me?

I opened the book again and studied my page. I examined the comments, trying to match the handwriting with signatures, but most people had disguised their writing.

During first bell, I gave the book to someone else and tried to put it out of my mind. But I found the phrases written on my page haunting me. Stuck up. Too intellectual. Teacher's pet.

At lunch, I told Jenny about Sandy's book and the comments I'd found. "I know," she said. "The popular kids really came down hard on everyone. Sandy's book wasn't even the worst one. You should read Pam's."

I couldn't believe it. Someone else's slam book actually contained worse things about me than Sandy's did? I was so hurt and angry that I couldn't finish my lunch. The rest of the day passed slowly because all I could think about was going home and having a good cry.

"I don't deserve those nasty comments," I told myself as I tossed on my bed. "I've never done anything to hurt them."

Then the thought entered my head unbidden: Those unpopular kids whose names showed up in my book didn't do anything either. How did they feel?

I didn't mean any harm, I thought as I picked up my slam book and thumbed through its pages. Yet reading it, I realized that even the design of the book lent itself to bad, rather than good, purposes. Not signing your name, disguising your handwriting, not giving the book directly back to the person who owned it—all these things let the writer be as nasty as possible without fear of being found out.

This is one of the stupidest things I've ever done, I thought. My slam book had encouraged gossip and hurt a lot of feelings—mine included. No more of that, I told myself. I took the notebook and stuffed it deep inside one of my desk drawers. That's the last time I take that to school.

The next step was one I knew I'd find even harder to take. First, I had to forgive the kids at school for their comments. I knew that wouldn't be as easy as closing my drawer and leaving the slam book inside, but it had to be done.

Then there was the matter of the unpopular kids whose names had turned up in my book. I need to apologize to them, I told myself. Besides learning to forgive others, I had to ask for forgiveness as well.

In the weeks to come, I realized that taking my slam book to school had taught me some unexpected lessons. The lesson of forgiveness was the one I most needed to learn.

~Teresa Cleary

Ricky

Act as if what you do makes a difference. It does.
~William James

I rushed in to the cafeteria desperately. It was yearbook day and I had waited nearly a week for my chance to see how many times my picture was in the school publication. I was a freshman in high school and we were given an hour to sign each other's yearbooks. I sat down at a table, and people started to come over in groups to get their yearbook signed and to sign mine. I played sports and was the president of my class of 300. The whole freshman class was in the cafeteria in their cliques, signing each other's yearbooks.

A frail boy came up to where I was sitting. I had seen him around, and I knew he was the target of a lot of teasing. He had buckteeth, glasses, and rocked back and forth nervously. He seemed painfully unsure of himself, and was so pale it hurt to look at him. I'm not entirely sure what was wrong with him, but I knew he spent his time with a "special" helper because he couldn't do everything himself. Little did I know that this boy would completely change my life.

He came up to me nervously and asked me in an almost pleading way "Can you sign this?"

I looked back at my friends, and they just shrugged and laughed.

I took his yearbook, not knowing what to write. I saw that there was the name "Ricky Sanders" etched into the front of it. So I wrote:

Ricky,

I think you're a really nice kid, and I hope you have a great summer. Have lots of fun on break.

~Will

I put down the yearbook and turned around to get some signatures from some of my friends when I noticed my yearbook was gone. I looked at a friend of mine in front of me and he was snickering. I glanced where he was staring and I saw that Ricky had sat down at the end of the table with my yearbook.

"What are you doing?" I asked this boy who I had just met.

He looked up calmly and just said "Sign!"

My friends exploded in laughter, and I saw that he was intently trying to put a signature in my yearbook. He hadn't even finished the "R" yet. I decided I wouldn't make a scene, and I let him sign.

It took him nearly five minutes to sign and when I got my yearbook back, there was a very shaky "RICKY" written in all capital letters. He hugged his yearbook and smiled, absolutely delighted. I couldn't help but smile back at him.

In that moment, my mood changed completely.

I gave him a high five and suddenly everyone at my table wanted his signature. He was getting requests from everyone to write in their yearbook. His yearbook wasn't going unsigned either.

"You're great Ricky," "Have an Awesome Summer Ricky!" and "You're so cool" filled up the signature pages of his yearbook. It was amazing, and Ricky was ecstatic. He was smiling so big it lit up the whole room. That's when I saw his special helper standing a small distance away from the table. She was wiping tears from her eyes and smiling, and she looked at me and mouthed the words: "Thank You."

I switched schools the next year, and I never saw Ricky again. I don't have a clue where he is, or what he's doing, but I'll never forget the day that he became the most popular guy in school. Whenever

I'm down, I still look back at that yearbook. There on the inside cover, is where a boy changed my life just by signing his name— "RICKY."

~Will Moore

A Flower for Leourn

We can do no great things,
only small things with great love.
~Mother Teresa

We were out to change the world. This was our time, our senior year. My best friend Beth and I had big dreams and big hopes for our last year at high school. We were ready for a miracle we knew we would see. With great anticipation, we started the year with my senior quote in mind: "But God and I have big dreams, and with big dreams you can't give up, you have to keep pressing on."

I would like to say that I was the first to notice her, but in my world of "big dreams," this one small, quiet freshman did not appear on my radar. My sensitive best friend Beth was the first to notice her.

"Kristi, did you see the girl standing by us in the lunch line? She looks so lost, so out of place," Beth said to me. We had heard of a family that had just moved to our town from Cambodia. We knew there was supposed to be a new girl at school from that family, but we had yet to meet her... until now.

Leourn was a small, dark-haired beauty. She was thrust into a new country where she struggled with the little English she knew, and it made it very hard for her to get to know people in our small town. She was starting her freshman year and was trying her best to blend in without attracting any attention.

We watched in the lunchroom at our "Senior Table." This table was reserved for our senior sport jock friends, and no one else. Leourn would get her lunch tray with the rest of the students, but she always kept her head down with her eyes focused on the floor. She would then head to the only table of girls she recognized. Unfortunately, it was the table for the most popular girls in the freshman class. Every single day, Leourn would sit at the very edge of her seat and eat as fast as she could. She kept her eyes fixed on her food and we never, ever saw her look up. We would watch in dismay at the interaction of the other girls at her table. They would make gestures to one another and laugh at Leourn while she ate.

As we paid attention over the next week, we never heard anyone so much as say "Hi" to Leourn.

We watched as Leourn walked, with her head always down, through the halls of a high school where most didn't even acknowledge her existence. She was a girl invisible.

Beth and I prayed and talked—what could we do to help Leourn? With love and faith, we decided to try our hardest to let one lonely girl know that there were people who knew she existed and, more importantly, that there was a God who knew and loved her.

As the weeks and months passed, Beth and I made an effort to let Leourn know that we cared. We sat with Leourn at the freshman girls' table. The other freshman girls tried to let us in on the joke that "nobody talks to Leourn." Their lofty glances and laughs were met with death stares from two upperclassmen.

We sought out Leourn in the halls and said "Hi" and tried to continue to engage her in conversation. I would like to say that, at this point, Leourn responded to us with smiles and small talk. But she didn't—Leourn still kept her head down and responded very little. We were okay with that, because we knew that God wanted us to keep trying to spend time with Leourn, regardless of her response.

When February rolled around, our school sold carnations that we could send to one another for Valentine's Day. I immediately thought of Leourn and decided I would send her a flower for the holiday. When I thought about what to write, it occurred to me that keeping it simple would be the best for someone just learning our language and customs. So I just simply wrote:

Happy Valentines Day, Leourn—

I want you to know how much God loves you.

Your friend, Kristi

I will never forget that Valentine's Day.

For the first time, Leourn was the one who sought me out. She found me in the hall with the carnation clutched tightly in her hands. Then she did something amazing. She looked up.

She actually took her eyes off the floor, looked up at me with beautiful beaming eyes, and in a low choked whisper said two words: "Thank You."

It was a life-changing moment for me.

You see, Beth and I were out to change the world, but instead God was changing me. I learned that I may never be president, be famous, or have a million dollars to my name. But I learned that what Christ wanted from me was for me to love Him with all my heart and all my soul so that I could spread that love to everyone around me—one flower at a time.

It's like walking out to a pond and throwing in one tiny pebble. Though that pebble is incredibly small compared to the pond, it still creates ripples that affect the water around it. As I learned my senior year, every word that comes from our mouths and every action we carry out affects the people around us, whether we realize it or not.

We ended our senior year not knowing how many people's lives we touched. However, Beth and I knew that our two lives were changed. Leourn went on to graduate from our small high school three years after us, and I went back for her graduation. As Leourn walked out of the gymnasium after the ceremony, I gave her a big hug and told her congratulations. As she looked up at me, the tears streamed down her face. I asked her if the tears were happy ones or sad ones, and she said they were both. I gave her another hug before she walked off into the crowd.

As I look back, I hope in my own small way that we helped to make her first year in a new country easier, and that we brought a little light into her world.

~Kristi Powers

"Ah! We're finally seniors! That's ALMOST as good as being teachers!"

The Boldest Girl in Class

Courage is what it takes to stand up and speak;
courage is also what it takes to sit down and listen.
~Winston Churchill

I'll never forget the first time I heard my English teacher, Mr. Barnes, make an inappropriate comment in class. He'd just handed out our first assignment and someone asked how long it should be. "Like the length of a lady's skirt," he said. "Long enough to cover everything, but short enough to keep it interesting." The guys howled and gave each other high fives. Mr. Barnes just sat there and smiled with an annoying little smirk on his face. It made my skin crawl.

As the year went by, his comments became more and more inappropriate. I began to dread his class. He could turn anything we studied into something negative and degrading to women. It was humiliating. How could he treat us like this? Each time he made one of his comments, I wanted to say something, but I was too afraid of him. Besides, everyone called me "Miss Quiet and Shy." I didn't like speaking in front of other people and I would never talk back to a teacher.

Toward the end of the year, we started studying *The Canterbury Tales*, a Middle English collection of stories about a group of travelers. Mr. Barnes made a generic, stereotypical comment about the traveler in each tale we were reading. When we came to the tale about the "Wife of Bath," I braced myself. Just as I suspected, he told us about how this woman was a typical wife. They only brought her along because they needed someone to cook and clean. I just couldn't take it anymore. What was wrong with us? Why did we all sit complacently, taking this abuse? The guys were laughing and acting like Mr. Barnes was a stand-up comedian. I looked at the girls and most of them just sat there with their arms crossed and their heads hanging down. It made me so angry. I felt like I was going to explode.

I don't know what came over me. Suddenly, I blurted out a "Hmm!" My teacher's head jerked up.

He glared around the room and asked, "Who said that?" No one said a word. It was so quiet that I heard the clock on the wall ticking for the first time ever.

I had a queasy feeling in the pit of my stomach, like I'd just gone upside down on a roller coaster. I could feel my face getting hotter as the blood rushed to my cheeks. My heart was pounding so loud and so fast that I thought it might jump right out of my chest. What was I thinking? I was "Miss Quiet and Shy," right? I was already in way over my head. Oh well, I thought, somebody has to stand up to this guy — here goes nothing. I opened my mouth and blurted out, "I said it." Everyone whipped around and stared at me with looks of horror. I wanted to crawl underneath my desk.

Mr. Barnes glared at me and said, "Do you have something you'd like to say?"

"Yes... I... do." I choked out. "I think your comments are stereotypical and rude. They are... um... inappropriate, sir." I stammered.

"Well," he said, "I'm sorry you feel that way. Thank you for your comments, Miss Westbrook."

I don't think I paid attention to anything else the entire class period. I couldn't believe what I had just done. Was that my voice I had heard? Did Mr. Barnes really just thank me for my comments? When the bell rang, I grabbed my stuff and ran down the hall to my locker.

By the end of the day, the entire school had heard what had happened. People I didn't even know were coming up to me and patting me on the back. All of the girls were so glad that someone had finally stood up to him, and so was I. I just couldn't believe that it had been me!

For the rest of the year, Mr. Barnes toned down his comments, at least in my class. He still told some awful jokes, but they were no longer degrading.

When I handed in my final exam, Mr. Barnes looked me in the eye and said, "You, Miss Westbrook, will go far in life. We need more leaders and fewer followers. Good luck next year." I was shocked — it seemed like he actually respected me for standing up to him. I smiled and felt proud. Who would have thought that "Miss Quiet and Shy" would have ended up being the boldest girl in class?

~Christy Westbrook

Troubled Influence

Be neither a conformist or a rebel, for they are really the same thing. Find your own path, and stay on it.
~Paul Vixie

My stomach was churning and my palms were sweating like crazy. I only knew one other person in the entire assembly, and we weren't friends in grade school, so I wasn't counting on us being friends now. As I scanned the room looking for someone I could be friends with, I had this feeling of enormity, this sense of "this is the first day of the rest of my life." And it was. It was my first day of high school.

I don't really remember how we became friends, but by the end of the first week of school I had a new best friend. Her name was Lindsay and she was so interesting to me. She was everything I was not. She had gone to public school for most of her life and her parents were divorced. She had a boyfriend who was older and had just stopped going to school. I had been in Catholic school my entire life and grew up with both of my parents acting as a combined force. I was desperate to grow up and feel older. Lindsay represented every freedom I had dreamed of. Plus, she was so smart and completely hilarious. We hit it off right away.

One day after school, Lindsay and I were walking to the mall where my mom was going to pick us up. We had walked just far enough away from school when Lindsay pulled it out — a pack of cigarettes. She took one from the pack and lit it. She was so nonchalant, like she'd done it a thousand times before. "You want one?"

I just stared at her wide-eyed. I began thinking of my parents' warnings, and how my mom would be picking us up soon. I was scared and nervous, but I wanted to be more like Lindsay. She seemed so much more mature than I.

"I would, but I'm just nervous about my mom smelling smoke on me," I said.

"Don't worry. I know what to do. I do this all the time." And Lindsay took off her sweater and stuffed it in her backpack. "Just take your sweater off and put it in your bag. That way it won't smell like smoke and you can put it on before you see your mom. Plus we're going to the mall. We'll just go in a department store and spray perfume on us. I always do that. My mom never knows when I smoke." It seemed so easy for her. So I did just as she told me, and my mom never suspected a thing.

My friendship with Lindsay opened up a whole world for me. Before high school, I had never really done anything "bad." But every day with Lindsay was a new lesson in pushing boundaries and getting away with it. She confided in me that she was having sex with her boyfriend. I couldn't believe it. We were only fourteen. It just seemed so grown up to me. I was still waiting for my first kiss. I felt so sheltered compared to Lindsay.

"Hi Lindsay, how are you tonight?" my mom asked as we picked Lindsay up for the movie. Lindsay got into our van and climbed into the backseat next to me.

"I'm good. How are you?" she replied as she slowly lifted her shirt to show me that she had a bottle of liquor under it.

"Put that away!" I urgently whispered. I was petrified my mom would see it, but I was also a little intrigued. I'd never snuck a bottle of alcohol before, and certainly wouldn't have thought to bring it to the movie theater in the mall.

After we were dropped off, Lindsay led us to the food court. "Just buy a big soda," she instructed. I bought a soda and then she led me into the bathroom. "Here, pour half of the soda in the toilet and then we'll mix the rest of it with the liquor!" It felt so wrong. I was so afraid of getting caught or getting in trouble.

"Umm, Linds, we are going to miss the movie. I don't know if this is such a good idea," I argued.

"Duh. We aren't going to the movie. We're just going to get drunk and smoke cigarettes!" I didn't know what to think. I knew my parents would be so disappointed if they knew what I was doing, but I figured, I'm a teenager and this is what teenagers do. And so that's how we spent many of our weekends that year.

Lindsay talked me into doing a lot of things that I would not have done on my own. I don't really know why I did some of them. We did get caught a few times, and my parents were terribly upset. Looking back, I know how much I hurt them and I wish that would have been enough to keep me from behaving as I did. I mostly did these things because I thought I had a right to and I thought it was what everyone was doing.

Lindsay didn't come back to school after our freshman year. She transferred to public school and we lost touch. I made new friends and got involved in extracurricular activities. I had to earn my parents' trust back. And like everyone, I continued to make mistakes, but I thought about my choices more and I learned to say "no" when I didn't want to be included in something that I knew was wrong.

After my freshman year of college, I was working as a receptionist for the summer. One day a package was accidentally delivered to our suite, and I brought it to the correct suite. When I entered the office, I couldn't believe my eyes! Sitting there at the receptionist's desk was Lindsay!

"Lindsay?! I can't believe it! How are you?!"

Lindsay jumped up and gave me a hug. It was wonderful to see her again. We made plans to have lunch together the next day.

At lunch, Lindsay told me that after she transferred she didn't stay in school much longer. She dropped out of school and got involved in some criminal activity. She even had to spend time in jail. She had been pregnant twice, and now had a little boy. She had recently completed her GED and started working at this receptionist job.

Then she asked what I had been up to. It had been four years since I saw her and I felt like I didn't have much to report, certainly not compared to what she had just told me.

"Umm, well, not much. I graduated high school and started college. I just finished my first year and I am planning to go to law school," I told her.

That was the last time I ever saw Lindsay. We had been two girls on a similar path four years ago, but there at that lunch table, we were two women with nothing in common. Lindsay showed me the thrill of living on the edge, but in the end she taught me the importance of staying grounded.

~Natalie Embrey Hikel

May I Have This Dance?

When we feel love and kindness toward others,
it not only makes others feel loved and cared for,
but it helps us also to develop inner happiness and peace.
~The Dalai Lama

My heart was beating ninety miles per hour as I approached her. I looked back several times to see if the boys from my class were still watching me. They had told me that Gloria wanted me to ask her to dance. I did not believe them but every time I looked in her direction, she would smile and wave at me.

I was fourteen years old and I had never danced with a girl. In fact, I had never even held the hand of a girl before. Talking to a girl, or even looking at a female, was strictly forbidden by the orphanage where I lived. Such actions would result in being sent off to reform school. I didn't want that to happen.

Just as I was about to reach the prettiest girl in our classroom, a heavy-set girl came running out onto the gym floor.

"Roger, they are going to make fun of you again. I heard the girls in the bathroom laughing about it," she advised me.

Once again, I looked back and saw the four boys motioning for me to continue.

I looked into Jackie's eyes and saw that she was very serious. She was a heavy girl and had a very bad skin condition. No one in the class liked her and they always called her "Fatty, fatty, two-by-four."

I stood there as Jackie turned around and walked back to the area where the girls were waiting to be chosen to dance.

Once again, I turned around to look at my friends.

"Go on," yelled Davis.

I turned back around and looked in Gloria's direction; she winked and then she smiled. I looked over at Jackie, who had never been asked to dance by anyone.

Slowly I walked over and stopped directly in front of the two of them.

I looked at Gloria and then I looked at Jackie. I bent down, in a bow and I said, "Would you care to dance with me?"

"Look, creep. I don..." Gloria started to say.

"I would love too," said Jackie, as she grabbed me like a rag doll and pulled me out onto the dance floor.

All I remember is Gloria stomping out of the gym with everyone laughing at her.

I was not a very handsome boy and Jackie was not the prettiest girl in school. However, she made me feel handsome that night. As I constantly stepped on her feet, I told her that she was pretty and she smiled at me.

That was the night I learned that you don't have to be handsome or pretty in order to feel good inside.

~Roger Dean Kiser

Walking Away

They cannot take away our self-respect if we do not give it to them.
~Mahatma Gandhi

I'm watching him sway as he traces my face,
His eyes are glazed over, not looking at mine.
A hand on my waist leads me into his bedroom.
He slurs and assures me I'm going to be fine.

Starts running his fingers through my hair now,
Caressing the nape of my neck with his lips,
Cradles my shoulders, the warmth of his breath
Comes in bursts as he steadies his hands on my hips.

I'm tasting the beer as we're starting to kiss,
Secondhand drunk off his liquor-dulled tongue,
He stumbles on words as he tries to be sexy
And just ends up sounding incredibly dumb.

He fumbles with buttons and grabs at my shirt,
Won't listen as I try to push him away
He's drunk and determined, it all feels so wrong
And he just doesn't hear anything that I say

I roll out from under the heavy embrace
Of this boy who just isn't himself anymore
He clumsily curses and struggles to rise
When I hold my head high as I walk out the door.

~Michelle Vanderwist

The True Meaning of Friendship

A friend is one of the nicest things you can have,
and one of the best things you can be.
~Douglas Pagels

I couldn't believe that I was here again, starting a new chapter in my life. It had only been three years since I was in the same situation. But those doors were much smaller and so was the depth of my knowledge. I heard a ring and in I went. It was time to face it—the first day of high school.

Compared to all the upperclassmen around me, I felt very small. It was honestly the hardest day of my life, and just trying to make it to class on time was difficult. I couldn't believe that so many people knocked over others to get to lunch. What happened to waiting in line? Looking for a lunch table was also tough. High school wasn't like middle school. It was much bigger and harder to make myself stand out. I was used to the attention and to people saying "Hi" in the hallways. Now all I heard was, "Move Freshie!"

The next week was better because at least I knew my locker combination. I hadn't gotten knocked over in the hallways and my schedule was coinciding with my friends'. All I saw around me was happiness—the seniors catching up with each other and bragging about new loves and new adventures. And then I saw her. The prettiest girl I had ever seen: Emily Butler.

Besides the fact that she was ranked number two in her class, took part in numerous activities, was the prettiest and most popular girl in school and a teacher's favorite, and already had a full scholarship to the college of her choice, she had class. She was a role model to everyone and wasn't afraid to tell it like it was. She was so lucky to be so amazing—I could only pray to come that close.

As she bumped me in the hallway, she smiled and apologized. Following her were numerous boys and girls. Her laugh could be heard for miles and her teeth were brighter than a cheerleader's positive attitude. I told myself that if I tried really hard, one day I could be just like her. She couldn't have always been perfect, right?

As weeks went on, I joined plenty of activities and got myself involved in numerous sports and volunteer programs. One club I stumbled my way into was Mock Trial. The captain, of course, was glamorous Emily Butler. She instructed and ran the meetings and was very nice to me. As time went on, we became close and she taught me a lot. She always hung out with me and put in the extra mile for me. It was weird, but she treated me like a little sister. The more we hung out, the closer I was to the seniors. I went to parties with them and even hung out one-on-one with them. I became more outgoing and well-liked.

In December, I became quite ill with mononucleosis and couldn't go to school for a month. After that, Emily and I stopped hanging out and again I felt alone. Then one day, she called me and asked me to chill with her. I gladly accepted. We began hanging out every day and I was more attached to her than I was to my own boyfriend. She lifted me up and again I became comfortable in my own skin. Each day, I found something more to love about her and myself.

When I would do something wrong, Emily would be there to pick up after my mistakes. When the year finally came to a close, we cried as we said goodbye. She had made my freshman year more than I could have ever hoped for. She said good luck and told me that I was beautiful and had a heart full of love. She told me that if I ever needed her, she would be there for me. She hugged me goodbye and left. Tears rolled down my face and I began to wonder how I could ever survive without her.

As my sophomore year began, I no longer heard people talking about Emily and how great she was, and I missed her loud laugh. We still keep in touch and I hope to become just like her one day. I have already vowed that I, too, will find a freshman to teach and treat like a little sister. Emily taught me that I can do whatever I want, and I will pass on her sweet lesson. She showed me the true meaning of friendship, love, and the courage to be myself.

~Amber Curtis

Teens Talk

HIGH SCHOOL

Love Gone Bad

Out of this nettle, danger, we pluck this flower, safety.

~William Shakespeare

27

Hideaway Friend

Never violate the sacredness of your individual self-respect.
~Theodore Parker

She liked him,
And he liked her.
But because of their friends,
They lived in two separate worlds.

He would talk to her when no one was around,
She would allow her walls to come tumbling down.
He hated to hurt her, but he wouldn't lose pride.
He'd pretend not to see the tears in her eyes.

For he was an athlete — a star of the school,
And for this one girl he wouldn't forfeit his rule.
She wasn't popular — no one knew her name,
She tried to blend in; she felt so ashamed.

Why didn't he like her? Why didn't he care?
How come he only came to her when no one else was there?
It didn't matter that he'd never felt this way before,
Or that her face lit up whenever he walked through the door.

He only thought of himself and how it should be,
Patiently she waited for him, dreaming of how it could be.
Finally, one day, she decided to chance fate,
She worked up the nerve to ask for a date.

She went shopping to find something new.
Ignoring the fear in her heart that continuously grew.
What if he doesn't show? What would that mean?
The "what ifs" were tearing her apart at the seams.

Sure enough, when eight o'clock rolled around,
That boy was missing, nowhere to be found.
She decided on Monday she would avoid him at all costs,
Another relationship failed, another friendship lost.

Later when he found her and started to apologize,
She listened to his excuses;
        her heart knowing they were all lies.
But it was easier to believe him and to just give in,
That's what she did, when they agreed to try it again.

She began to feel worthless and totally lame,
Once again he had done exactly the same.
So as she sat home alone, again that night,
She decided to give up the fight.

Knowing it's a battle she could never win,
Her heart just couldn't go through that pain again.
The next time he walks up, she'll hold her head high,
She'll quickly turn away, and try not to cry.

That's just what she did, but he called after her,
As he started to speak, silent teardrops fell down her cheeks.
She didn't look back, but continued on her way,

She didn't stop when he said he was sorry for his mistakes.

It took all her strength to keep walking away,
She knew what would happen, if she chose to stay.
The pain and the hurt would start over again,
And she would continue to be his hideaway friend.

~Tiffany Caudill

28

My Own Path

*One half of knowing what you want is knowing
what you must give up before you get it.*
~Sidney Howard

I broke up with Josh three weeks before the senior prom. We had been dating for almost a year. He had graduated the previous year and landed a good job. Josh was ready for marriage and a family.

I wasn't.

His dreams included two children, a boy we would name Joshua, a girl named Jessica. We would have dogs, horses, boats, cars, and of course, live happily after. Each time we discussed our future, I became more nervous. I thought we were too young for marriage. My room was filled with college applications and towers of books. I dreamed of becoming a lawyer, or maybe a veterinarian, not a wife and mother. I wanted him to wait while I walked my own path for a while. I didn't want to break Josh's heart, but I did.

Emily handed me tissues as I told her about the break-up. Of my four friends, she was the one I came to when I needed comfort. Emily understood that I wanted to pursue my dreams. She nodded and agreed with my decision. I thought the rest of my girlfriends would support my decision. I never dreamed that they would take his side.

But they did... even Emily.

Once news of the break-up spread I was somehow transformed from best friend to heartless villain. One by one, my friends stopped speaking to me. Two weeks before the prom—four weeks before graduation—during what was supposed to have been the best year of my life, I walked the halls of my high school without a single friend.

I didn't mention the break-up to my parents. Looking back, I should have. At least I would have had someone to talk to. Instead, the day before the prom I announced that I would be going stag.

"What about the party?" Mother had asked, referring to the pre-prom party she and I had been planning for weeks.

"We decided to do something else," I replied.

Mom frowned but said nothing.

When you're a senior in high school, the worst thing that can happen isn't breaking up with your boyfriend, it's posing for prom pictures alone. Or so I thought. After the humiliating photo, I entered the ballroom just as the lights dimmed. I tried to ignore my ex-friends who were gathered in the corner of the room. The music started, and a sea of taffeta gowns parted, revealing a smiling Josh. Excited dancers jostled against me as I stood frozen to the floor, my mouth ajar.

Then reality hit me.

My ex-boyfriend Josh was at the prom with my ex-friend Emily. Their matching tuxedo-taffeta ensemble was my first clue. Emily attached at his hip was my second. I acted like it didn't hurt.

But it did.

Anthony, a graduate from three years ago, who was majoring in law enforcement and moonlighting as prom security, took pity on me and asked me to dance. Then the foreign exchange student followed his lead. The rest is a blur of tear-drenched memories.

After my ex-friends had surrounded me and danced with my ex-boyfriend, I left the prom. The temptation to drink away my worries was great. Everyone knew where the after-prom party was. In fact, several of the students had bypassed the prom and gone directly to the party after having their picture taken. I was already the laughing stock at school. I was in no mood to embarrass myself further by getting drunk and ruining the only thing that remained intact—my good name.

I drove home, took the stairs two at a time, and slammed my bedroom door. I ignored Mother's worried knock and spent the rest of the night in bed with my face buried in my stuffed animals.

I awoke the following morning, a mess of blue silk and black mascara.

Mother cracked the bedroom door wide enough to extend the telephone. "It's Lisa," she whispered.

I sat up and held a stuffed Garfield to my stomach. "Hey," Lisa said the moment she heard my wilted corsage rustle against the phone, "I'm sorry about what happened at the prom."

I nodded on my end, but didn't respond.

"Look. I don't understand what happened," she said. "Everyone was upset because Josh seemed so hurt about you breaking up with him. Things got out of control. I'm really sorry."

From where I stood, Josh hadn't looked upset last night.

I wiped a tear. "You know Lisa," I said my voice breaking. "I didn't break up with my friends. I broke up with him."

I imagined the discussion Lisa had with my ex-friends on my behalf. Even in elementary school, when the school bully sought me out, Lisa had been the peacemaker. We had been together since kindergarten. Deep inside, I wanted to ask how many minutes had passed before Josh asked Emily to the prom. But it didn't matter. Right now nothing mattered.

"I just wanted you to know I'm sorry and I would like to put this behind us… if you're okay with that." Lisa said.

An hour later, Lisa arrived at my house with a box of Heavenly Hash ice cream. Our friendship resumed where we left off. Gradually, my ex-friends returned, except for Emily.

She and Josh walked down the aisle shortly after graduation, and I started walking my own path.

~Renea Winchester

"Ever since my heart was broken
it grew back a lot stronger."

Like Glass

Your work is to discover your world
and then with all your heart give yourself to it.
~Buddha

He could see through me, just like glass.

When I met Rich, I was young, confused, and ready to explore the world. I was twelve, soon-to-be thirteen, counting down the weeks until I entered high school.

Rich and I met through a mutual friend, and though he was the quietest, most mysterious person I had ever met, something about the intensity of his shyness intrigued me. The chemistry between us was gravitational: soon, we were the best of friends, and in three years, he became my unrelated brother, my other half, my confidant.

One night, when we had our usual Friday night sleepover, which consisted of watching Disney movies and playing Metallica songs on his many guitars, something went wrong. As I settled into my nest on the top bunk of his bed, I felt something stir in my stomach—like something bigger than me and beyond my control was about to happen. Partially scared and mostly curious, I hopped into Rich's bed and asked him if he felt this overwhelming anxious feeling, too. He looked into my eyes deeply, pulled me close, and we kissed.

And we didn't stop kissing for years after that.

Our relationship grew rapidly—too fast for either of us to try to stop it. Our close friendship became a codependent, borderline-unhealthy teenage marriage. Since we were best friends years before we dated, he already knew me completely: he had my flaws pinpointed to perfection, my every move memorized. Sentences I hadn't even thought of yet were already being mouthed by him.

Just as he had learned to study me, I, too knew him inside and out. I knew the reason for the sad look in his brown eyes. I had listened to countless stories of his family's past, and never questioned the screaming from his parents in the other room of his house. From the tender age of twelve, I had been exposed to the truth his walls had hidden—the rest of the world, including our friends, never knew about his abusive father or cocaine-addicted mother. Those secrets were kept between us.

When I told him the truth, the words pricked and cut my throat, just like glass.

Though my feelings for Rich were strong, I somehow knew they were not durable. I began to realize that although I truly did love him, what I felt for him was not true love. He was my best friend, my world, and while my arms wanted to protect him, my heart wanted to be free.

Rich's disheartening past was beginning to catch up to him—his home life was destroying his confidence. He had dropped out of high school and lost all motivation to pursue his dream of being a musician. His abusive father had finally broken his hardened exterior and Rich was now becoming bruised from the inside out.

Whenever I talked to him, he was miserable. He cried all the time and cut his wrists constantly. The only thing that ever made him happy, the only reason he would stop drinking himself into unconsciousness or stop carving his flesh, was me. Every night he would hold onto me so tight, as if I were his last bit of hope and I might quickly float away. His intensity began to scare me—I was his everything, but unfortunately, I didn't feel the same. During high school, I had other friends, activities and clubs to keep me busy, while Rich just sat at home and cried and waited for me to come over.

Soon, the stress Rich piled upon me became unbearable. I was the only source of happiness Rich had, and the responsibility of keeping him sane, blissful, and alive was too suffocating.

At this point, high school was almost over and I realized days before graduation that I had spent the prime four years of my life taking care of my best friend. I needed to take care of myself.

I got up the strength and courage to talk to Rich and finally release myself from the web of attachment I had allowed myself to get caught up in.

I drove to his house, and as he met me at the door with bright eyes and an overwhelming smile, I felt nauseous and dizzy at the thought of how he would react to the truth I was about to unveil: I was leaving him, and things would never be the same.

When I left him, his heart fell to the floor and shattered into millions of pieces, just like glass.

From what his family told me, Rich was on suicide watch the first few weeks after I left him. From what his friends told me, Rich didn't talk to or see any of his friends for months after. From what he told me, he lost the one thing he lived for, and no longer felt the need to live.

I know that Rich would never intentionally hurt me, but the severe depression he endured broke my heart, and the pain between the two of us was too much to bear.

It hurt me more than anything to leave him, but I know for my own happiness, my own life, and my own future, I couldn't be tied down by him any longer. I was going off to college soon, and had to let go of my high school commitments. Finding a social niche and making solid friendships is hard enough in high school, and doing it with a depressed, estranged boyfriend attached at my side made it nearly impossible.

Every once in a while I still cry when I think about Rich. I feel guilty and angry and sad for hurting him, but I know I ultimately feel better knowing no one but myself is depending on me for happiness.

Looking back, I can hardly count how much Rich has truly given me: he taught me how to read music, how to properly hold a pet snake, and how to laugh at myself in embarrassing situations. He taught me the importance of self-reliance, and the consequences of codependency. He taught me why honesty is better than lying, and that sometimes taking care of yourself can unfortunately be at the expense of someone else.

I learned that, in life, sometimes letting go of the past is the first step to moving toward a future. Years later, we have glued the pieces of our friendship back together, but the scars from our relationship years before are still visible.

Just like cracks in broken glass.

~Alexi Leigh

Too Much to Sacrifice

We are all primary numbers divisible only by ourselves.
~Jean Guitton

I'm so horribly sorry
But I can't live life this way
To fall in love, I've sold myself
A price too high to pay.

My interests became yours.
And your interests became mine.
And from the outside in
We were doing fine.

This warm comforting net
I fell into with a sigh.
But I awoke so startled
That my world was passing by.

Somewhere along the line
I lost what made me "me"
It seemed like I had given up
My own identity.

Countless hours talking
And late nights on the phone.
I realize we were both afraid
That we'd wind up alone.

Clinging for the wrong reasons
"In love" we thought we were.
It pains my heart to say
That I'm not really sure.

There will always be a place for you
Right here in my heart.
But I have to let you go
To let my own life start.

We're sacrificing way too much
Our hopes, our goals, our dreams
To make this thing work out
It's not as simple as it seems.

Living solely for each other
We're standing still; so still.
And we've both got a hole
That only we can only fill.

So this goodbye is not a final one.
I love you as a friend.
But I just need to let you go
To let our lives begin.

~Katie Hankins

The Broken Boy before Me

Fear is the father of courage and the mother of safety.
~Henry H. Tweedy

Jake and I dated for three years, during which his home life fell apart. When his parents failed to show him the love he needed, he clung to me, believing that I was the only person who would ever love him. It was this conviction of his, I'm sure, that forced him to see me as both a mother figure and a girlfriend. He began to speak of marriage and harassed me for my grades that outshone his. While I knew that logically this was wrong, I stuck by him and hoped things would pass.

Finally, in our last week of tenth grade, I reached a breaking point as I evaded questioning stares on my way out of the school auditorium. I'd just won an academic award, and my name echoed over the applause. As I shuffled up on stage, I burst into tears. I was ashamed of my achievements and myself. And I knew that was just... wrong. Finally, I knew.

The confrontation that followed was ugly, ending in his decision to dump me because I refused to fail on purpose. I felt hollow and empty, but I couldn't take him back. Not even when he began to beg for forgiveness.

I found comfort in family and friends who I knew would be there, but finding no sympathy in his home, Jake resorted to desperation.

Verbal insults turned to physical threats—not to me, but to himself. He'd wait for me outside school, pounding his head into walls, carving my initials into his ankles with scissors, and sometimes snarling suicidal threats. The hopeless anger that blazed in his eyes frightened me, and I couldn't bring myself to fight back when he slammed me up against walls and threatened me in the hallways. In complete denial, I watched his decline until a friend alerted the office. When hospitalization failed to reverse things, he transferred schools.

A few weeks had passed since his transfer, and each time he had called, it took every ounce of self-control in my body to ignore him, telling myself it was for his own good. I had managed to avoid him pretty well so far, but when I attended a concert featuring a mutual friend's band, I wasn't sure how much longer I could hope to elude him.

Leaning against the wall of the venue with my friend Nina, we chatted until the first loud notes rang out. The crowd surged together, and in the brief moment that I was caught in the flow of people, my heart froze, gripped by the icy fingers of a sudden observation:

His hat.

His Metallica hat. It had to be his. In the flickering lights and pulsing strobes, it bobbed around on a head that I couldn't quite see but was sure belonged to him.

Charged with adrenaline, I shoved my way over to Nina, who turned and frowned at the panic on my face. Leaning to shout into her ear, I suddenly felt her stiffen and grab me by the arm. Confused, I looked down and realized that the hand closed tight in a rigor mortis grip around my forearm was much larger, broader, and hairier than hers....

I whipped around and was suddenly face-to-face with desperate, bloodshot eyes and an unkempt, stubbly beard. Wordlessly, he dragged me off towards the entrance, pulling me by my arm as I struggled against him, digging my feet into the wooden floors and clawing at his unrelenting grasp.

Finally, in a less crowded section of the venue, Jake turned sharply and pinned me up against the wall in one fluid spin. As my shoulders hit the rough bricks, I squinted back tears and leaned away from him, in a futile attempt to guard myself from what I knew I was about to hear.

"Michelle." His voice was a strange mix of crazed anger and naked despair. "Michelle!" he repeated. The word was demanding and hopeless all at once. He gave a shuddering sob and his eyes blazed with fury, locking onto my tear-blurred gaze as he bellowed, "I GAVE YOU THREE YEARS OF MY LIFE! WHY WON'T YOU GIVE ME THREE SECONDS OF YOURS?!"

"Stop!" I yelled. "Stop! STOP IT!" I hung my head and slumped, crying out of frustration and helplessness.

"Hey, kid! Let go of her!" a security guard moved toward Jake.

In that one moment, his grip loosened slightly, and I jerked away from him as Nina grabbed my hand. We ran, confused spectators blurring into black shadows as we raced down the hallway, hearing Jake's pounding footsteps behind us as he gave chase.

Nina and I hesitated when we reached the sidewalk, and as Jake caught up to us I braced myself for his rage. To my surprise, he continued straight past us, zigzagging madly around as though he was unsure exactly where he was going. He stopped beside a rusty parking meter, the tarnished metal caked with mud and grime. Nina and I watched, confused, and he met my gaze for a moment with an intense and yet alarmingly empty stare. Suddenly, he turned toward the meter, grabbed it by the metal limbs, and began to bash his forehead into it.

Frozen by dismay and horror, I stood helplessly as the sickening thud of skull on metal sounded over and over and over again, like the pounding of a sordid drum. Finally, he looked up and met my stare dead-on once more, his hood casting an eerie shadow over his face. A dark river ran down the center, oozing over his upper lip and into his mouth.

"This is what you like, isn't it?! Do you like it when I'm in pain?!" he demanded, the heavy trail of blood seeping between his brows from the gash in his forehead. Too paralyzed with shock and revulsion to respond, I simply gaped at him.

He spat at my feet, the bloody saliva landing in a nauseating puddle on the dirty sidewalk. All of my limbs felt suspended—I couldn't think, I couldn't move, I couldn't breathe... As my world started to spin and I started to fall, his bloody face and fiery eyes were the last to fade into blackness. I felt the security guard's arms hold me up, and vaguely heard him shouting for someone to call an ambulance. None of it mattered, though. All I could think about was the broken boy before me and the crimson stains spreading in vivid contrast to the pale cement below.

Since that night, his eyes have haunted my dreams, never quite fading even as his desperate calls and threats slowly tapered off. Although those nights were torture beyond my wildest imagination, I can honestly say that somehow I emerged a stronger person. Looking back, I can clearly see the emotional abuse Jake put me through, even though, at the time, I didn't recognize it for what it was. The scariest aspect of this entire ordeal, however, may be the other girls I've since met who face the exact same situation. All I can do is offer my story and a helping hand, since the hardest things to see are often directly in front of your face.

~Michelle Vanderwist

Without a Trace

He who fears something gives it power over him.
~Moorish Proverb

We were in her apartment, sprawled on her bed watching the TV flicker with the constant movement of the people on the screen. Our eyes were halfway closed when the phone rang. We both looked at each other. I prayed it wasn't him. I looked at her and the sadness in her eyes reappeared and was as tangible as ever.

"Do you want me to answer it?" I asked her, and she nodded. "Hello?"

"Let me talk to her, Lauren," he demanded. It was Rubin.

Amber and I had come home from a friend's party and Rubin, her boyfriend, must have found out. According to Rubin, Amber wasn't allowed to go anywhere unless it was with him, so going to our friend's party was a major violation of the rules.

"No," I coldly responded. I had been through this with them too many times, I knew what was coming if I allowed him to talk to her.

"Okay fine, I'll just ask you. Did both of you go to Matt's party?"

"No," I said with the same iciness as before.

"Let me talk to her!" he commanded.

Amber took the phone from my hand and put it to her ear. I could hear him screaming and I could see the pain in her eyes. He was telling her what a lousy girlfriend she was and how she was an alcoholic. He called her hurtful names for going to the party and talking to guys.

That was the thing about Rubin—he was excessively jealous and overprotective. Amber and Rubin had been going out for almost a year. At the beginning of their relationship, things were "flawless," as Amber had put it. He would buy her flowers and do nice little things for her. But over the last few months, things seemed to be going downhill. Amber would come to school with swollen red eyes as if she had been crying all night. I had asked her what was wrong and she had told me everything.

"Rubin keeps calling me and yelling at me for no reason," she told me after school one day. "He keeps saying mean things to me and I break up with him every time. Then he calls back an hour later crying and telling me he'll never do it again. But he does it a few nights later. Lauren, I don't know what to do."

Weeks followed and things seemed to be getting better. They had an occasional fight here and there, but nothing too big. That is, until the night of Matt's party. Rubin had called before we left for the party and told her that there would be people watching Amber to make sure she didn't do anything wrong. Someone must have given him incorrect information, because he was yelling at her for no reason.

"I'm coming over right now! The door better be unlocked!" I heard him scream right before he hung up.

"Do you think he's serious?" she asked me.

It pained me to see her with someone who was always treating her like this. The constant verbal abuse was apparent on her face, and tears swelled in her hazel eyes. The tears ran down her face, leaving black mascara marks on her rosy cheeks. Then we heard a pounding at the door.

BANG! BANG! BANG!

"Open up, Amber!" he screamed. "I'm not messing around! OPEN UP!"

My heart dropped to the bottom of my stomach. He had really come. I was struck with instant fear and my heart sank even deeper in my stomach. The door opened and he pushed himself through. His eyes were bloodshot, and his breath smelled like alcohol. He was drunk. He grasped Amber's neck and pushed her into the wall.

I stood in the doorway stunned. What was he doing? I worked up my courage and jumped on his back, making him fall clumsily to the floor with a thud. He quickly got up, clearly unbothered by the fall and my attempts to subdue him. He saw me coming after him and pushed me against the wall.

Then he went back to Amber. Still scared and confused, I watched. His arm lifted above his head into a fist and I watched him pound Amber hard in the face with all of his might. I screamed. The impact of the punch made Amber's head hit the kitchen cabinet and she collapsed onto the tile floor.

I kicked Rubin out of Amber's apartment and called an ambulance. Amber woke up in the hospital eleven hours later with her mom and brother by her side. Her mom was fuming mad and I couldn't blame her. I told the story to the cops and they quickly arrested Rubin. Weeks passed and I still hadn't talked to Amber. I called her house and a voice recording told me to check the number and dial again. I went to her apartment and knocked on the door. When no one answered, I contacted her landlord. I was told she had moved without notice.

Rubin served a month at a juvenile detention hall but he was able to get out early when he agreed to take anger management classes. Sometimes I see Rubin in the hallways and I cringe. The very sight of him brings back terrible memories and makes me sick. I see him with another girl, and I wonder if she knows or if she'll ever find out.

Amber's gone now, and I'll never be able to talk to her again. I'm glad she won't have to go through anything like that night again, but I wish I knew where she was. I'm really going to miss her.

~Laura Castro

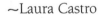

33

The Persuasion of Him

Never violate the sacredness of your individual self-respect.
~Theodore Parker

I said I didn't want to
And he said he understood.
He said it didn't matter
But I knew it probably would.
He told me it wasn't important
That he'd love me either way.
It felt so good to hear that,
But he tried again that day.
He said, "But I'm your boyfriend
We've been together for so long.
It's been two weeks since I've seen you
I don't get it — what's wrong?"

It's not as though I'm innocent,
But the timing wasn't right.
He told me not to be self-conscious
As he turned off the light.
I lay down submissively
Hating myself inside.
He asked if I was okay,
I looked at him and lied.

When I told him I didn't feel well
He said he'd make it quick
I wanted to feel love
But all I felt was sick.
After it was finally over
I walked to the bathroom mirror.
The vision that was once a blur
Had become a whole lot clearer.
As I tried to rationalize my actions,
I took one look at myself and knew
That what was left was a small fraction
And there was nothing I could do.

I still believe he loves me,
My words just weren't so clear.
My voice can be so soft
Maybe he just didn't hear....

~Laura Campbell

34

Against My Will

You may be deceived if you trust too much,
but you will live in torment unless you trust enough.
~Frank Crane

People say time heals all wounds, but it's been a year since that night with Bobby, and the memory of what happened is still as fresh and painful as if it were yesterday.

Everyone always told me that Bobby and I were the perfect couple. I think they meant we looked good together. His dark hair and olive complexion contrasted with my blond hair and fair skin. He was a football star; I was a cheerleader. He was outgoing and liked being in charge; I was content to follow his lead. Bobby decided what parties we went to, who we saw there, and which fast food restaurant we'd stop at on the way home.

I never gave much thought to the fact that Bobby always got his way. That is, until the night Bobby wanted something I wasn't prepared to give him. We were in his car on some deserted road when I realized things were out of control. We'd gone there before, but Bobby always quit when I put up the stop sign. That night he ran right through it. I fought him, but it wasn't enough. Bobby said he'd get what he wanted, and he did.

I can still hear the squeal of car tires as Bobby pulled away from the curb in front of my house. He ran the stop sign at the end of the street in his hurry to get away. I was crying so hard I could barely see to get my key in the door. After letting myself in as quietly as possible, I headed for my room. Even though it was May, I piled on clothes—long underwear, winter pajamas, my bathrobe—then I pulled the covers up over my head. Still, I couldn't stop shaking. That night I dreamed the whole thing was happening all over again.

I woke up early the next morning and headed for the shower. I turned the water on so hot it burned, and then I scrubbed my skin over and over until it was fiery red. I didn't feel any cleaner. I remember wishing I could reach into my brain and wash away the memory of what happened. After my shower, I took a bath. Then another shower. None of it helped. I could still feel and smell him on me. I still felt dirty, violated.

As I was drying myself, I stared at my body in the mirror. I kept thinking I'd look different somehow, that there'd be a physical sign of what had happened. I didn't even have a bruise.

I was startled by a knock on the bathroom door followed by my mom's voice. "Honey, are you all right? What are you doing? You've been in there over an hour."

I told my mom I had a headache and that the steam from the shower seemed to help. Lying to her just added to my feelings of guilt. She and my dad thought Bobby was wonderful, but they'd warned me against parking and spending too much time alone with him. How could I tell her that Bobby had raped me? She'd probably be mad and just yell at me for letting him take me out on that deserted road. I thought she'd say I was asking for trouble.

I wrapped a towel around myself and headed for my bedroom. As I got dressed my mind whirled from thought to thought. What do I do now? Who can I talk to? Will anyone believe me?

I realized the importance of my last question because of something stupid I'd done a few weeks before. I was sitting around with my girlfriends talking about the guys we were dating when the topic of sex came up. I was astonished to hear my friends all say they were sleeping with their boyfriends. They acted as though it were the most natural thing in the world for a fifteen-year-old girl. Then someone—Debbie, I think—asked me if I was sleeping with Bobby. Well, with eight pairs of eyes on me, I did the dumbest thing I've ever done in my life. I lied. I said I was.

While everyone around me nodded their approval, I longed to take my words back. "It's a lie!" I wanted to scream. "I only said that because I was afraid you'd laugh at me if I said I've been trying real hard to hold Bobby off. He's pressuring me to go all the way, but I don't want to do it."

Now it was too late. I knew after what I'd told them that none of my friends would believe me if I said Bobby had raped me last night.

The tears came as I realized the trouble I'd gotten myself into. There was nowhere to turn, no one to talk to. What was I supposed to do? I didn't have any answers.

I faked being sick on Monday so I wouldn't risk running into Bobby at school, but Mom saw through my act. She thought I'd forgotten to study for a test and made me go anyway. I saw Bobby in the hallway between classes. He just grinned, waved, and kept on going. I was angry and relieved at the same time. I wanted to confront him, to expose him in front of all our friends for the scum that he was, but at the same time I was relieved he just passed by.

Days, then weeks passed, and I never heard from Bobby. I tried to put the memory of that night out of my mind. When my friends asked what happened with me and Bobby, I would feel the battle begin. Part of me wanted to tell them everything, hoping they'd believe and sympathize with me. The other part of me knew they'd never accept the flip-flop in my story. I'd be called vindictive, and I'd be accused of trying to hurt Bobby's reputation. In the end, I just told them we split up. It was the simplest way out.

As more time passed, I withdrew from my friends and family. I'd sit in my room with the lights out, replaying that night over and over in my mind, trying to figure out a way to make things end differently. I went over my words and actions trying to find something that indicated to Bobby that I wanted to have sex with him. I couldn't find anything, but I still felt guilty.

If only I'd fought harder, I told myself. If only I'd screamed. If only I hadn't gone with him in the first place. I knew I couldn't change what had happened, but I put myself through this torture day after day. I took long, hot showers as often as I could, but still there was no washing away the reality of what had happened. Even after a year the wound was as raw as ever.

Yet I know now it's time for the healing to begin. I've heard there are counselors who can help you deal with something like this. And I should finally tell my parents the truth. They've been there for me all the time, even though I've pulled away from them. I'm ready to learn to trust people again, so I take the first healing step by trusting my story to you.

~As told to Teresa Cleary

Chapter 5

Teens Talk

HIGH SCHOOL

Fitting In...
or Not

*I've learned to take time for myself
and to treat myself with a great deal of love and respect
'cause I like me... I think I'm kind of cool.*

~Whoopi Goldberg

Chicken Soup
for the Soul

Ingrained

You don't get harmony when everybody sings the same note.
~Doug Floyd

Our shoes,
all the same kind.
Our pants,
all the same cut.
Our shirts,
all the same style.
It's how we've been conditioned:
to all look the same.
We're told, in school,
to "be ourselves".
But our peers
never let us forget
what's "in",
what's "trendy",
what's "cool",
so as not to
Stand Out.
So much so
have we been taught
to blend in

that even the snowflakes,
when they land on the window
with their intricate designs,
know to discard their unique patterns
and morph into
tiny, identical
droplets of water.

~Jennifer Lynn Clay

Library Sanctuary

The eternal quest of the individual human being is to
shatter his loneliness.
~Norman Cousins

I'm sitting alone on the steps, eating cold pizza from my brown paper sack. Actually, I'm not entirely alone. If someone were to look at the group of students on the steps, it would appear that I was sitting at the side of the pack. But the truth is that I really don't know these girls that well; I only wish I did. And it's not as if I am new to this school, although I often feel like that's the case. No, I've known these girls for almost ten years, and yet I feel like I can't talk to them. My friend Tracy is sick today and I have no one to eat lunch with. So I sit at the outside of this group and just listen, pretending that I belong here.

Never has a slice of cold pizza seemed so large or taken so long to eat. I want to finish it so I can remove myself from these steps of torture, and yet I never want to finish it because I have no plan for the rest of lunch. I have nowhere to go and no one to hang out with because Tracy is gone. I have an entire half hour to fill. I envy people who have friends and things to talk about with them, and the irony is that no one would ever guess that I feel totally alone. I'm in the school plays, on the track team, I wrote for the school paper for a while... but I feel as if I don't know anyone at all.

I chew. Do I even like cold pizza? It actually tastes sort of rubbery, doesn't it? I always fancied myself as a cold pizza lover and now

I'm not sure that I am. I don't think I ever noticed the pools of oily fat that congeal in the pepperoni. I relate to those pools of oily fat. They're always on the pizza, but no one likes them, and everyone sort of wishes they would go away. But they're accepted as part of the pizza-eating experience. I am congealed oily fat.

"Hi." Movement behind me. It's Kathryn and Courtney, two girls who never seem to be aware of or ruffled by their own less-than-popular status in any way. And neither one ever seems to be sick either, stranding her friend.

"Hi," I say, unable to think of anything else worthy of conversation.

They turn to each other and talk about the upcoming weekend. I've lost my window of opportunity to join the conversation. I turn my body slightly so I'm sort of facing them, but not too much in case they get annoyed that I'm hovering. I really don't have anything to say. I never have anything to say.

I'm finished with my pizza and can't bring myself to eat my apple. I'm not hungry at all anymore, and this anxiety is making me sick to my stomach. I stuff everything back in my bag, and give a halfhearted wave to Kathryn and Courtney ("KayandSee!" as they're sometimes called—I can't decide if that's cute or cringe-worthy) and head to the bathroom, tossing my lunch sack on the way.

In the bathroom, I lock myself in a stall and just lean against the wall. No one is in here, so I don't feel any pressure to leave. I hate when I hide from the world in the bathroom only to find people there, forcing me to enter and leave at a normal rate lest I appear to be having digestive problems. Peace, to me, is an unoccupied bathroom. I really want to pull out a book but that's probably too weird. I don't want people to wonder why I'm in the bathroom with a book—I don't want to be that girl.

Ok, now what? I've only been in here for three minutes. But if someone saw me go in, then it's about time for me to leave. Seventeen minutes until the end of lunch. It's time to bring out Plan B: Library.

I find sanctuary in the library, where I hide among the stacks pretending I'm looking for something for class. I grab a literary-looking tome and take the long way through the stacks to a table. If I time this right, I'll never have to sit down at all. I pass slowly by the books, pretending as if I'm looking for something, noting all the titles. There are so many books that I've never read. It's as if they've all been published simply to keep me occupied during this Tracy-less lunch hour.

The bell rings. Fifteen minutes is over already. I feel as if the weight of the entire school has been lifted. I'm safe. Relieved of the burden of carrying this heavy book that's masking my insecurity. I toss it onto the re-shelve cart and head to biology. I'll be dissecting a frog today. Nothing like the innards of an amphibian to get my mind off my lonely lunchtime.

~Karen Woodward

"Got time for a friend, or are you overbooked?"

Finding My Way

He who sings scares away his woes.
~Cervantes

Don't drink, don't smoke—what do you do?

From the outside, I was a goody two-shoes in high school. I never had a sip of alcohol, never tried cigarettes, and the only parties I went to were parent-supervised. I didn't even date boys.

Instead, I spent my four years with men twice my age, ruining my hearing.

I was a concert junkie.

I'm a loner Dottie, a rebel.

"So are you straight edge or what?" they would ask. My fellow class-mates assigned labels to me at will, puzzled by my nonconformity and non-partying. Sometimes the popular kids perused my concert pictures, but their weekend activities consisted of drinking beer and flirting with cute quarterbacks. While they would see large pop acts like *NSYNC once a year, I addictively attended concerts bi-monthly. My cynicism told me they thought I was weird, but I'll never know the truth.

Pretending not to care what they thought was a satisfactory defense mechanism. All I wanted to do was listen to music. Concert venues were the only place I felt free. No parents, no restrictions, just me and the music ringing in my ears.

When the first guitar chords rang out, the adrenaline was so addictive I could fly. Crammed against one hundred strangers, I'd let the music take me away for hours. For the first time in my life, I found I belonged somewhere. My heart was at home in a run-down, badly lit room with a makeshift stage and an unknown band.

Many of my concert experiences were extraordinary: backstage at the Warped Tour, onstage at the Grove of Anaheim, meeting a member of Green Day (my favorite band), but those were merely moments. The one experience that continues to stand out, inspire me, and shape my world is more than an event worth flaunting. His name is Scottie Somers.

You're the meaning in my life, you're the inspiration.

Towering over my 5'2" skinniness, Scottie was a cool bassist in the band Lefty. I was an awkward, rock-loving fifteen-year-old. We met after a concert he had just played with another band I loved. Scottie and his bandmates were the only musicians I'd met who treated fans like friends. They talked to me and my best friend for hours, and their music was great, too. I was hooked.

I stumbled upon Scottie's e-mail address a few months after the concert, which commenced my Scottie Support System. Anytime I had a bad day, his encouraging words always lifted me up. "Hope you're doing great, you're beautiful." "Hope to see you soon, My Melissa Baby." I cherished every e-mail—I still have each one printed out, kept safe inside a journal.

When 9/11 happened, Scottie reminded me to stay safe. When I was applying for college, Scottie hoped I would get into my first choice. Scottie was there through my change in best friends and the inevitably hard fallout.

Nothing cheered me up more than watching his band onstage, and as soon as he saw me at every show, he enveloped me in the biggest hug possible. But he spread his warmth to more than just me. I watched Scottie talk to his fans, and his selflessness restored my faith in people. Scottie accepted others for who they were, and he had no desire to make me something I wasn't. He was the first genuine person I felt that I'd ever met. I now had something to strive towards.

...Until you shared your secret with me.

Scottie never told me he had Cystic Fibrosis. He was always in the hospital, but I never knew why. One day I deduced the truth, and suddenly all the hospital trips made sense. As a concerned seventeen-year-old wanting to learn more, I wrote my report for health class on Cystic Fibrosis.

What I read concerned me: Cystic Fibrosis, a genetic disease with no cure, affecting the lungs and digestive system. Most don't live past age thirty. I secretly worried about Scottie from then on, but never told him I knew. "I had my gall bladder taken out," he would write, and I prayed he was okay. When I saw him, I'd hug tighter, smile wider, and appreciate him more. It was my first real life lesson: the people you love aren't going to be around forever, so cherish them.

Eventually, Scottie's band broke up and I didn't get to see him anymore. Our friendship was strictly through e-mail, probably because of the formidable age gap between us (even more pronounced when I was underage). I graduated high school and didn't get into my first choice college after all, but I ended up at one that suited me better. I was Scottie-less for years. He stopped writing me uplifting e-mails and I had no other way of contacting him. All I hoped was that I would see him one more time.

Better thank your lucky stars.

Miraculously, years later, I found Scottie thanks to the wonders of the Internet. Reunited at last, we were like pen pals who had lived on opposite sides of the world. And I have seen him more than once since then. Today, my tiresome high school days are long over and he no longer plays in a band. Much has changed for both of us. At twenty-four, I am helping adults with developmental disabilities, and he, at forty-one (a CF miracle), founded Living the Dream and is making dreams come true for children with terminal illnesses. Turns out our passions, although new, are still the same.

Even though I didn't do everything the popular kids did, I am further ahead in finding my place. I hardly go to concerts anymore, but Scottie is still family to me. My experiences in those days shaped how I see the world today. I have no regrets. While taking a different path, I learned that it's okay to stray and find your own way. After all, the road less traveled has better music.

~Melissa Townsend

Having, Losing, Finding Myself

It's all right letting yourself go,
as long as you can get yourself back.
~Mick Jagger

I t is ironic that my academic downfall began with an official school form. One little checkmark in one little box can change everything.

All of my life, I have embraced the neat, the structured, and the planned. I have basked in my ability to excel at almost everything I have attempted. My grades have been high, my extracurriculars have been impressive, and my volunteer sheet has been overflowing. Up until last semester, I was every parent's dream child.

And I was all right with this. Why wouldn't I be? All of my friends were like me. We would get together to study over popcorn, and congratulate ourselves upon scoring a 100% or getting chosen to make a speech for student council. I thrived on positive attention and busy schedules, and so did everyone I chose to associate with.

Imagine my surprise when I discovered we were a minority. Newsflash: most high school students would choose a concert over extra math homework. They would choose the mall over volunteering to sell fair trade coffee. They would have, in their words, a life.

This is where my story starts—upon the realization that I was, in fact, not cool. The thought occurred to me the first day I walked into my drama class. I had checked the little box beside "drama," instead of the one marked "foods" back at the end of the ninth grade when I had been asked to choose my future courses. To this day I don't know why, but I'm glad I did.

As I stood in the doorway to my new class, I took in a strange sight. A group of people I didn't recognize were sprawled on the black boxes and the dirty carpet. One boy was alone in the middle of the room, dancing to his music and strumming on an imaginary guitar. A girl was flicking a lighter on and off, and the guy next to her was painting his nails black. I was scared.

As the weeks wore on, I got to know my fellow drama students, and a second mind-blowing realization hit me hard; they were genuinely nice. I started spending more and more time with them, entranced by their sense of humor, their ability to listen and care, and just who they were in general.

My new friends were completely different from anyone I had ever known before. They knew who they were and didn't care what others thought: So what if I only wear black and draw tears on my face? So what if I ride around on transits without a destination because I like watching the people? So what if I'm gay? So what if my shoes never match and I wore the same sweater every day this week? This is the way they thought, and as I slowly got to know them, I liked them even more for their quirks. They weren't freaks; they were people who refused to surrender to the norm, and were therefore rejected by the people who followed more mainstream lifestyles. Unfortunately, another one of their favorite phrases was, "So what if I'm failing?" That one quickly began to make an impression on me.

By December, I was spending most of my free time with the new clique. I no longer seemed to be able to complete the things my parents and teachers felt were important. Namely, my homework. My average plummeted and that created tension at home.

"Why?" my parents cried, their eyes bulging and arms flailing dramatically, "You've never been the one with school problems before! Where did we go wrong?"

I tried to explain that my outlook on life had changed: "Stop making such a big deal out of it. Nobody went wrong anywhere. But I'm not going to waste my time with schoolwork... it's not teaching me anything useful anyways!" I yelled impatiently, "I don't need school! I want to go to concerts and write poetry! And then I want to work for Greenpeace and travel and write and play the guitar and...." I stopped. "Dad? Are you alright?" As it turns out, he wasn't.

I was grounded for two weeks, and was expected to pass my next precalc test with a 95%. If I didn't do that, I was grounded for another week. Parties were banned, as were shopping and going to friends' houses. Basically, there was no point in living. My whole newly created life came crumbling down around me.

At least, that was my initial reaction. However, all of the time cooped up at home gave me plenty of studying time. I managed to pass my precalc test with the 95% demanded of me, and was freed from my parental prison. Now I could see my friends again! Except... I had enjoyed returning to my old ways. The pull of order and routine countered the pull of hanging out and having fun. Suddenly, I didn't know what to do.

As it turns out, I could have the best of both worlds. I managed to pull my grades up while maintaining my social life. I was forced to give up a little of each, though. My average went down 2% (a miraculously low amount, due to a lot of make-up work) and my number of outings decreased as well.

So what have I learned? That the drama room is messy and probably should be cleaned. That although my dad "supports Greenpeace and many of their endeavors," he "doesn't think it is the best career path" for me (we'll see about that). Oh, and that there is such a thing as a happy medium—that last one is pretty important. I've been successfully dividing my time between school and friends and prioritizing accordingly. I still believe in most of what I told my parents. High school isn't only about learning from a textbook. It's also about learning who you are as a person, developing social skills, and discovering what you want to do with the rest of your life.

I understand all of that now, thanks to a little check mark in a little box that changed everything.

~Annie Summers

Boomerang

Where thou art — that — is Home.
~Emily Dickinson

"**N**o way in hell am I coming! You can't seriously expect me to leave this place," I raged on and on. "Why doesn't anyone care about what I want?!"

My parents had just told me that we would be leaving Delhi. It wasn't the first time that we had been transferred to a new place. My dad was in the Indian Navy, and moving from place to place was pretty much a part of our life. But I had lived in Delhi during the best teen years, the years of "firsts" — first girlfriend, first kiss, first razor, first temptations, and so on — and it was especially hard leaving the place. I was extremely angry with my parents for being so insensitive to my needs. I threw tantrums and stopped only after I realized that they weren't having any positive effects and were spoiling my last days with my friends. However, that didn't lessen my resentment towards my parents, who I thought were being unreasonable.

A week passed and we were finally in Mumbai, the place I was sure I would hate. Pretty soon, we had settled into our new home, but I still only felt attached to Delhi and all I did was mope around the house. My parents encouraged me to get out of the house, find new friends, get familiar with the new city, and so on, but I was determined not to like the place and was also determined not to make my parents happy. I knew it was stupid, but I still wanted to prove a point. The two months during my summer vacation were the most boring two months I had ever endured. And they only further convinced me that Mumbai could never compare to Delhi.

School started soon, and my first few hours were spent cursing my fate. Then I met my classmates who, despite my pretty awful behavior, welcomed me into their circle of friends. School was the reason my perception of Mumbai changed, and it became the place where I acquired a new positive outlook. Soon, I opened up and even made friends in my colony. I was drawn back into the highs and lows of being a teenager.

The memory of Delhi faded away and was replaced by my new experiences in Mumbai. There were plenty of new firsts that I discovered in Mumbai—going to my first dance and performing on stage with my guitar for the first time were two of them. There were too many things to do, like flouting my parents' rules and hanging out with friends, that didn't allow me the time to miss Delhi. So life went on.

Until one fine day...

I was at home, strumming my guitar, when my Dad came home with a sheepish expression.

"What now?" I asked instinctively, sensing danger.

He told me.

"No way in hell am I coming!" I yelled. "You can't seriously expect me to leave this place." I raged on and on, "Why doesn't anyone care about what I want?!"

We had been transferred to Delhi.

~Siddart Rangachari

Without Limo, Luck, or Love

It took me a long time not to judge myself through someone else's eyes.
~Sally Field

Prom is a word fraught with symbols for any girl: the dress, the limo — and, obviously, the handsome date. In February, the whispers started. "I think Chris is going to ask me," Claire passed me via contraband note in English. My other best friend, Jess, was a hot commodity. Flipping her long highlighted hair over one shoulder, she never even thought about May 22nd, that date that loomed so threateningly on my horizon.

Potential boys were being gobbled up like unattended Rice Krispies treats. The New Boy, whose name I never bothered learning, but who hovered within my date radar, was taken by a short, round-faced girl from my Anatomy class. My friends were already planning their couples' limo ride. Claire giggled with Jess over seating charts, "Don't put me next to Rachel! I can't stand her!" They invited me dress shopping, but it was more of a token offer than a serious proposition. After all, I was still dateless.

Then it was April. Tickets were on sale. The real boyfriends were buying the whole $70 couples bill, the friends couples were splitting it $35-$35. I was eyeing the single person's ticket and wondering why there was a monetary penalty for being undesirable.

Jess and Claire fawned over their Nordstrom gowns. Jess was

going short and chic, in a tradition-breaking pink silk dress. Claire was going long and black with flashy jewelry. I obligingly looked into their closets and sighed, wondering when I could head home to a long, self-pitying wallow.

Why didn't I have a date? I wasn't sure, exactly. I'd never been really popular with the boys, always feeling that awkward teenage tension clamp my tongue in their presence. I could never seem to come up with the bold, clever remarks Claire did or the sweet normalcy of Jess. Halfway between the "I care too much" and the "I don't care at all" approach, I hung in dateless limbo.

With May drawing near, and desperation mounting, I drew up the courage to ask the only boy whom I could describe as a friend, James, after history class. "Just as friends," I hastily tacked on, my stomach churning with my morning bagel and cream cheese.

"I'm sorry," he replied, shouldering his book bag. "I'm not going."

"What?!" I squawked. "Why not?!"

"It's just a big waste of money that I don't have," he shrugged, heading out the door. "I'm not interested."

His philosophy intrigued me, but it didn't stifle my burning desire to go. I used it as a sort of ego armor, saying I was too conscious of prom's commercial consumption to go, but I knew the real reason: I was too afraid to go alone.

What would everybody think? Obviously, that I was a loser, that I wasn't pretty or cool enough to get even an average guy into my limo. I would show up, all gangly 5'10" me, and the music would stop just in time for the snickers and whispers to start. No thanks!

I came home from school with the same desolate look on my face for two weeks before my older brother, always the philanthropist, came up with the solution. Grinning ear to ear, he held up the phone. "Michael Fisher!" he exclaimed.

"What?" I asked.

"My friend, Mike," he said. "He says he'll go with you, no problem."

"No way," I replied. "I don't want to be the girl with the weird old guy who nobody knows. Plus, we can't go with any of my friends. They don't know him!"

"So go just you two!" my brother exclaimed, exasperated. "Take the minivan!"

All the self-consciousness in me rebelled. This whole plot reeked of weirdness. Prom was supposed to be a certain way — you were supposed to go in a limo, with your boyfriend or the senior quarterback, stopping for a nice dinner beforehand and heading to the coolest party afterwards. Saddled with Mike, I'd be ostracized: the girl who couldn't find anybody else.

But some small spark of defiance lit up in me, fed by my brother's insistent enthusiasm. "Really? He'll go?"

"Dude, he's on the phone right now! You just have to ask him!"

I pulled the receiver over, quickly blurted — before tainted reason could set in — "Mike, will you go to the prom with me?"

"Absolutely!" my brother's perpetually exuberant friend answered.

Yes, we split the ticket. And yes, Mike showed up in a pink tuxedo with a corsage the opposite color of my dress. And finally, we did take my parent's dented blue minivan.

Did my friends give me the time of day? No.

But did I have the time of my life? In the words of Mike, one of the truest people I've ever known because he stepped into that ballroom hoping to give me a memorable experience, not caring if anyone thought he was out of place or too old — "Absolutely!"

That was what he taught me: that only you can embarrass yourself, and only by being someone other than yourself. I'll never forget my limo-less, after-party-less prom, where I took a step to the left of the crowd — and didn't look back.

~Laurel Jefferson

The Academic Jock

I know not what the future holds,
but I know who holds the future.
~Author Unknown

I hate crutches. They slow you to a snail's pace and make your armpits ache. In elementary school, I always wanted to be on crutches, because they got special attention from all the teachers and looked really cool. Once I was actually on crutches, my body ached all over and my dreams of playing on the high school soccer team had been completely crushed. It was my sophomore year of high school, my last chance to at least be a benchwarmer, since all the starters would be the girls who played on the freshman team. The previous year I hadn't even had a chance to try out for soccer—tryouts started right after I busted my knee for the first time.

To say I'm a stubborn and willful person would be an understatement. After I first landed on crutches, I returned to the soccer field in two weeks, and within two minutes of the first half I dislocated the same knee. However, I wasn't deterred just yet. I harbored the hope that if I rested my knee for the remainder of the year, I would be able to try out for the high school JV soccer team the next fall. So I waited patiently and even finished a good season without injury. My optimism was high. Tryouts for the JV team started off with a bang, and the coach noticed me enough to use me as a demonstrator in some of the drills.

Then it happened. On the fourth day of tryouts, we were doing a simple passing drill when my turn came and I made my pass. I quickly turned around, pivoting on my twice-injured knee to return to the line—big mistake. My breath caught in my throat and my left leg went numb as my knee quickly popped abnormally. It was so quick that no one noticed. I was able to hobble my way through the rest of the tryout. The next day, I made an emergency doctor's appointment to make sure I could continue with tryouts. It turned out I couldn't—I was done. The towel had been thrown in for me.

Tryouts weren't over yet, but I knew what I had to do. I slowly made my way on my crutches to the coach's room and explained my situation; I wasn't going to be able to finish tryouts. He was nice enough about it. He told me he was sorry and thought I would've been a great asset to the team. Of course, I didn't want to hear that last part—now that I knew I would've made the team, I was in an even darker mood. What did I have now? Soccer was my pride, my core. Now I had nothing—no real future other than graduating high school, since I still wasn't sure if I wanted to go to college.

I hobbled my way to my English class and scribbled in the last couple of paragraphs to an essay that was due that morning. I was one of the few people who turned in handwritten essays, but it was the easiest way to do it and I didn't care.

"Ms. Bermudez, your essay please," snapped my English teacher. I ignored him as I wrote my last sentence and quickly held it up to his crossed arms.

"Sorry." I gave a weak smile, but I was in no mood to make up an excuse. He gave me one last glare and continued with the rest of his lecture. Just what I need, I thought. Someone else who thinks I'm a failure. The rest of the week passed in a blur and I spent the weekend sulking in bed, my knee iced and propped up.

Then Monday rolled around and I had a pleasant surprise waiting for me on my desk in English: an A- on the paper I had written partially in class the day it was due.

However, my triumph was short-lived. Before class ended, my English teacher told me I had to stay and talk to him after everyone left. I sulked in anticipation of the lecture I was about to receive.

Couldn't he see I was on crutches? Give me a break! It took me almost ten minutes to get from class to class.

"Ms. Bermudez, have you ever heard of the Academic Decathlon?" he started.

"No, I haven't. Why?" I asked suspiciously.

"Basically it's a competition with other schools in ten different academic tests including speech, interview, essay, literature, etc. I think you would be a great asset to our team. I'm one of the coaches and we meet twice a week after school. We expect you to study on your own in the meantime." He must have caught the face I made at the thought of taking tests and studying for fun, so he continued, "Ms. Bermudez, your half-ass work always gets you an A. You think quickly on your feet and you retain information like a sponge. I have a feeling you'd definitely place and win some medals in a few of the subject areas."

I laughed at his "half-ass" comment and said I'd give it a shot. Might as well. What else was I going to do with myself? Plus, it would be pretty cool to win some awards for the school, and it would look great on college apps if I decided on that route.

I can't lie and say that I didn't have fun over the three months of prep work before the competition. The team was an eclectic group of students because, as it turned out, the competition required students with all levels of GPAs—2.0, 3.0, 4.0. I was in the 3.0 group and carried my weight easily.

The day of the competition we were up against six other schools in our region. It was an all day event and my parents even showed up for the Super Quiz, which required students to sit on stage and answer questions in open competition. I couldn't help but smile as I heard my Dad cheer us on from the audience. It really was exciting.

I went home with three medals—two for second place in speech and first place in super quiz with the rest of the team. Who knew academics could be so rewarding? I had a gift for learning that I had never realized before, and now I was ready to exploit it. My time as a jock was over—not that I couldn't enjoy the occasional recreational sport—but I knew my future now revolved around academics, honors classes, AP courses, and eventually college. It turns out that when I lost the chance to play soccer, I found a new future for myself.

~Tanya Bermudez

Have Pump, Will Travel

Empty pockets never held anyone back.
Only empty heads and empty hearts can do that.
~Norman Vincent Peale

When I was in high school, I had a raft that I wrote "S.S. Rampage" on. I kept it alive in my garage with a bicycle pump, and moved it on the mooring by the New Haven Yacht Club with one big plastic oar. Despite the fact that if it overturned I would not even be able to tread water for a minute, I would career through the wakes of the yachts, a seaman at heart but a landlubber by nature.

The older kids would cruise by in hand-me-down canoes or paint-chipped rowboats and mock the S.S. Rampage, but I didn't care. The sun would be beating on my face, seagulls singing to me, and I decided I would just call the Coast Guard and tell them the other kids had cases of beer on board when I got back to shore, anyway.

Throughout the summer before my senior year, I worked at the yacht club. The job title was coxswain, which, according to Webster's Unabridged is, "a seaman in charge of a ship's boat in the absence of the officer." Little did I know that this would be only the first of several positions I would hold in my life where the words "in charge in the absence of" played an integral role.

Essentially, my duty was to bring yacht owners back and forth to their docked yachts on a tiny boat powered by what appeared to be a toy outboard engine. Getting this thing started was more difficult than the lawnmower back home that was passed down from my great-grandfather. My arm would ache so much after starting the engine every day that I could barely adjust the lawn chair that I would sleep on until the club members began to file back in.

Bringing these pompous yachtsmen out to their vessels was one thing; bringing them back in was something else altogether. They would cruise in, drop anchor, and blast their obnoxious boat horns three times as a way of alerting the coxswain to their needs. I was then to dash to the dock, hop into the yacht club boat, and fetch them and their freckled, debutante daughters.

One particular ride in, a snob of a fifteen-year-old spotted the S.S. Rampage, remarked that it was "sad," and then asked where the little boy was who must be its owner. I told her he was mowing lawns.

In the meantime, I had been spending the entire summer telling every girl I met that I had a boat. When one finally said that she wanted to go for a ride in late August, the words of that stuck-up teenage girl, no doubt at some cotillion at the time, resounded in my head. I wound up taking my new friend out in the yacht club boat, after hours, claiming ownership and signing someone else's name in the yacht club log. In short, I had forsaken the S.S. Rampage.

Why this girl never questioned me naming my boat the "New Haven Yacht Club I" is beyond me.

I retired the S.S. Rampage at the end of that summer, mildly embarrassed, especially as other kids my age were not only now tooling around town in beautiful, brand new cars, but seemingly did not have to work either.

However, many years later, the girl I was dating and I were in my garage and she spotted it, lifeless and hanging on a nail. "What's that?" she inquired, laughing. I told her it was a raft I used to take out as a boy, plain and simple.

"Well," she continued, "where's the bicycle pump?"

~Vinnie Penn

Material Girl

Be beautiful if you can,
wise if you want to, but be respected—
that is essential.
~Anna Gould

"Let's try out together!" my best friend Rachel suggested. We were hanging out by our lockers after third period and I had just finished P.E. class with Ms. Jockson. We were in the middle of a swimming unit in P.E. and I had been officially demoted to the "Tadpole" class. Me, and a half a dozen other freshmen who couldn't tread water for thirty seconds.

"Aren't cheerleading try-outs this Friday after school?" I squirmed. "I have a church thing Friday. Besides, I wouldn't stand a chance as a cheerleader. Cheerleading's for the popular girls. I'm just not cheerleader material."

"Pleeeeease! Please just try out with me! Even a poor unpopular freshman deserves a chance at happiness!" Rachel begged.

"Alright!" I said, sticking my index finger way in my ear canal, trying to eradicate the residual water from P.E. class. "But stop quoting *Fiddler on the Roof*, would you?"

Maybe Rachel would make the cheerleading team. She was coordinated, cute, and she didn't have flat feet. I, on the other hand, was simply not cheerleader material. I hung around the wrong group. I had braces. I had glasses. And my hair just wasn't... big enough. But if my BFF wanted me to try out....

For the rest of that week, Rachel and I stayed after school to learn the try-out cheers. We learned "A" jumps and "C" jumps. (Thank goodness there was no thing called a "Z" jump). We (ouch!) practiced splits. We even (no lie) practiced smiling our best cheerleader smiles.

Then, doomsday—Try-Out Friday.

"Come show your school spirit and try out for cheerleading in the gym after school!" read the magic marker bubble-lettered sign taped to the high school gym door. Unfortunately, I had to make it to church right after school, so I got special permission to try out first. First out of all the fifty bouncy, giggly, perfect cheerleader people. People who never needed braces and had never had to fasten an eyeglass safety strap to their head to keep their glasses from falling off during an especially energetic cartwheel. Rachel waved at me from the back of the line, all smiley. "Good luck," she mouthed. Or was it "You stink?"

"Cristy L?" the first of six judges called my name.

Or maybe it was God.

I could hear myself sweat. Trudging what seemed like a half-mile through wet cement, I made it to the center of the cavernous gym.

Smile. Keep your head up. Point your toes. Don't worry that fifty other people are watching you make a fool of yourself. And most importantly, don't throw up on the panel of distinguished judges....

I cheered.

I left.

I cried.

Then I ran out of the high school to catch my ride to my church event and agonized through the weekend alone. Just me and three chapters of geometry work.

Monday morning.

An especially rigorous Tadpole gym class was over, so I met Rachel at my locker.

"Cheerleader try-out results are posted on Ms. Jockson's door!" Rachel squealed. "I couldn't bear to look at the list without you. Come on!"

Arm in arm, Rachel and I held each other up on legs of Jell-O as we wobbled to Ms. Jockson's room. "Congratulations High School Cheer Team," read the list on the door (where the whole school could see). Names, like little black tadpoles, swam before my bespectacled eyes. "Anderson, L. Baumgaard, D. Green, A. Jackson, K. Miller, R..."

"That's me! That's me! Miller, R!" Rachel screamed in my ear, the one with chronic swimmer's ear. Assorted classroom windows shattered. "I maaaaaaade it!" Rachel bounced and kicked and cheered just like any good cheerleader-type person should. Then she dragged me into the cafeteria where she treated me to a trayful of over-cooked peas, a slice of pale meatloaf, and a super-size serving of despair.

My name, of course, was not on the list.

Then someone with really big blond hair, a senior girl wearing a too-tight miniskirt, barged in line ahead of me. "Some girls are just not cheerleader material," she sneered.

She's right, I thought, as I watched the big-haired blond walk away towards the popular table with my best friend. Some girls are just not cheerleader material....

Ten years later, at a class reunion, a really big bleached blond with a too-tight miniskirt came bouncing toward me. "Cristy! Is it true? No, it can't be! I heard that you were a Minnesota Vikings cheerleader! A professional cheerleader! I was wondering because, of course, you remember I was a cheerleader in high school and you... weren't."

For ten entire minutes I listened as the blond lady reminisced about her high school cheerleading days and bemoaned the fact that a bothersome bunion kept her from performing in college. "You're so lucky!" she exclaimed. "I can't think of anything better. Everybody looks at you. You're on TV. You meet pro football players and...."

"I quit in the middle of the season," I said.

Jaw drop.

"But why?" she asked, as though I had just told her I single-handedly euthanized my own cat.

"I didn't like the way people looked at me when I was a cheer-leader. People were more concerned with how I looked than who I was. I had a 3.8 GPA in college but no one thought I had a mind of my own. Plus, I had to miss church on Sundays during the season to cheer at games. So now I'm a writer and a mom."

The blond lady's big hair bobbed up and down as she consoled me. "I just can't believe you quit! I mean, you got free tickets to the games! You got to be on the field with pro football players! You got to have photo shoots and complementary hair styles at the best salons and...."

I tuned out the blond lady babble as I thought about the stories I wrote, the children I was raising, the faith I had been given, and my passion for learning. I just smiled as she talked on and on like a human text message gone bad, her too-tight miniskirt bunching up in all the wrong places. I smiled, thinking about my husband, my family, my future.

"Yeah," I said, hugging my husband. "I guess some girls just aren't cheerleader material."

~Cristy L. Trandahl

The Football

A successful person is one who can
lay a firm foundation with the bricks that others throw at him or her.
~David Brinkley

Julia Fiorucci disappeared one day and none of us noticed. She sat by herself in class and stared into space. If someone asked her a question, even her name, she shook her head in confusion. It wasn't long until the words "weirdo" or "zombie" were sniggered around and they soon stuck. Julia was a football everyone wanted to kick.

I tried to stay away from her, of course. My position in the popularity stakes was pretty low as it was; I didn't want it to fall any lower. But it seemed that everywhere I turned, she was there. When I sat down in class, she'd sit behind me; when I hung out with my friends at lunch, she'd be hovering on the edge of the group.

One day, I'd had enough. I was walking to my locker and Julia was a few steps behind me when I spun on my heel and glared right into her vacant looking eyes. "Julia," I said slowly and clearly. "Why don't you just disappear?"

For a moment, her face didn't seem quite so expressionless. There was a flash of pain in those pale brown eyes and it made me feel ashamed. But then I turned around and kept walking. I told myself I was relieved when she stopped following me, when she started melting into the background. After all, I didn't know that she was going to take my words literally.

It was during athletics training that Julia finally disappeared. The first day out on the oval made me feel sick. Running was something I tried to avoid. Not only was I slow, but I'd been told I ran like a duck. The words "Quack, quack" followed me for an entire summer until people started to forget. I hadn't, though.

That afternoon, the new tracks stood out starkly in the lush green grass. You could smell them—that fresh sweet scent of grass when it's just been cut. The sky was an amazing shade of blue and there wasn't a cloud in sight.

I watched as the first line of girls stood up and got into starting positions for the 100 metre sprint. Sandy Jackson was the first in that heat and it was pretty obvious she was going to win. She usually did; it was something that had shot her right up into the popular crowd.

"Get set... GO!" Mr. Shields yelled, jumping up and down like the sports freak that he was. "Go Sandy!" some of us cheered, or "Go Jess," "Go Trace!" I didn't notice Julia was in that heat until she was suddenly out in front. The way she ran was amazing. It was like watching a crane in flight, completely effortless. When Julia got out in front, the cheers evaporated. She crossed the line a few steps ahead of Sandy. As they walked back, Sandy threw Julia a dirty look that broke the silence. "The zombie can run," someone laughed. "I guess you don't need a brain for that." There were a few sniggers, a few grins, and Julia's shoulders slumped. The class football was kicked again.

The next time we had Phys Ed, I didn't have the usual sick feeling. Instead, I was buzzing with excitement. Nobody had dared to take on Sandy before; nobody had been crazy enough to mess with the popular group. Mr. Shield's eyes were shining as he grouped Sandy and Julia together. This combination was a Phys Ed teacher's dream. "Right," he boomed cheerfully. "Now we need one more...."

"I'll go!" I said, and had to smile at Mr. Shield's amazement. Usually I had to be dragged onto the tracks.

"Okay, get set, GO!" Mr. Shield yelled. I ran. But something wasn't right. Instead of shooting out in front, Julia was lagging just in front of me. She looked like a doll whose legs were too stiff for running.

"What are you doing?" I gasped. She looked back at me and I knew. The injustice of it made me blurt out, "You can't give up! You can't let her win!" Julia stopped so suddenly I almost fell against her. "What the hell do you know, Kristie Jones?" she spat out. Her look, as she ran off the track, made me feel about five centimeters tall. I hurried to finish the race even though I was dead last. Julia had gone.

Julia never came back to school. I had wanted her to disappear, but now that she finally had, I couldn't forget her. Sometimes my sleep was painted with dreams of Julia: Julia on the streets, Julia doing drugs, Julia with a broken and bruised face.... However, time passes, and soon I stopped thinking of Julia altogether.

High school finished and soon I was at Uni. My group of friends was ripped apart and flung into different departments. I was pushed along by the stream of students, reaching out to the few familiar faces I saw. Uni was like being on another planet. I didn't understand the lectures or even the tutorial discussions. Worst of all, not everyone was adjusting as poorly as I was. There was a student who sat at the back of the lecture theatre who would interrupt the lecturer every now and then with an intelligent sounding question. She wore short black skirts with knee-high boots so complicatedly laced she probably slept in them.

One afternoon, I was waiting outside the lecture theatre when she passed me. I glanced at her and there was something familiar about that face....

"Julia Fiorucci?" I whispered. She paused, and an icy shiver went down my spine. Could this sophisticated woman really be slow, zombie-like Julia? It was, and she was looking at me in puzzlement.

"Kristie Jones, remember...? You spent most of ninth grade in my class and then you... well... disappeared." Julia's frown smoothed into a wry smile, "Yes, that's when I was living with Dad and his girlfriend. I got sick of it, so I went back to Kingston to be with Mum." Julia looked away as the lecture theatre doors opened and a rush of students burst out. "I want to ask the professor something," she said distractedly. "See you."

Julia strode into the stream of students with such confidence that they stepped aside. I knew now that I had been wrong. Julia hadn't been the class football after all—it had been me all along.

~Kristie Jones

Teens Talk

HIGH SCHOOL

That Was Embarrassing

Comedy is tragedy plus time.

~Carol Burnett

The Test

I think the next best thing to solving a problem
is finding some humor in it.
~Frank A. Clark

This was it. The moment of truth. It was right there and then that the rest of my life was going to be determined. This over-the-top, life changing experience was my driver's test.

If you ask adults about their driver's test, they'll say something along the lines of, "Oh, it's no big deal!" or "There's always next time." Well, not for me. I don't fail—whether it's a final exam or a quiz in class. For me there was only one chance. There was only one try.

There I was, in my grandmother's Pontiac Grand-Am, alone. I watched my mother walk into the building and I began to worry. As I look back on it now, I am—well—embarrassed. I sat there, hands tightly grasping the steering wheel, knuckles white, with beads of sweat dripping down my cheeks. My left leg was shaking, not one of those fun, overly-excited shakes. No, it was a shake brought on by the complete and utter fear of failure. I checked everything. "Lights, check. Mirrors, check. Seat belt, check." I was ready. As I looked around for a final time, I noticed that my lip gloss had faded. Instinctively I reapplied my gloss and, while I was at it, my blush. Hey, a girl always has to look good. For all I knew, my instructor could have been a gorgeous twenty-year-old.

"Tap, tap," he knocked on my passenger window, gently. It was time. I turned to my right and there he was. He was tall... and scary.

I unlocked the door and he let himself in. "Hello," he said. I had no idea what to say. A mellow "Hi" would be too casual. Of course at the same time a stern "Hello" would have seemed too forceful and possibly angered him. I sat there. After a few moments that felt like minutes, I replied with an "Um, hey." After the typical exchange of "how are you" he asked me the big question: "Are you ready to get this show on the road?" Hmm, well let's think about this—NO! How could anyone be ready for this test? I know I sure wasn't.

Deep breath. Okay, I was ready. I can remember it so vividly. As I went to put the car in drive, I accidentally hit the windshield wiper fluid bar. I quickly fixed it and put the car into gear. I turned to over to Mr. Lewis and, to put it simply, he did not look happy. I began to move forward. As we came up to the first stop sign, I stopped. I began to talk to myself, "very good." As I did this, Mr. Lewis turned to me. He gave me one of those quizzical looks. How rude! So what—I was talking to myself, just giving myself a little encouragement. He had no right to make me nervously rethink what I just did! Oh well. I moved on.

We turned the corner and I saw it—the flags arranged in a square. I knew what that meant: parallel parking. Parallel parking is, as someone wise once put it, stupid. How often will a driver need to parallel park? I surely knew that I would never have to. Needless to say, I hate parallel parking. Once I pulled up next to the flags, I stopped.

Mr. Lewis looked at me: "Come on now, get to parking." I looked at him. Knowing I could not ignore the inevitable, I began to park. I unbuckled my seatbelt and began to turn my right arm behind the passenger seat next to me. As I reached for the headrest behind Mr. Lewis, "SMACK!" I hit him in the head. I hit him in the head. I HIT him in the head.

Oh my gosh. I quickly pulled both of my hands to my mouth, partly in shock and partly to cover my giggling smile. He turned toward me. "I am so sorry. I had no idea. I am so, so sorry. Can I start over?" I can't believe I hit him in the head. Not only did I hit him, but I also had the nerve to ask if I could try it again. "Let's just keep going," he said. I put the car in drive.

I hit him. This thought kept on running through my mind. But I had to stay focused. I had to pass this test. Deep breath. The next few minutes went well. I did not run over anyone, or hit them for that matter. I stopped at all the right times. I watched my speed and did not forget to use my turn signal. I kept on repeating one simple phrase in my head for moral support: "Go me." Then as we approached what I thought was our last turn, I saw them again—the dreaded flags. They were a bright, fluorescent orange, a color one usually only sees on Halloween. It is a cringe-worthy orange that upsets the stomach. These flags were my enemy. While I was evaluating these repulsive flags, Mr. Lewis spoke for the first time since our little incident, "Ninety degree back-in up ahead."

There we were again, parking. At least this time I could understand the purpose of ninety degree parking. It could come in handy in many different situations, like loading a boat onto a trailer or going into a driveway. Despite the many uses of this method, I still decided I was never going to do it once I had my license.

I pulled up next to the flags. Here we go again. As I turned my head a few times, I was mindful of where my arm was. I didn't hit him this time. Right as I began to think I could actually successfully finish this task, it happened again. This time, I hit the flag instead of the instructor. As my eyes began to tear up, Mr. Lewis spoke: "We're done." After my twenty minutes with this man I had concluded two things. First was that he was a man of few words. Second was that he had an unusually hard head.

I choked back my tears and began to drive forward. "Screeeeeech." My car was making a noise. I turned to Mr. Lewis, "Did I break it?" I asked. "No, you're dragging the flag under your rear bumper," he replied. Before I could yet again apologize, he stepped out of the car and went to fix the flag. After a few minutes of Mr. Lewis weaving the flag out from under my car, he sat back down in his seat and I drove back to the parking lot—without any accidents.

Before he exited the car, I turned to Mr. Lewis and began to cry. I thought that maybe I could play the sympathy card. It did not work. He said, and I quote, "Maybe next time kiddo." Maybe next time?

There was no next time! This was it! After I was sure the door was closed, I broke down in tears.

Once my mom came to the car and sat down, I told her about the whole ordeal. Contrary to what I had expected, she laughed. No, she didn't just laugh. She had a laughing attack. Somehow, through my tears, I began to laugh also. Now as I look back, I realize how funny the whole thing actually was. So what? I didn't pass. Oh well.

I did eventually go back and take the test again. I passed — and I didn't even hit anyone.

~Julie Pierce

Freshman Zit Girl

At fourteen you don't need sickness or death for tragedy.
~Jessamyn West

It was the eve of my very first day of high school and I had spent the entire night planning my outfit for the next day. I had arranged the books and supplies in my new book bag. (I completed several experiments that tested how full the bag looked with different combinations of textbooks and notebooks. A wise friend had warned me about the mistake of looking "too much like a freshman," which included lugging around an overstuffed, heavy-looking bag.)

Right before getting in bed, I stood in front of the full-length mirror that hung on the back of my bedroom door. I scanned from the top of my scalp to the tips of my toes for any major issues that needed to be addressed. Everything looked okay. No split ends. No chipped nail polish. No blemishes. It was time for a little beauty sleep....

"RING, RING, RING," buzzed the alarm clock next to my bed.

I sprung from bed, grabbed my hairbrush, and scurried over to the mirror. As I lifted the brush to the top of my head, I raised my chin; the gaze of my eyes repositioned to the center of the mirror. Something caught my attention. There was a strange shadow cast on my right cheek. My reflection was slightly odd. A weird thing was on my face.

"Aaahhh!" I shrieked.

There it was. On the tip of my nose had sprung the world's largest zit. I had never seen anything like it before. It was big and round and pointed. It looked as if tiny aliens had landed on Earth and had chosen my nose as the site for their little spaceship. It was shiny and bright and red. It made Rudolph's nose look pathetic. It was a new super breed of zit. It was the mother of all zits—she had chosen my nose to start her colony.

"Why?" I pleaded to my reflection. "Why does this have to happen on my first day of high school?" I begged as tears began rolling down my flushed cheeks. "I can't go to school!" I sobbed.

Despite all of my pleas and cries, my Mom said that I had to go to school—zit and all. The time I had planned to spend curling my hair and fixing my outfit in front of the mirror was now devoted entirely to covering up my Monster Zit. Unfortunately, like some strange mutant force, nothing worked on it. Concealer was powerless against this beast.

As if being a freshman were not bad enough, I had to start my high school career with Mt. Everest's evil twin on my nose. People were going to know me as the "freshman zit girl!" I was mortified. I thought it would be the most embarrassing day of my whole life.

Fortunately, I survived that horrible day. No one pointed and laughed at me. No one called me the "freshman zit girl."

However, for the rest of the year I believed that people still remembered the first day of school when I entered the high school hallways with the Abominable Zit riding on my nose. I was convinced that all of the other students would always remember me as Zit Girl.

This changed, though, at the beginning of tenth grade.

On the first day of tenth grade, as I arranged the contents of my locker before school, I was talking with one of my good friends. "At least this year has already started better than last year," I said.

My friend turned and looked at me quizzically. "What do you mean?" she asked.

"I don't have the same humiliating problem as the first day of freshman year," I replied. Still, my friend looked at me blankly.

"My huge, mortifying zit!" I yelled, pointing to my nose.

"Hmm. I don't remember," she said. She continued, "Oh my gosh, do you remember that ugly shirt I wore on the first day of freshman year?" she asked, making a disgusted face. "I don't know what I was thinking!" she cried. "It's sooo embarrassing."

"But that blue shirt is cute," I said confusedly.

"No. That orange one with the buttons," she stammered.

"Really?" I asked. "I don't remember."

I had totally forgotten my friend's embarrassing moment, and she had forgotten mine! That meant there was a good chance that everyone from my high school had forgotten about my Zitzilla on the first day of school.

I can remember almost every embarrassing blemish, outfit, and mistake from when I was in high school. But, when I think about it, I cannot remember a single embarrassing blemish, outfit, or mistake from another person—not even my best friends in high school. What I have realized is that most people are only worried about their own life's blemishes. They have no spare time, or spare memories, for caring about other peoples' blemishes.

I survived the attack of the Killer Zit, and I won. Now I now have a funny memory that reminds me to laugh... and to clean my skin regularly.

~Anna Kendall

A Most Embarrassing Date

Humor is merely tragedy standing on its head with its pants torn.
~Irvin S. Cobb

The end of summer and beginning of the school year was definitely a change of seasons. Long summer days and hot sultry nights gradually became dusky evenings with cooler breezes. The sounds of a Friday night football game could be heard from miles away as the muffled roar of the crowd and the fight song played by the band was carried by the West Texas wind. Weather could be dramatic. It could be a cold and windy night when the crowd snuggled together under shared blankets of textured woolen plaids and quilts. That would be followed by the next Friday evening of almost spring-like warm weather, clear skies and a stillness that made our small town feel even smaller.

It was on a night such as this that I had a first date with Doug. I had never noticed him before, though we had been at the same church and school for years. Why I hadn't paid attention, I don't know. I suppose I was just preoccupied with someone else.

As first dates go, there is generally a bit of nervous anticipation and a feeling of awkwardness. Internal dialogues such as: Will he walk me to the passenger side of the car or will he lead me to get in on his side and slide to the middle? If he leads me to the passenger side, do I polish the door on my side, scoot to the center or somewhere in between?

Each body language position sends a message. If I am assumptive and scoot to the middle, he might think I'm pushy or, worse, too forward. Polishing the door would be prudish or indicate we weren't "hitting it off" and that I wasn't having a good time. There was so much for a girl to consider and "read between the lines," so to speak, on a first date—not to mention what to wear!

Doug came to my house, went through the quick introduction of the parents, and we were out the door headed for the football game. He was so relaxed and natural, as if we had known each other forever, making me feel so at ease I forgot about those worrying details. We went to the game and who knows if we won or lost—I was in a daze. I just followed the crowd, standing and screaming at every cue, supporting our "Fighting Bulldogs."

The game ended at 8:30 or 9:00, too early to return home from a date. Our small town didn't have many options. The drive-in was about it and then we thought of the City Park. Doug parked the car along the curb and headed for the seesaws while I went for the swings. I was wearing a pair of printed cotton pants that zipped up the front all the way to my waistline. There was no waistband. My shirt was a solid color pullover that ended at the waist and though my clogs were clumsy for running, they could be easily slipped off and dropped below the swing.

Doug started walking the long, heavy seesaw from one end to the other, something I never was brave enough, nor coordinated enough to do. Though I had mastered the swings well enough to get really high, then shift my weight twisting and turning as I swung to and fro. And then it happened....

As I leaned back, feet straight, and tightened my abdomen, I blew the zipper right out of my pants. What could I do? There I was with my pants gaping open. I quickly bolted from the swing and held each side of the zipper together while embarrassingly telling my date that I must go home.

As he drove, I sat in the middle of the seat next to him holding my pants together for the never ending seven minutes it must have taken to drive from the park to my house.

Doug, still at ease, parked the car in the driveway, got out and held the door open for me. As I slid towards his door holding my pants together, I slid right out of the car and fell onto the driveway. I was so humiliated I wanted to find a crack in the concrete and crawl in it.

I stood up and kept my head down in agony. Doug put his arms around me, consoling me in my despair. I confessed my embarrassment as I buried my face in his chest. He walked me to the door to say goodnight and I entered, knowing for sure that this guy whom I had never noticed before, but wish I had, would never ask me out for another date.

He called the next day and asked, "Do you want to go to the movie tonight?" I didn't know for sure what he was expecting to be the entertainment — the movie or me.

~Belinda Howard Smith

Girl Most Likely to...

A laugh is a smile that bursts.
~Mary H. Waldrip

D o people really die of embarrassment? I've heard that expression often. But do you think actual death certificates say that? I've always wondered, because mine almost read:

Age of death: 16.
Cause of death: Embarrassment.

"What a pity!" teary-eyed mourners would have whimpered. "What a senseless loss!"

It was the summer before my junior year. Several friends and I decided that it would be fun to enroll in an eight-week drama class that would culminate in a full-scale theatrical production. Some of us acted (marvelously, I might add!), some constructed amazing scenery, some handled a gazillion props, others made magic with their make-up, costuming, or audiovisual skills.

I barely recall the play's title or any of my lines, but the memory forever branded on my brain, fresh as if it happened last week, is one particular day... I mean, one particular scorching hot day. Eight of us were gathered together on our hour-long lunch break, sitting around, commenting on the sweltering heat—fantasizing about how refreshing an ice cream cone would be. Kathy gleefully announced that she had her parents' car that day and could drive us to the nearby ice cream shop, ensuring that we would return before rehearsals resumed. Everyone loved the idea, so Kathy told the drama teacher that we were racing to the store. Mr. G said okay, but that only one person could accompany her. I volunteered, so we wrote down everyone's "orders" and collected their money. Kathy made a beeline for a shiny blue car, opened the doors, and slid in. "Hurry," she said, patting the passenger seat.

"Wow!" I exclaimed, whiffing that brand-new-car smell as the A/C fought with the stifling heat. "I can't believe your parents let you drive this!"

"It's my reward for getting good grades," Kathy purred. "Pretty cool, huh?"

"Cool reward, indeed! And thank God for these cloth-covered seats. Can you imagine what the sun would have done to leather seats? Ouch!"

We arrived at the ice cream shop within minutes. "Rats," I gasped, springing from the car. "I should have peed before we left school."

"We'll be fast," Kathy promised.

Lesson #1: Never believe promises about anything over which the person making the promise does not have complete control.

(I always make "mental notes" of life's important lessons.)

Apparently, everyone in the whole neighborhood had decided to cool off with ice cream. The line was a mile long. Okay, I'm exaggerating. But when you've gotta go real bad, it just seems like a mile. "Listen," I whispered. "You wait in line while I go pee."

I approached the cashier, saying quietly, "Excuse me, ma'am. May I please use your restroom?"

"It's for employees only," she grunted.

"I've really gotta go," I softly begged. "Would you please make an exception?"

"I SAID the BATHROOM is for employees ONLY!" the woman snapped. Several nearby customers snickered.

So much for asking discreetly. I slunk back into line with Kathy, but the wait seemed endless. We decided to abandon our mission so we wouldn't return to school late, thereby holding up the whole rehearsal. Our friends would understand. Just as we started leaving, the line miraculously sped up. The clock was ticking, but Kathy hurriedly ordered a variety of eight double-scoop cones while I politely paid the cranky cashier. Smiling, she responded, "Sorry about the bathroom. It's a strict company policy."

Lesson #2: Don't shoot the messenger.

(Maybe Miss Sourpuss was cranky because someone else had already shot her.)

One-by-one, the ice cream scooper-outer man carefully placed each colorful order into the plastic cone holder on the counter. Kathy and I thanked him, grabbed two cones in each hand and sprinted back to the car. Needing to retrieve the keys from her purse, she asked me to take the cones from her right hand. I somehow managed to do so, precariously juggling six cones. She opened her car door, then mine. Holding three cones in each hand, I obviously couldn't close my door after getting in. "Help!" I called after her. Kathy raced back. We looked at each other and started giggling like crazy. Kathy attached my seatbelt for me, and closed my door. She bounced into the driver's seat, reached over, closed her door with her right hand (given that she was still holding two cones in her left one), and single-handedly attached her seatbelt. If I hadn't already been strapped in, I would have been rolling on the floor. Kathy thought that she was being so careful, but she got ice cream everywhere.

My sticky friend pretended to glare at me, but cracked up. "How am I going to drive? This is a stick shift! For two people on the honor roll, we're not very bright, are we?" We laughed harder than ever before we caught a glimpse of the dashboard clock. We had seven minutes to drive back, distribute the cones to our sweltering classmates, and hop on the stage. And I still had to pee—bad!

Kathy thrust some "chocolate mint" and "peppermint surprise" at me. "Here! You've gotta take these!"

"How?" I howled, tears streaming down my face. "I can barely balance three in each hand."

Assessing the situation, Kathy took charge. "Just hold them here." She reached over and wedged her two cones between my wobbly, bony knees.

The tires and I squealed in unison, but my shrieks were in response to the rapidly melting ice cream that was dripping all over my hands and lap. By now, my ribs ached. Unfortunately, this unique situation reminded Kathy of a joke... which she decided to recite. In retrospect, this was more poor judgment because we were already in hysterics. When she said the punch line, I completely lost it. Literally. I lost all the pee that I'd been holding in for the past forty-five minutes.

The next few minutes are a blur. I vaguely recall that Kathy screamed, but I don't know if it's because we were almost in an accident from her splitting a gut or because she was horrified to suddenly realize that she'd have to tell her parents why the passenger seat was so soggy and sticky. At that moment she probably didn't care that I would certainly die from embarrassment when we had to get out of the car at school. In fact, this scenario was pretty much a given. I mean, I had light colored shorts on, and there was no way I could hide what had just occurred.

When we pulled into the school lot, I could see our friends eagerly awaiting their specially ordered cones. They started walking over to the car after spotting us. Little did they know that their double-scoop ice cream was half melted all over my lap. Little did they know that their sixteen-year-old friend (moi)—who was holding their cones—had just wet her pants. Something told me that they wouldn't want their treats anymore.

Worse than that, as nice as my friends were, I knew that "the word" would spread rapidly and I'd be the laughing stock of the school for weeks or months or even years ahead. Kathy's parents would probably warn other parents at upcoming PTA meetings to never let me in their cars. They would probably put notices in the school newspaper and on bulletin boards.

I had obviously stopped laughing by then, and was fighting back tears. My heart started pounding so fast that I thought it would burst. Hmmm, I concluded. That's probably how people die of embarrassment. The stress just makes them have a stroke or heart attack. Well, rats. I sure had a lot more to do in life, but at least my inevitable end would be quick.

I looked over at Kathy and mumbled, "I'm soooo sorry! Will your parents freak out?"

She smiled at me sweetly and said firmly. "I have a strange feeling that they'll believe this was an accident. And you've gotta admit — this will make a great story! You will survive this and even laugh about it one day. So ya know what? You might as well start laughing now!"

What kind of line was that?!

I scanned my storage of the "mental notes" I keep, and something sprang to mind:

You teach people how to treat you.

Kathy was right. I turned to her and grinned. "Open my door, undo my seatbelt, and get those damn cones out from between my knees." She did so, and I fumbled out of the car, my hands and lap completely covered in melted ice cream, a very obvious localized "wet" spot on my shorts. Our six friends burst into laughter, and so did I.

Kathy said, "Apparently, you can't take her anywhere!"

"You can if I'm wearing a diaper!" I replied indignantly. "Ice cream, anyone?"

Woohoo! I will certainly make the school yearbook as "the girl most likely to wet her pants...."

Lesson #3: I'd be so ashamed to die of embarrassment... I'd MUCH rather die laughing!

~Karen Waldman

Humble Pie

The finest clothing made is a person's skin,
but, of course,
society demands something more than this.
~Mark Twain

Two weeks before my fifteenth birthday, early in June, I bought my first bikini. White cotton eyelet and trimmed in lace, it did nothing to detract from my newly acquired figure. Our family vacationed at the lake the same time each year, and my purchase was calculated to attract Rodney, the sixteen-year-old boy whose parents rented the cabin next to ours. I'd had my eye on him since I was thirteen, and I was determined that this summer he would notice me, if nothing else.

Within an hour of unpacking, I found myself knee-deep in the muddy bottom of Bass Lake, the ski rope clenched in one fist. Dad was at the wheel of our rented boat, my little brother next to him as the spotter, and Mom sat in an umbrella chair on the sand holding a life vest for my use. Proudly sporting my snow-white bikini and a new tan, I was acutely aware of Rodney and his friends seated at the end of his dock, all taking a special interest in my starting technique. My mother leveled one eye on them and the other on me. Ignoring her, I signaled "ready" to my brother and we took off just before Mom could toss me the vest.

The boat cut smoothly through the water pulling me atop my freshly waxed slalom ski. I leaned right, and then left, dipped low, and skimmed the waves, finding my balance and gaining the confidence I needed for my first ride of the season. As I jumped the wake, a sense of freedom and a deep joyfulness soared through me. I felt beautiful, alive, deliriously happy, and in control of my destiny. Dad circled the lake and I dashed across the wake, each time jumping higher and higher until I was pretty sure Rodney and his friends were held captive by my performance. I gave Dad the thumbs-up sign and he pressed down on the gas. As we circled around again, flying past our cabin, I waved at the guys on the dock who were standing now, watching me. My cheeks glowed with pure pleasure from all the newfound attention I could command with just a simple bikini.

As we made the final circle towards our dock, I signaled to "cut" at the boat, pointed my ski at the shoreline, and with a grand flourish, tossed the rope away from me. I held my arms in the air like a diva in demand and let the momentum glide me towards shore when suddenly my ski fin snagged a lake plant and stopped dead in the water, ripping me from my boots.

I shot forward, skimming and bumping belly first across the top of the lake like a skipping rock. My missile-type body headed straight for Mom's chair, with nothing to slow me down except the muddy section of shore ahead. I hit the beach straight on and face down, coming to rest in two inches of water. Caked from head to toe in black goop, my cheeks didn't glow any longer. They were burnt crimson—but lucky for me, my mud facial covered that up nicely.

With all of my cocky bravado sunk to the bottom of the lake like a shipwreck, I courageously pulled myself to a standing position. I ignored the obnoxious laughter and the hoots of "Nice show, Sarah Jo!" coming from the dock next door. With as much dignity as I could muster, I turned my back on them and swam out into the lake to rinse off the best I could, wishing I could stay submerged until my audience went home for dinner. Apparently, they were waiting for the final curtain call. So, with my head held high, I again emerged from the lake, wobbling my way to solid ground. The mud glued to my feet had created a suction cup effect with each step I took, emitting a loud slurping noise. I zeroed in on Mom, who was there, walking towards me holding out a beach towel, like a beacon in a stormy sea.

It was during this infamous grand finale that I felt the back clasp of my bikini snap and looked down in time to watch my top roll up around my neck like a Venetian blind when its cord is pulled too hard. I yelped in pure mortification. Wiping the image of Lady Godiva from my mind, I reached out to Mom hurrying towards me and accepted without comment the towel that was lovingly draped over my shoulders, shielding me from my snickering fan club.

I spent the rest of the afternoon begging my dad to take me home. I threw my former accomplice turned traitor, the white bikini, into the fire pit. Looking in the mirror after a hot shower and blow dry, I found the smug look I wore earlier in the day wiped clean off my face. Sighing, the words from the old adage my grandmother often quoted, "Everything that doesn't kill you, makes you stronger," popped into my head. Well, I thought, I'm not dead.

Later that evening, as I walked alone on the grassy bank, cringing at the memory of my earlier misadventure, soft music drifted through the night air. My eyes adjusted to a dark shadow sitting at the end of the dock next door. I watched silently as Rodney put down his guitar, stood up, and walked towards me. Smiling kindly, he asked, "Do you know somewhere around here where a guy can buy a lady a Coke?"

~Sarah Jo Smith

Hair Don't

Life is an endless struggle full of frustrations and challenges,
but eventually you find a hair stylist you like.
~Author Unknown

I looked in the mirror. "Oh my God," I thought. "I look like a brachiosaurus."

You know—those dinosaurs with the nostrils on top of their heads? That's what I resembled. Immediately, a picture of a brachiosaurus popped into my thoughts, its big, bumpy, dumb-looking head looming from some prehistoric lake. It was hideous. I was hideous. My hair was pulled back, flat at the sides, with a monstrous teased bump of hair on the top. It was unflattering in every possible way.

"Oh wow!" said a passing hairstylist as she admired it from the back. "That looks fabulous!"

I smiled weakly, feeling like each of my cheeks weighed one million pounds and was resisting the smile with every ounce. "Thanks," I said softly. Look pleased! Look happy! I screamed at myself. "I have to leave now."

I got up from the chair and looked at the lady who'd just done my hair. She was smiling smugly, and the look on her face said, "Wow, I'm so good at my job." I needed to get out of there. I paid the money my grandma had so generously given me to get my hair done for prom, money I knew I could have spent on a hundred better things, and practically ran from the salon, my leaden cheeks weighing down my already wilting smile.

I sat in my car and looked in my rearview mirror. Not so bad, right? Wrong. It was terrible. I smiled and mugged for the mirror. Sometimes if I turn my head a different angle it helps me look—no. No way. It wasn't getting any better.

So I did what I always do in a tight spot. I called my best friend.

Natalie!" I cried, "I'm not sure about my hair!"

"It's okay," she assured me, "I bet it looks fine. Just come and get your make-up done. It's not a big deal."

I hung up the phone and swallowed, breathing deeply, in and out. It was going to be fine. The night would turn out fine.

I hadn't been really particular about prom. I bought my dress months in advance, but only because I'd happened to wander across one I really liked early on. It was simple and beautiful—blue and shiny and elegant. I figured I'd wear my hair up since the back was low-cut, and when my grandma insisted she'd pay for a professional to do it, I said okay. I didn't expect prom to be the best night of my life. My boyfriend and I had decided to forgo a limousine for his parents' car and had made our corsage and boutonniere by hand with some flowers we'd gotten at Stop & Shop (believe it or not, they actually looked pretty nice). All I had wanted was to be able to walk down the stairs of my house, like in all the movies I'd seen as a kid, and see the look in my boyfriend's eyes. "You look beautiful," he would say. And I'd smile, stepping down to meet him and be enveloped by his tuxedoed arms.

My smile now was slowly disintegrating as I walked into the department store where my best friend was. Taking down the umbrella (it was raining on prom night), she could finally see my hair. I saw it in her eyes—she knew it wasn't good.

"It looks fine," she said, but she didn't mean fine. If I can read anyone, it's my best friend, and the tone in her voice said "Not fine! Not fine!" Still, she didn't want to rain on my promenade.

"It's not fine," I said, and suddenly I couldn't control it anymore. I started to cry in big heaping sobs, feeling absolutely idiotic for caring so much about a stupid hairdo. Was I really a prom-zilla? Was I that superficial eighteen-year-old whose life revolved around prom? The tears rolling down my cheeks at the Bobbi Brown counter said so.

The lady who was supposed to do my make-up looked at me with pity. Even she told me it wasn't that bad, although she was clearly lying. I looked at Natalie and told her I had to leave, even if it meant I wasn't going to get my make-up done. She wholeheartedly understood.

I got in the car and called my boyfriend. He told me to come to his house and his sister would do my hair. At this point, I didn't care. I just needed to get rid of my hump-head. I started ripping out the bobby pins.

Driving in the rain to my boyfriend's house, I had a high school breakdown. I was pulling the bobby pins from my hair, crying my eyes out and mumbling about how I just wanted to look pretty. The hairspray made my hair stand on end, sticking out every which way. I looked terrible.

In retrospect, my meltdown wasn't really about the hairdo. It was about the time — second semester of senior year. I had worked so hard for so long and was beaten down by the pressure I had put on myself. Prom was my chance to relax, to take a breath, to dance and have fun. It was my farewell to high school, my opportunity to dress up with my high school boyfriend one last time before we went our separate ways. And I had paid money to look terrible. It just didn't seem fair.

Everyone in my life came through for me that night. My boyfriend's sister did a wonderful job with my hair and the woman at the Bobbi Brown counter told Natalie she could fit me in later, once my hair had been fixed. After I got my make-up done, I sat down in my car and looked in the rearview mirror. My eyes weren't teary anymore. Instead, they were shiny and pretty, the way only a professional make-up artist can make them. And my hair didn't look so bad. I drove home to put on my dress.

Later, I walked down the steps of my house to meet my

boyfriend. There he stood in his tux, looking dashing, his vest a deep, shiny blue to match my dress. I stepped off the last step and looked shyly into his eyes. "You look beautiful," he said, sincerely. I smiled and thanked him, not because he had fulfilled my childhood prom dream, but because he loved me regardless of my little prom meltdown. Sometimes in high school, little things like a bad hairdo can seem like the end of the world and the absolute worst thing that can happen. If you had asked me if the world was conspiring to ruin my life when I looked in the mirror at the salon, I would have given you a resounding "yes." But looking back on it, I know how silly it was to wail in the car because my hair was bumpy. As you grow up, you face much more difficult challenges—and you learn that there are worse things than narrowly avoiding going to prom looking downright Jurassic.

~Madeline Clapps

"Bad hair day."

Beauty Comes from Within

Wise men ne'er sit and wail their loss,
but cheerily seek how to redress their harms.
~William Shakespeare

"I am not going to cry, I am not going to cry." I whispered over and over as I stood stunned in the doorway. I was so embarrassed and humiliated.

I was a sophomore in high school and I was flattered that a senior girl, who I had always admired, had asked me to join a group of seniors who were getting together to celebrate the last week of school. It was a beautiful spring evening and Lacey told me to wear casual clothes—cut-off shorts and a T-shirt—since they were planning on having hamburgers and afterwards just having fun. We were to meet in front of a restaurant that I'd never been in.

I was elated to be invited to their party. I liked a certain senior boy who had been friendly and seemed to like me too. I was really looking forward to spending the evening around him. I took extra pains with my long, dark hair. Since Lacey had said it was casual, I wore a new pair of jean shorts with my favorite T-shirt and a new pair of slip-on canvas shoes.

Since I didn't have my driver's license yet, Mom dropped me off in front of the restaurant where Lacey said everyone was going to meet.

"Mom, I'll call you if I don't have a ride home," I told her. I was hoping a certain boy would take me home afterwards.

I didn't see anyone, but I could tell by the cars that everyone was there. Maybe they decided to wait inside, I thought. I hurried to the restaurant door not wanting to be late and having everyone wait for me. I was smiling when I stepped through the door, but in an instant, I froze.

The whole group of seniors was dressed up. The girls all wore soft, pastel spring dresses and the boys were in dress slacks and shirts. With my shorts and T-shirt, I stood out like a sore thumb.

The group of boys stood there with their mouths open and I realized they didn't even know I had been invited. I spied Lacey standing with a group of girls who were all laughing and snickering behind their hands. She had a malicious smile on her face and was being praised by the other girls for having played such a "funny joke" on me, a lowly sophomore.

I stood and stared at her. Why did I ever admire her or think she was pretty? Sure, she came from a well-to-do family, had plenty of pretty clothes, and her hair and nails were always perfect, but now I realized how ugly she was. She was ugly on the inside.

I wanted to cry, to run away, but I had nowhere to go. Mom wouldn't be back to pick me up until ten if I didn't call her. She would be so hurt for me. What was I going to do? Then, I remembered something Mom was always telling my sister and me:

"Beauty comes from within. If you're beautiful on the inside, then it will show on the outside."

At that moment, I certainly didn't feel beautiful inside or out. My stomach felt sick, my heart was beating fast, and my knees felt shaky. "Well, you're not going to have the satisfaction of seeing me cry," I muttered to myself.

I knew Lacey was waiting for that kind of reaction. Right then and there, I decided I was going to make Mom proud of me. I would be so beautiful on the inside, it would have to show. I took a deep breath and put a smile on my face.

I slowly walked toward Lacey, smiling the whole way. When I came to her group of giggling friends, I said to her, "Thank you so much Lacey for inviting me tonight. I'm afraid I misunderstood and wore casual clothes, but that shouldn't bother anyone. I'll just make the rest of you look better."

Still smiling, I turned and walked toward the group of boys. The one I liked stood there and looked at me as though I was a freak. I couldn't help but get the impression that he was embarrassed for me so I veered toward a guy I didn't know who stood a little to one side of the group. At least he wasn't laughing at me.

"Hi. My name's Patsy. What's yours?" I held out my hand to shake his.

He took my hand and held it. "Grant. I'm very glad to meet you Patsy." He had a warm smile that went all the way to his eyes.

We chatted for a few minutes and I joked in a loud enough voice for everyone to hear, "You need to speak up, Grant. I'm not hearing very well it seems. I must need a hearing aid or maybe I just need my ears cleaned out," I laughed. I wasn't about to give Lacey the satisfaction of knowing how deeply she'd hurt me.

Lacey stepped forward to announce that our tables were ready, and she actually had a sneer on her face as she glanced toward me. My face turned pink as I marched into the dining room. This certainly wasn't a hamburger joint, but I held my head up high.

I felt someone take my arm. It was Grant.

"I think you look great. You're the prettiest girl here tonight," he said.

I smiled and squeezed his hand. I was grateful for my new friend. As for the guy who I thought I liked, Connie had grabbed his arm and was leading him to another table.

I ate very little that night. I didn't bring very much money with me so I only ordered a salad. My smile felt frozen on my face, but I was kind and gracious to everyone. I have to admit, though, that it was one of the longest dinners I've ever sat through.

After the dinner, everyone wanted to go to a favorite teen hangout to dance. While they all went to their cars, I tried to slip away to call Mom. I felt someone take my arm.

"Do you need a ride home?" Grant asked.

"Yes, I was going to call my mother."

"I'd be happy to take you home, after the dance, of course." Grant grinned at me.

"Thank you. I'd love that, too."

We had a great time, dancing and getting acquainted.

The next morning, every time I thought about Lacey, I became angry. I realized she had done everything on purpose. I thought about ways to get even, but when I glanced at myself in the mirror, I noticed the frown and the look of anger. I sure don't look pretty now, I thought.

I thought about it most of the day, and even though I was deeply hurt, I decided to pray for Lacey. At first the prayer stuck in my throat, but it got easier in time. I felt better knowing that God was taking care of the matter.

I never knew why Lacey did what she did. Was it because she liked the same boy and was jealous of me? Did she have a cruel streak, or did she think it was cool to pick on a younger student? I learned later that several of the other girls turned against her for fear of her pulling a cruel joke on them. The few times I saw Lacey afterwards, I would smile and say hi, but I never wished to socialize with her again.

I never told my mom what happened—I didn't want to hurt her. When she asked if I'd had a good time, I said yes and told her all about Grant, my new friend.

I did learn a valuable lesson that night: No matter what kind of situation you find yourself in, if you hold your head up high and are kind and gracious, you'll get through. Grant told me he admired the way I'd handled the embarrassing situation Lacey had put me in, but I was grateful to him for being so kind to me. After that, I vowed I would never let anyone else suffer what I did that night. No matter where I am, if I notice someone alone or looking ill at ease, I do my best to make them feel welcomed and comfortable.

As my mom would say, "Act beautiful and you'll be beautiful, because beauty comes from within."

~Pat Kane

Worrywart on the Dance Floor

Life is the art of drawing without an eraser.
~John Gardner

Before my sophomore year homecoming dance, I spent countless agonizing hours worrying about the event. I worried about my dress. I worried about my hair. I worried about getting something in my teeth at the pre-dance dinner. As I lay in bed at night, I cringed while embarrassing scenarios played out in my head—wearing the same dress as another girl, or tripping over someone's foot and falling flat on my face, mooning my entire class.

Eventually, the night of the dance came, and the first part of the evening went as planned. My date picked me up, we went to the restaurant, and we went to the school's gymnasium for the dance. Everything seemed to be going well. There were no duplicates of my dress. And I hadn't tripped. After about an hour, as I was talking with some girl friends, I glanced around for my date.

"Has anyone seen my date?" I asked my friends as I scanned the gym.

"Not for a while," one friend replied. "We can go look for him?" she suggested.

"Okay," I relied." "He's probably getting some punch."

As we slowly pushed our way through the crowd, I felt my friend's hand jabbing me in the back.

"I see him!" she yelled, jerking my head in a different direction with her hands.

I was wrong. My date couldn't have been getting punch, because he was too busy kissing another girl!

I stomped up to him, smacking the shoulders of the other students who stood in my path.

"What are you doing?" I sputtered.

"I'm spending the rest of the dance with her," he coolly replied, taking the other girl's hand and walking away.

My jaw dropped down to my collarbone as I watched my date officially ditch me at the homecoming dance. In disbelief that this high school tragedy had happened to me, I stayed at the dance talking with my sympathetic friends until the limo picked us up to take us home.

The following year, junior year, I was getting ready for my first-ever prom. I had survived my junior homecoming dance, but, once again, I was on worry overload. I worried. I fretted. I agonized.

And, once again, the big day eventually came. Fortunately, the very beginning of the prom went as planned. My date picked me up and we went with our group to the Italian restaurant for dinner.

As I had already strategically planned out, I ordered ravioli without the sauce, because I didn't want to risk spilling bright red tomato sauce on my lavender dress. As my plate of food was placed in front of me, I noted that the sauce had been omitted; however, in lieu of sauce, it had been prepared with oil. Therefore, I carefully adjusted the napkin over my lap as I picked up the fork. I cut one ravioli in half and poked the fork through one of the halves. I pulled the ravioli up to my mouth, and as I leaned in... SPLAT!

"Aaahh!" I exclaimed.

Quickly plucking from my lap the ravioli half that had landed on my napkin, I realized the oily pasta had hit my chest before sliding down onto my napkin, leaving behind its oily path.

"Can someone come into the bathroom with me?" I whispered across the table to two of my girlfriends.

I slid my chair out and darted over to the washroom.

I pushed open the washroom door and ran over to the sink. As I grabbed for a towel I glanced at my reflection in the mirror, cringing at the large, oval-shaped dark stain that prominently appeared in the middle of my stomach.

"What's wrong?" my friends asked in unison as they pushed open the door.

I turned to face them, and they both gasped.

"What is that?" the first friend asked.

"You ruined your dress!" the second friend declared.

"I know. I ruined my prom!" I sobbed as tears filled my eyes.

"Try wiping it off with water," the first friend said grabbing a towel and soaking it under the faucet. She tried dabbing the oil spill, but it only made it appear darker.

"No, you need to dry it," the second friend said pointing to the hand dryer. With the help of my friends I slipped out of the dress and held it up to the heated air. Nothing changed.

"That's it," I sighed. "I have to leave."

"You can't leave!" both friends urged. "You can't miss the prom."

Reluctantly, I agreed.

So, I entered the prom halls with a huge stain on my dress. My only defense was positioning my date's hands over my stomach so I could hide the stain in the prom pictures.

After my junior prom, I began organizing the pictures from all of my high school dances. In my junior prom pictures, it's as if that evil stain never existed. And, in my sophomore homecoming pictures, it's as if my date never left. However, I wished I did have pictures of my dateless self at the dance and of my stained prom dress.

I got ditched at a high school dance and I spilled oil all over my dress at the prom. I survived not one, but two embarrassing high school moments!

More importantly, though, these two incidents remind me that it doesn't help to worry, because we really can't control most of the embarrassing things that happen to us in high school. We don't know in advance that our dates will ditch us, or that we'll spill oil on our dresses.

We need to tell ourselves that we will mess up; we will suffer embarrassing situations. And, we need to remind ourselves that the dance will go on.

~Anna Kendall

Teens Talk

HIGH
SCHOOL

Consequences

Mistakes are the usual bridge between inexperience and wisdom.

~Phyllis Therous

The Power of Saying I Was Wrong

Keep your words soft and tender
because tomorrow you may have to eat them.
~Author Unknown

Mike's face looked like I'd just punched him in the stomach. His eyes widened with shock, and all the color drained from his cheeks. I hadn't touched him. In fact, I hadn't even noticed him standing in the doorway of the wardrobe room, watching my friend Megan and me sew costumes for the upcoming school musical. He wasn't in any drama classes, and that was the only reason anyone ever came down this out-of-the-way hallway. What was he doing here? Mike was the last person I ever expected to pass this open door. Maybe that's why I'd felt so free to answer Megan's question about my date with him: "Yeah, I only went to the movie with Mike because he asked me and I didn't want to hurt his feelings. I'm not really interested in going out with him again. He's kind of... well...."

That's when I glanced up and saw Mike in the doorway. He looked like I'd slapped him, and instantly my hand stung just as if I had. I desperately wished I'd been standing over the trap door on stage, so I could've dropped out of sight. Instead Mike spun on his heel and dashed back down the hallway. I knew I should run after him and apologize, but my cute Mary Jane's felt like lead on my feet.

"Oh, really cute," I thought ironically as I stared at my shoes, my own face flaming. I was embarrassed, and the worst part was I knew I should have been. I could tell Mike I was sorry, but what could I ever say to undo the pain my flippant words had caused him?

Megan's face was flushed, too. "Maybe we've done enough for today," she offered, and without a word we put away the costumes, gathered up our books, and headed home.

All the next week I couldn't even look at Mike in the three classes we shared every day. I had to do something, had to say something, but a wrestling match was going on inside my head. "Which is it?" I kept asking myself. "You feel humiliated that you acted like a jerk, but do you feel that way because it made you look bad, or because you hurt Mike's feelings?" I knew I had to answer this question before I could honestly apologize.

The time to decide landed right in my hand in speech class. On Wednesday, Mr. Kincaid had announced we'd be giving three-minute extemporaneous speeches on Thursday and Friday. He had already written out topics on slips of paper, so there was no way to prepare what we would say. Thursday morning, Mr. Kincaid passed down my row handing out topics. "No problem," I kept repeating to myself to calm my nervousness. Like a sprinter in the starting bock, I mentally focused on the finish line: "I can do this. I can do this." I opened the folded paper Mr. Kincaid handed me and suddenly sucked in my breath: "Tell about your most embarrassing moment."

My knees shook and my mouth went dry as I walked to the front of the classroom, but I knew what I had to say. Without naming Mike's name or giving details that would only embarrass him more, I confessed before thirty people—who, until now, all considered me "Miss Perfect"—my unkind, thoughtless act, my deep regret, and what I'd learned as a result. The room was deathly silent as I finished. Well, there it was, as public an apology as I could possibly give, no more "Miss Perfect," and I'd probably made my first D in speech class as well, I thought ruefully. I could only stare straight ahead toward the back of the room as I returned to my seat, my stomach turning somersaults: relieved, afraid, glad, foolish, hopeful somehow, embarrassed all over again. Suddenly one person clapped, then another, then another, and finally, amazingly, the whole room was applauding. For me, though, this was a moment not to be proud of, but to be humbly thankful for.

Mike and I never spoke about the incident. He moved out of state soon after when the semester ended, so I never knew if he accepted my apology. Mike had never asked me out again, and I surprised myself when I felt genuinely sorry about that.

Mr. Kincaid didn't know how much he helped me. He gave me an A on the speech, but what I learned was much more than how to speak off-the-cuff. I realized that if I wouldn't say something to a person's face, I shouldn't say it about him or her to anyone else. Just because what I have to say might be true, I didn't have the obligation, the liberty, or the "right" to say it unless my words were also help-ful, kind, and necessary. Those four "filters" for my conversations about others—is this true, helpful, kind, necessary?—have certainly saved me and others I know from more mutually embarrassing and destructive moments.

Did Mike ever realize what I tried to do in speech class that day and accept my apology? Well, not long ago I got a note from him through a website on the Internet. Occasionally, we write to catch up on each other's families. Even though we've gone separate ways, I'm grateful for the healing that came for both of us from my admitting I was wrong. After forty years it's nice—really nice—to know that despite your failures, at your high school reunions you can still be friends with the people who called you a friend so long ago.

~Rose M. Jackson

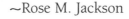

But I Never Spoke

Unless someone like you cares a whole awful lot,
nothing is going to get better. It's not.
~Dr. Seuss

We were only acquaintances really.
Not quite at the friendship level,
But not at all considered enemies.
We smiled in the halls,
Talked a little on the Internet at night.
But I never spoke.

She was much prettier than I,
Much more popular than I ever wished to be.
More friends, better grades.
But that was only half of what I could see.
And as I watched her that one morning,
I wondered silently where she was going.
But I never spoke.

I would hear the rumors,
But I would turn my head.
Why should I care?
Rumors are nothing more than lies.
And I continued to talk to her,

Admire her for her brains and beauty.
But still I never spoke.

I wandered aimlessly one morning,
To the bathroom where she had gone.
And I couldn't help but cry,
As I listened to her vomiting in that stall,
As I realized it was all true.
But as she walked out,
I quickly rubbed my eyes.
And still I never spoke.

And now I stand here at her funeral,
Listening to some guy speak,
About all of her accomplishments.
In my head I hear what the doctors said,
Malnutrition, underweight, bulimic for too long.
And still, even after it's over and done,
I do not speak.

~Monique Ayub

Middle Ground

A slip of the foot you may soon recover,
but a slip of the tongue you may never get over.
~Benjamin Franklin

I n the middle of my junior year, I had to transfer to a new school—a school much bigger than my old high school—and I was terrified. It meant having to find my way around a whole new campus with a semester already in progress. However, I was met with acceptance in Journalism class from the moment I walked in, primarily because of one group of girls and one girl in particular.

The J-I classroom contained rectangular tables, and the students sat around them in groups of four. I was assigned to the very first table, where there was an empty seat. I was immediately welcomed to the class by this one girl, Roxanne. Our other two tablemates, Sarah and Chrissy, seemed to like me too, but it was Roxie I grew closest to. Roxie smiled often, laughed more, and had the prettiest blue eyes. Her eyelashes were long and thick and separated, framing her eyes just so, which gave an effect of sparkling stars. To this day, when I think of eyes that twinkle, I think of Roxie's beautiful sea-blue eyes.

So I became a part of their table, and it delighted me. Sarah and Chrissy were cheerleaders, and Roxie was in the school drum corps. In my last school, I had been grouped with the studious, brainy kids, so to be deemed part of a foursome with these popular girls pleased me immensely. As the weeks went by and autumn became winter, our table consistently turned in good stories and layouts. We worked well together as a team, and most of all we had fun.

Meanwhile, in algebra class, I made another new friend. Deanne was a bit rough around the edges, but she was funny and smart. She wasn't a well-liked girl, though, and I noticed right away that many of the kids actually shunned her. I tried not to let this affect me, even when she sometimes acted hostile toward our classmates. She was still my friend, plus she understood algebra, and since it wasn't my strongest suit, she made the class more tolerable. There came a time, however, when Dee realized that Roxie and I were close. I've often wondered, looking back, whether what happened later that year was something Dee had planned all along.

It seemed that Dee liked the boy Roxie was dating. Of course, I didn't know this at first, but both girls promptly brought it to my attention. For Roxie, it was a matter of sharing information, for Dee, a growing obsession. Dee had a class with this boy, and during class they got along well. Perhaps, like me, he was just trying to be her friend, but whatever his motivation, Dee took it to mean that he would have asked her out, if not for Roxie. Dee soon began grilling me: What does Roxie say about him? How serious are they? Does she ever talk about me?

As time went on, the pressure of Dee's continual questions got to me. Words tumbled out of my mouth as if by their own will. I was disgusted with myself for talking about Roxie, for reporting a play-by-play of her status with her boyfriend, but when I tried to ignore Dee's inquisition, she grew increasingly hostile. Talking about Roxie with Dee turned into a coping mechanism of sorts, the only way I was able to keep Dee pacified.

It didn't take long for Roxie to become aware of Dee's jealousy. To my dismay, Roxie then began asking me about Dee: What's she saying about me? What's she saying about him? Why does she hate me?

All too quickly, I was in the middle with no place to go, wondering how in the world I'd gotten there. I tried to ride in that middle ground for as long as I could, to appease both girls. I tried being a friend to them both, but they put me in the middle and I caved. The questions they fired at me came more rapidly, more pointed, more loaded. The situation volleyed out of my control, swiftly becoming combustible. Who knew that Dee would soon go ballistic?

It happened in a gym class that the two girls shared. Dee attacked Roxie in the locker room, screaming, spitting, pummeling—so full of rage that she tore one of Roxie's hoop earrings completely down through the flesh of her ear, leaving a ragged hole. Both girls got suspended for fighting, even though Dee was the one who started it.

News of the fight traveled quickly around our school. When I heard about it, I was mortified. I couldn't sleep at night. Roxie had been nothing but kind to me and I knew that, in part, what I'd said to each girl had fueled this. Shaken, I was called into the counselor's office to give my side of the story, but my side felt so incredibly lame. Instead of standing up for Roxie, I'd done her irreparable harm. I'd done Dee harm too, by letting her use me as a way to focus her hostility. Instead of refusing to talk to one girl about the other, I'd taken what I thought was the easy way out, only to find it wasn't easy at all. I wasn't suspended, but in my own court of law, I should have been. I had been complicit in the whole miserable situation. The guilt I felt was oppressive, like a sudden fog that strangles you, leaving you unable to breathe as it settles in around you for days.

The fog didn't soon lift, even though outside temperatures were moderate. It was early spring, and my dad's daffodils were already approaching full bloom in our yard. We were on our way to the end of the school year, a year that had been going so well until that awful fight. It had been rumored that I would be chosen as yearbook editor for our next year's J-II class, and I knew Roxie's encouragement had had a lot to do with that. She'd helped me shine, she'd helped me find confidence. In her absence, I felt lost.

I'll never forget the look in Roxie's eyes when she returned to school after her suspension and sat down at our table. "You really got me in trouble," was all she seemed able to say to me.

My eyes filled with instant tears, and within seconds we were both crying. "I'm so sorry, Rox," I said, choking on the words. "I never meant to hurt you."

Roxie forgave me and we managed to stay friends, while Dee only spoke to me long enough to call me a traitor. There was no middle ground for me in all this. I should have kept my mouth shut and I blew it. The pain in Roxie's blue eyes told me just how much I'd messed up, a far worse punishment than if she'd snubbed me. Her kindness and her forgiveness hurt worse than any suspension ever could. What happened that year still bothers me, even now. It served as a powerful lesson about the damage that gossip and talking about others can do.

~Theresa Sanders

Regretting My First Kiss

You will do foolish things,
but do them with enthusiasm.
~Colette

I wish I could take back my first kiss. I wish that it hadn't been out of spite and jealous revenge. I wish that I hadn't been stupid and drank that night. I wish for a lot of things, but most of all, I wish that I had dealt with everything differently, so I wouldn't be stuck with this memory.

A sixteenth birthday party, especially your own, is supposed to be cherished. It's supposed to be something to look back on with fondness and say, "Wow. That was great." The night started out perfectly. My best friend Katie and I were sharing our party, and she arrived at my house to get ready. We pulled on our dresses and applied our make-up to the blasting tunes of Justin Timberlake and 50 Cent. An hour before our party, Katie pulled out a bottle of vodka.

"It's our sixteenth!" she said, unscrewing the cap. "Have fun and drink up!" Although it was diluted with cranberry juice, the alcohol still burned my throat and my stomach, and immediately gave me a buzzing sensation in my head. I felt like I wasn't myself, but that wasn't such a bad thing. I was usually a wallflower, the shy girl in the back of the classroom who knew the answers but wouldn't raise her hand. So maybe not being myself was good, especially on the night of my birthday.

That was my first mistake: Not being me.

The second didn't occur until the guests started arriving. Since Katie and I don't live in the same state, the coffee shop we had rented was soon packed with teenagers from New York and Connecticut. Katie and I enjoyed ourselves and began making regular trips to the bathroom to finish off the rest of the vodka in doses from the little plastic cups. We never got through the whole thing, and we didn't need to. I was tipsy from the first sip, and I was probably drunk by the time the party was halfway through. It was that night I found out I was a lightweight.

With the flow of partygoers, my friend Chris finally arrived. I had known him since we were both three, and our relationship had been complicated ever since I started liking him as more than a friend. That summer, though, he had gotten a girlfriend, and when I called him to get together, he was always busy. Maybe I was being immature then, but he was my first real crush, and he was dating a girl who none of his other friends liked, and who hated me.

That was the second mistake: Letting my jealousy get to me.

I was going to make Chris see that I could be fun and beautiful, as well as intelligent. I already felt the part, with my hot pink dress, elegantly curled hair, and boosted confidence, so all I needed was to act like it. I danced and laughed and flirted, but he didn't notice, or didn't seem to care. In the middle of it all, I spotted the one who would make Chris experience the heartbreaking envy that I was feeling.

His name was Sam, and I hadn't seen him in forever. When I still lived in an apartment about eight years ago, he lived in the room below me. Back then, though, he was an innocent boy who used to do everything with me, from skating to seeing movies to going trick-or-treating during Halloween. Now? He smoked, he drank, and he did drugs.... He was the complete opposite of me, and the epitome of the guy I was taught to stay away from. Despite that, I felt if anyone could help me, it would be Sam. No one knew him, he didn't know anyone, and, best of all, he didn't know the real me.

We were on the couch before I knew what was happening. I was curled up next to him, his arm around my shoulders, as we yelled to each other above the pounding music. Everyone was stealing glances in our direction, gossiping unbelievingly that I was actually with a boy, while Katie tried to avert their attention. There was some novelty to the moment, something that compelled me to actually start to like it. I had never had a boyfriend, and I had never had a boy pay this much attention to me before. I couldn't believe it. Sam, who had probably had numerous girlfriends and partied every night, actually seemed like he was interested in me... Or, at least, the person he thought I was.

Which brings us to my third mistake: Letting it get too far.

When he leaned in to kiss me, I must have known on some level that it wasn't really me he wanted to kiss. He wanted to kiss the vision I had created for myself. And I knew that I hadn't really wanted him to kiss me anyway. I just wanted Chris to look over and see us talking and having a great time in the hopes that he'd realize we were meant to be together. But that's not how it happened.

I leaned away as he was leaning forward.

"Are you going to kiss me?" I asked, which I immediately regretted. What was I doing, asking him that? How much of a loser could I be?

"Uh, yeah... I was thinking about it," Sam said, looking perplexed—and rightfully so. I felt bad. Here he was, this cute boy who obviously wanted to kiss me, and there Chris was, already taken. I didn't think about the consequences or the aftermath. In fact, I didn't think much at all... my thought process was limited at the time. So I just smiled and leaned in, kissing Sam.

I felt nothing.

I had always imagined the setting for my first kiss to be somewhere romantic, like a beach or a park, or the front steps of my house. I had also imagined feeling something, like that flow of happiness to the heart that's supposed to come with a kiss, but I didn't feel that either. My first kiss, I realized with a shock, had just happened, and it was not at all as I pictured it. It had been on a worn leather couch at the back of a crowded room, with the music so loud I could barely hear and with a guy who I hadn't seen for years, and didn't know very well.

My plan hadn't worked. By the time the night was over, I realized three things: Chris didn't like me anymore than he had before (if anything, he probably lost his respect seeing me kissing a random guy), Sam and the rest of the teenagers there thought I was "easy," and alcohol may seem like it can solve any problem, but when the effect is over, it leaves you picking up the pieces of your mistakes... alone.

~Nicollette Alvarez

Lines Leading Home

Keep your promises to yourself.
~David Harold Fink

It was my best friend Karen's eighteenth birthday. She and all of our friends had been planning a huge river lot party near her dad's house, complete with a rope swing and campfire. Earlier that evening, as I was leaning into my mirror to apply my mascara, I heard Yung Joc's "It's Goin' Down" blast from my cell phone. I quickly ran to it, knowing it was a text about tonight's festivities.

"HURRY UP! WHERE ARE YOU?!" I read.

"Chill. I'm leaving my house now, so sit tight," was my reply to her impatient message. I gathered all that I needed for the night. My dad helped me load my tent into my car as he gave me a long lecture about partying at my age.

"I know you're going to drink. I'm not stupid, Whitney," he started. "But you need to do it responsibly and safely. You're a smart girl and I trust you not to do anything that can hurt you or anyone else." I rolled my eyes and tried to defend myself by saying that not all teenagers need alcohol to enjoy themselves. I don't know why I wasted my time—he isn't stupid, he was right about that. He knew my plans. Go there, drink enough to make myself look cool, then crawl into my tent and pass out. Although those plans don't sound very responsible, I wish that's all I had done that evening.

The ride to the river lot was almost an hour. The trip was nothing but steep hills, sharp turns, deer bounding out into the road in front of us, and rain pouring down so hard that it sounded like gravel was bouncing off my windshield. If I had had any sense at the time, I would have turned around, gone home, and spent my evening with popcorn and my *Boy Meets World* DVD. Looking back, I wish I had done just that. When we arrived, I was so stressed from the rigorous drive that I quickly twisted the lid off a handle of vodka and toasted the birthday girl.

The party got out of control fast. Most of our friends kept calling and bailing on us and most of the guests were uninvited strangers. After about four hours of drinking, falling and sliding in mud, and goofing off, all of us were about ready to crash. I stumbled my way up the big hill I had to park on and attempted to get my tent out to set it up. Completely not happening. I was in no condition to carry the tent down a muddy hill and attempt to put it up. Considering I wasn't even able to bring the tent down, I should not—and I put so much stress on that "not"—have thought I was in any condition to drive home.

After countless shots of vodka and numerous Mike's Hard Lemonades, I let all the alcohol I had consumed do my talking. "I'm fi-fi-fine to drive home. I promise. I can drive so much better when I'm drunk, just watch and see!" Shortly after that, my long Jackson High School lanyard, with my keys attached, ended up in my hands and I was headed home. No, the rain hadn't stopped—nor had it died down at all, and my eyes kept wandering to my fluorescent red clock. With all of the distractions I was dealing with, the worst was the "I trust you" repeating in my head that my dad had said just hours ago.

I tried regaining all focus by promising myself everything would be fine in the morning, and every second we were one inch closer to Karen's house. Cars passed me as I prayed I wouldn't swerve over the line and hurt anyone because of my horrible actions. The time dragged like molasses and I felt as if I were the only one in the car who actually cared that I was committing so many dangerous crimes in one car ride. Everyone was so infatuated with their chain-smoking and my boyfriend's stupid jokes that I almost wanted to pull over and walk myself to safety, not worrying about how my friends got home.

I couldn't see anything except four yellow lines. Or maybe they were white lines—I don't remember and I don't really care. I certainly know my boyfriend didn't care, as he giggled in the backseat, sandwiched between my two best friends. The strange guy in my passenger seat wouldn't stop caressing my leg as he whispered, "everything will be okay," in my ear. Gross. I guess my boyfriend didn't care about that either. He was the last thing on my mind at that moment.

I had to stay focused on trying to keep the half-eaten strawberry phyllo cake from falling off my lap as I swerved through the whatever-colored lines. I would have loved to have been able to glance in my rearview mirror to keep a look out for any red and blue lights that might have been approaching, but an obnoxiously oversized mylar balloon obstructed my view. I tried to listen to sirens, but belligerent singing and talking clogged my ears. I was screwed for the next forty-five minutes as I tried to stay within my allotted lane space.

Finally, I reached Bruce Road and pulled into my friend's driveway. I don't think I'll ever in my life forget what I did next. I opened my door, threw out that gross cake no one even liked, and cried. I cried and cried and cried. I cried for so long that the next day my eyes were swollen shut.

After I cried for what seemed like a lifetime, I did something I never thought I'd do. I called my parents. "Hello?" my dad answered with a raspy voice as if the phone had just awoken him. "Dad, I don't want to talk about it now, I just want you to come to Karen's and get me. Bring mom so she can drive my car home. I love you and please drive safely," I said as I slammed my cell phone shut. I didn't talk to any of my friends that night; I just left when my parents arrived.

What happened with my parents was what I expected, and deserved. I will never forget the lives that could have been lost on that rainy October night. I am strongly reminded of this every time I get in my car or attend any event serving alcohol. Luckily for me, my passengers, and all the innocent drivers on the road that night, those lines that I vaguely remember led me to safety. Absolutely nothing can justify my actions and make my choice to drink and drive acceptable, but I'm glad that I learned my lesson without hurting anyone. Never have I been so scared in my life. I also now realize the true impairment of alcohol and vow to never repeat my actions.

~Whitney Smoot

A Hard Lesson

Wisdom consists of the anticipation of consequences.
~Norman Cousins

I t happened on an Advanced Placement English class trip to England in my junior year of high school. My classmates and I were having a grand time in jolly old England, seeing the sights, soaking up all that rich history, attending plays, visiting museums, and still it wasn't enough—we decided to up the ante.

One night we snuck out of our hotel, bought way too much alcohol from a corner shop, and proceeded to turn the top two floors of the hotel into a scene from *Animal House*. What they don't show you in the movies are the real and long-lasting effects of too much alcohol on an inexperienced young adult—not yet seventeen—such as myself.

Our English teacher and chaperone, Ms. Overdale, stared at me for a long time when I sat down shakily at her little breakfast table rather early the next morning. This was a teacher with whom I had formed a strong bond. I was developing a passion for literature, for writing, and she was an encouraging voice, a valuable presence in my life. And here I was, in the grip of the king of all hangovers, held together by a thread that might snap at the slightest touch.

She did nothing to mask the disappointment on her face and I could do nothing but wither further under her strong gaze. She was not unsympathetic, but told me firmly that I was going to have to deal with the fact that my parents would have to be told, that the school board would be notified, that I might be suspended, that I might very well have jeopardized trips for future classes, and on and on. As she spoke, my temples pounded, my eyes bulged, and my world absolutely collapsed. I nodded, said I was sorry, vowed it would never happen again, and then I looked into her kind eyes and saw the disappointment there—that's when I truly apologized. And I meant every second of it. And then I ran for the bathroom. Apparently, my tender constitution was not yet ready for apologies, or for the orange juice she had insisted I drink.

Most of what she had predicted that early morning in a darkened London hotel dining room came true. My parents, hard-working dairy farmers who had to work extra hard to send me on the trip, were of course told, and were suitably and justifiably mortified, angry, and disappointed. I would have done anything to change the situation. The disappointment in their eyes brought to mind immediately that in Ms. Overdale's, and was more punishment than I could imagine. I would have gladly shouldered twice the load of farm chores I was given if only it could have erased that look from their faces.

It didn't end with my parents. I was suspended from school for several days, my grades were affected, and the entire population of the school seemed to know more about the incident—and the night of revelry in question—than did I. Which, I suppose, is only fitting, since my own memory of the episode is spotty at best. And it was not yet over. I was informed that I would not be allowed to attend the prom—the prom that my date had anticipated for months. My date's parents had spent much time and hard-earned money on buying and altering a dress for her, to say nothing of the tuxedo rental on which I had already laid out a good deal of non-refundable deposit money.

My one night of poor judgment was setting in motion an entire series of unfortunate events that seemed to have no end. The worst of it was that innocent people were being affected by my behavior. I decided to take matters into my own hands. I attended the school board's next meeting. I still remember the odd feeling of going back to the high school at night, the dim, after-hours lighting reflecting off the corridors' polished linoleum, the teachers' dining room as the light at the end of the tunnel — a light toward which I wasn't so sure I wanted to head. But I did.

Just like in a movie, I swallowed hard, knocked, and looked in the half-open door. Nearly a dozen middle-aged men, plus the vice principal, the bulldog of our daytime hours, the enforcer of the school's policies (and the father of one of my classmates who happened to have participated in the revelries of that ill-fated night in London) all turned their tired, bored eyes on me. Not a smile among them. They had been informed as to why I was there.

I was given a nod, and so I began explaining my situation, how I believed it was unfair that my prom date should suffer for my dumb mistake. I'll do whatever it takes, I said. Is there any distasteful task the school needs done? Anything at all? As a farm boy, I was used to long hours and hard work.

I was forced to wait outside the room for what seemed like forever. In the end, the vice principal told me that they had decided I could go to the prom, but that I would be on probation for the remainder of the school year. And that they would indeed take me up on my offer of work. I was to help the curmudgeonly old janitor, Mr. Kirby, strip and re-wax all the floors in the school. Well, I thought, sighing inside — I asked for it. The vice principal then did a strange thing. He smiled and shook my hand.

"You know," he said, looking serious again. "In all my years in this job, I've never had a student do what you did here tonight. I'm glad you did." He turned to go, then looked back at me and said, "I hope you are, too."

The next year, while applying to colleges, I needed a letter of recommendation from a teacher. Ms. Overdale agreed to help. And reading that letter made me swallow hard again. It read, in part, "He is not afraid to accept responsibility for his actions." It is a simple sentence, but it made me feel good inside that someone I respected so much had recognized one of my better qualities, despite the ample reasons I gave her not to. It is a quality I can thank my parents for. By trusting my gut feeling (which by then had recovered from its London escapade), I had unwittingly done the correct thing.

A reemergence of breast cancer took Ms. Overdale's life a couple of years later. I was not aware when I knew her that she had already been through so much in her own life. Her continued faith in me is a gift for which I will always be grateful.

I would like to say that since the incident I have abstained from overindulgences of any sort, but I cannot. What I can say is that whenever I sense myself beginning to indulge in excessive behavior, I hear a little voice in the back of my mind—not unlike that of my favorite teacher, Ms. Overdale. That voice is saying something like, "Don't forget about the people who may be affected by what you do or don't do. Never forget one person's importance to others."

By the way, my date and I had a great time at the prom. And no, we didn't go to any parties afterwards.

~Matthew P. Mayo

Girl Stuff

An ounce of blood is worth more
than a pound of friendship.
~Spanish Proverb

When I was fifteen, I was invited to pledge for a high school sorority. The girls who formed it modeled the sorority after ones their older sisters were members of in college. Three of my friends were also invited to pledge. We thought it was a big deal at the time.

We went through all the stupid stuff that was required, like going around looking goth and wearing purple lipstick and black nail polish. My mother hated the whole thing and thought it was totally dumb. But I guess I felt a need to belong. I tended to be on the quiet side, a good student, but not as outgoing. Still, I was attractive enough and had my share of friends.

Our school principal was angry about all the hazing and called the two girls who were running the sorority into his office. He had caught the pledges on their knees bowing down to the sorority sisters in the hallway. The principal was furious. He called sorority hazing "out of control" and vowed to end it in our high school. The sorority sisters were threatened with suspension if the hazing didn't stop. Our principal was a tough guy, and his actions ended one of the many forms of torment.

Somehow, I managed to make it through all the yucky stuff. We pledges were told we had to go to an installation ceremony. This was going to be a fancy party where we got all dressed up and came with dates. I didn't have a boyfriend, nor did my two best friends. An older friend, Barbara, told us that she would set us up with the most popular seniors from her high school.

"These guys are football players. They're terrific. You've never met anyone like them," she told me.

But things like this never seemed to go smoothly for me. It turned out that on the exact evening of the installation, my favorite cousin on my mother's side was going to have a big engagement party. She was twenty and didn't plan to be married right away, since she and her fiancé were both still in college.

But a really great engagement party was still planned.

I knew I had a very difficult decision to make. I wanted to go to both functions, yet I realized that wasn't possible. I explained the situation to Barbara, who urged me again to go to the installation.

"It's going to be so great. You'll really regret it for the rest of your life if you miss it," she said.

I told my mother that I couldn't go to my cousin's engagement party. She was, needless to say, very upset.

"This is a family affair. It's more important than some club function. Please reconsider. You're making a big mistake."

Well, I thought about it. I really did. But it seemed to me that being a teenager, I should be with friends rather than family. Besides, I'd been promised I was going to have a really fantastic date.

Using the babysitting money I'd carefully saved, I paid for a party dress, matching heels, the cost of the installation dinner for myself and my guest, and getting my hair done. It bankrupted my savings. I was paying a high price for the honor of being installed into the sorority. In fact, it turned out to be a higher price than I realized. My mother was really disappointed in me. So were my aunt, uncle and cousin.

The big evening finally arrived. I was looking my best and felt very grown up. My parents left for the engagement party while I was waiting for my date to pick me up. He showed up about an hour late. I was beginning to have some qualms, when I finally heard a car horn honking. I went outside and saw my two girlfriends in a car with two boys.

My date barely looked at me. "Get in," he said.

Right away, my heart sunk. He was rude and he wasn't even all that attractive. My friends and I were seated together for the installation dinner, which was a good thing. My date and their dates were friends and spent the entire time goofing around together. They didn't look at us. They didn't even speak to us. When I tried to make conversation with my date, I was ignored.

I got the distinct impression these guys had only agreed to come to the dinner because they were promised a free meal. My date didn't dance with me and was an immature jerk. I felt like murdering Barbara, who had managed to get herself a very nice date for the party.

I finally decided to say something to her. "So what's the deal here? I thought you said this guy was going to be terrific, someone totally special."

"Well, he's really popular," she said.

"Hard to believe," I responded. "How could anyone so obnoxious be liked?" Frankly, I was more than ready to go home.

It was truly the worst date I ever had in my entire life. But that was not the most terrible part. When my parents came home from the engagement party, my mother said that a lot of family members had asked for me.

"It was such a shame," she said. "Your cousin had planned to seat you with her fiancé's cousin, a very handsome, charming boy from a wealthy family. I met him and thought you would have liked him. He's going to college next year."

I knew for certain I'd made the wrong decision. But when you're a teenage girl, you want to think for yourself. You don't want to do just what your mother tells you to do. I don't know if Barbara deliberately set me up with a totally awful date on purpose. I doubt it. I believe she had a different perception of what made for a good date. At least, I'd like to think so.

But I did learn something about thinking for myself. Giving in to peer pressure and doing things just because another teen tells you to do it isn't really thinking for yourself or making your own decisions. And I never went on another blind date.

~Jacqueline Seewald

Center Your Life

Not until we are lost do we begin to understand ourselves.
~Henry David Thoreau

My sophomore year in high school, I discovered ceramics. I had always been interested in art, but too afraid of failure. It wasn't until after I had enrolled in ceramics that I would find a passion for it. I signed up for the course thinking it would be an easy grade. As the year progressed, I realized my potential. My teacher, Mr. Yoshida, always had words of encouragement.

We were taught to center our clay on the wheel. Centering our clay not only made the process of throwing, or the forming of a pot on the wheel, easier, it helped keep our product from being wobbly and unstable. I can remember one day having a hard time centering my clay and wanting to quit. Mr. Yoshida approached me and said, "Center your life." I thought to myself, "Yeah, that doesn't help." It wasn't until two years later that I found the true meaning behind this saying.

It was December and I was with some friends, drinking, hanging out, and just celebrating that it was winter break. It was then that I made the decision to drive home after drinking. I was pulled over, and the last thing I remember is seeing my parents crying at the sight of me with my head smashed up against the back window of the squad car. I was arrested for DUI, possession of a controlled substance, possession of a fake ID, and a few other charges. I was taken to jail and booked without hesitation. In jail, I had a lot of time to think and reflect on what I had done and how it was affecting not only me, but my family as well.

When I was released on bail, I went home. As I was about to lie in my bed, I saw a Bible with a note attached to it. The note was from my parents, saying they wanted me to read a few passages they had marked off. After reading the New Testament, I came to the conclusion that the drugs, sex, and alcohol were only a temporary form of happiness; once the high wore off, I wasn't happy. I was seeking happiness in all the wrong places. I wouldn't be totally happy until I was willing to accept God and devote my life to him. That is when it hit me. Mr. Yoshida's saying rang through my head like a church bell on a Sunday morning, "Center your life." He wasn't just speaking about ceramics; he was imparting a life lesson. Just like centering your clay stabilizes it and makes for a better product, until I could fully accept God as my center, I wouldn't be stable or happy with myself.

That night, I could not sleep. It was all so simple—why hadn't I thought of this before? I hadn't realized the power of the saying. I was so one-dimensional, I thought it only applied to the clay that was in front of me. As I tossed and turned, I realized that I was giving in to temptation. It was easy to get that temporary release and happiness, but true happiness is hard to come by. Even though giving into temptation may seem easy, I had to overcome temptation to "center my life." Three simple words were the entryway to the beginning of my new, better life.

I now look back and reflect on that dreadful early morning incident, but not in a negative way. I use my arrest as motivation and inspiration for young people, to show that good people do make mistakes. It's what you do afterwards that truly helps you "center your life."

~Thomas Schonhardt

I Thought I Had Time

You may delay, but time will not.
~Benjamin Franklin

I thought I had time.
The first day of school
Went smooth and cool.

I met the teachers
Ignored their assignments,
Scoffed at their rules,
Laughed at their shoes.
I had time.

I sat sideways
During instruction.
Talked to my friends.
Chewed gum to no end.
I had time.

I had a few disagreements
That led to fights.
I got suspended a few times.
I tried to be bad with all my might.
I had time.

I wasn't prepared
When standardized tests came.
I figured listening in class
Was so very lame.
I had time.

My friends lined up
To graduate.
I had flunked.
It was too late.
I had run out of time.
I thought I had time.

~Jacqueline Perkins

Pomp and Happenstance

Wherever there is a human being,
there is an opportunity for a kindness.
~Seneca

'm walking to my high school's commencement exercises. My family isn't coming because I'm not participating, and why would anyone subject themselves to a commencement ceremony unless obligated to? I'm not sure why I'm even going. I guess for some reason I want to see all these people one last time. That, and I told Mr. Larson I'd sing with the choir.

Graduates pass me in cars with their families, all wearing their caps and gowns. Every commencement ceremony I've gone to before has made me envision my own graduation. I go to this one knowing that this is supposed to be it, but it's not. My graduation won't ever come with "Pomp and Circumstance" and a cap and gown. It will come after I complete the summer school course of the computer class that I failed because I didn't turn in enough of the assigned work. I spent the class time sleeping, surfing the Internet and trying to break my record on Typing Tutor.

I arrive at the Marriott Center on Brigham Young University's campus, descend the endless flight of stairs to the floor and take my place next to the juniors in the choir. I look through the audience to see who I know.

I spot Mrs. Koffard, the dance teacher whose class I failed because I only showed up during the first two weeks. I see Mrs. Clifford, my

Spanish teacher. Hers was the only class I liked going to this term. I remember when she taught us the preterite tense verb conjugations to the tune of the Mexican Hat Dance. Some of the other students thought she was goofy and eccentric. She is—that's why I like her. She's taking next year off from teaching because she's expecting her first baby in October. I went to see her earlier today. We had our first conversation in English while she cleaned out her room. Somehow it came up that I didn't have a yearbook. Mrs. Clifford was a bit taken aback by this. Immediately she offered to buy one for me. I accepted and thanked her profusely as she signed it.

I'm remembering the D- Mr. Brower gave me in drama. I know it's more than I earned. After I figured out that I didn't need his class to graduate, I quit caring or trying, just like I quit caring in computers. But I need that credit in computers, so now I'll have to go to school during my vacation. I'm more upset about that than I am about not being able to participate in commencement.

The audience rises in rippling waves as the members of the graduating class file in and take their places. They all look the same in their caps and gowns, like huge, royal blue ants, hundreds of them. I think the caps are pretty funny looking, but it could have to do with the fact that I'm not wearing one.

Everyone remains standing while senior class vice president, Tabitha, leads the Pledge of Allegiance. Tabitha is the embodiment of the high school world that I'm not a part of. She has money and looks and boys trailing after her like tin cans on the back of a honeymoon car. All year I've watched her in her pristine world of primping and prom and friends and football games. She seems to find satisfaction in these things. I can't understand why. The frivolity of it all makes me crazy and I've wanted out for months. Commencement is the final fiery hoop I have to jump through before I can leave.

Now the orchestra has to play a piece. As if inflicting "Pomp and Circumstance" on us wasn't enough! This stupid program is already going to be too long. I feel a blister forming on my left heel because I walked a mile and a half in my Sunday shoes. I wish I were home soaking in the tub and listening to Sarah McLachlan. The orchestra's song ends and the school principal, Mr. Merrill, begins to drone. I tune him out. He's not talking to me anyway. I'm not a graduate.

"As you go out to make your way in this world," Mr. Merrill begins, "I want you to take this as your creed: 'I am a nacho, and the world is my dip.'" Everyone else laughs hysterically. I look at my watch for the millionth time.

The valedictorian and salutatorian give their speeches and now we get to sing. I watch Mr. Larson's hands closely, trying to make every note perfect. Our song ends and I sit down with a tinge of sadness. High school choir is officially over now, and I don't know when I'll be singing again.

Finally it's over. Everyone rises and the Marriott Center floor is suddenly flooded with people. I want to leave as quickly as possible, but I'm drowning in a sea of weeping relatives and bobbing blue, square caps. I try to swim toward the tunnel that leads outside. Suddenly, someone is touching my arm and I turn to see who it is.

"Congratulations, sweetheart!" Mrs. Clifford gives me a big hug, squishing me against her pregnant belly. "You're all through. Now you can call me Michele." She's treating me like I'm wearing a cap and gown and just walked through with the graduates. I don't know what to say. Why am I getting choked up? Her pretty green eyes look concerned. "How are you doing, Hon?"

"I'm alright," I answer weakly.

"Are you going to the senior all-night party?" she asks. Of course I'm not. I don't have the thirty-eight dollars for that, or anyone to hang out with even if I did.

"No," I say in that same small voice.

"Do you wanna go?" she asks.

I think about it. What would it be like to actually belong and participate in something to do with high school for once? "Kind of," I answer.

"You're going!" she says. And with that she takes my hand and begins pulling me through the crowd.

Now the tears that have been brimming in my eyes spill down

my face. She sees them and pulls me back into another hug. "Thank you," I manage to get out of my tightening throat.

She can't possibly fathom how much this means to me. I always participated and excelled in her class and she didn't know me in any other setting. We only spoke Spanish in the classroom, so the deepest conversation we ever had was about the color of my carpet. She has no knowledge of my depressive episodes or anxiety attacks that began in third grade and have increased exponentially throughout high school. She doesn't know that I've never felt like I belonged anywhere in my entire life and my peers have never had any use for me. But now my funny, beautiful, free-spirited Spanish teacher is showing me such compassion and acceptance. Why is she doing this for me?

"Annette," Mrs. Clifford calls out. One of the assistant principals comes over to us. "Annette, this is Leah. She wants to go to the party."

"Alrighty," Annette says smiling. "We'll take care of her."

I look at Mrs. Clifford in disbelief. She sees the uncertainty on my face and tries to reassure me. "Have fun," she says. "That's all I ask."

"Okay," I reply. Annette takes me to a phone so I can let my parents know that I'll be home late. My dad answers, hears my still-shaky voice, and asks what's wrong.

I feel my throat tightening and new tears coming to my eyes. "Everything's fine," I tell him. "Do you know what Mrs. Clifford did for me?"

~Leah Elliott Hauge

Chapter
8

Teens Talk

HIGH SCHOOL

Going for It

Clear your mind of "can't."

~Samuel Johnson

The Unlikely Queen

Leaders don't create followers,
they create more leaders.
~Tom Peters

Ever since I was fourteen years old, I knew that I wanted to be her. She was everything that I was not: tall, beautiful, smart and seemingly perfect in every way. She was Amanda Harrison, a senior at my high school who was great at just about everything. She was a star basketball player, a member of the National Honor Society, Senior Class president, and Homecoming Queen.

Although, she never knew it, I looked up to her. I aspired to be her and was proud of everything that she did. Whenever I heard her name during the morning announcements congratulating her on scoring the winning basket, I beamed. Whenever I saw her walking towards the podium to make a speech for accepting academic achievement awards, I applauded as loud as I could. Whenever I crossed her path in the hallways, regardless of how my day had been, for that fleeting moment, my day was made instantly better.

She was my role model and the woman who I one day hoped I would become. She had everything that I ever wanted and always appeared to be living the life that I could only dream of.

Realistically, I knew that her life was not perfect and that she probably was going through struggles, unseen to me. But, from the outside looking in, I believed in her, and loved her as the older sister that I never had or even thought that I wanted.

Over the next three years, I walked in her footsteps. Using her as an example, I strove to be the best student, the best friend, and the best daughter that I could be. I wanted to show that her legacy lived on in me and I wanted her to be as proud of me as I was of her.

If this were an ideal world, I would have tried out for the basketball team and had the perfect season, culminating in making the state-championship-winning shot, the same shot that she missed her senior year. I would have run for Student Council President and won, revolutionizing student life and bringing about much needed changes. I would have been valedictorian and given an awe-inspiring speech on how we were on the cusp of changing the world.

Unfortunately, this is not an ideal world. I was far from being an athlete; I was not the brightest; I was not the most popular. In order words, I was average. Better phrased: I was not extraordinary.

I was completely unlike Amanda Harrison, who had more athletic ability, popularity, and charm in her pinkie than I had in my entire being. She had it, and I did not.

There was just an indescribable feeling that radiated from her and could catch you off guard every now and then. One such moment came during the week of Homecoming, my freshman year. Every year, my school holds a toilet paper fashion show to crown the new Homecoming Queen. Any interested senior is required to wear a dress fashioned entirely from toilet paper in front of the entire school. A panel of judges votes on the best one and the winning senior is then crowned Homecoming Queen at the dance later that evening.

In hindsight, the whole idea seems designed to elicit humiliation and embarrassment. If a misplaced, loose, or fragile bit of toilet paper somehow comes undone or breaks, its wearer ends up showing a lot more than she would like. However, everything usually runs smoothly and people have a good time.

That year, just like every other, the school cheered and applauded as each senior paraded into the gymnasium. Some of the dresses were short and cute while others were long and elegant. One, in fact, was not a dress at all. One senior wrapped herself up like a mummy and left the whole school in uproarious laughter. Even though it was funny, the toilet paper show seemed to be missing something.

And that's when Amanda Harrison walked out. There was a collective audible gasp when she appeared and quite literally took our breath away. She had a regal and radiant quality about her that I wished I could have.

So, with that in mind, during my senior year when the opportunity presented itself, I immediately decided to partake in the toilet paper contest. That entire week, I prepped for the fashion show. I debated the color choice (white, pink, blue, or beige), style (plain or patterned), and ply count. I designed the perfect dress, an off-the-shoulder formal gown with a longer train in the back. At home, I made one practice dress. I felt ready for Friday.

During school that day, I was in a tizzy. I had sequestered a room in the guidance counselor's office, where I made the skirt, layering each taupe section to give maximum coverage. In the hour or so before the event, I grabbed my two best friends at the time, so they could help me with the bodice. Before I knew it, it was show time.

When I walked out onto the lit runway, all I could see was a sea of faces, none of which I could pick out from the crowd. Staring out at them, I smiled.

Other than that, I don't remember anything. It was almost surreal, as if I was walking in a fog or a dream. My friends later told me my dress actually looked real, and not as if it had been made entirely out of beige toilet paper. When I came home that afternoon to get ready for the Homecoming dance that night, I already somehow knew that I had won. Later, when my name was announced as Homecoming Queen, I was not surprised. I was given a plastic gold crown from Party Town and a candy necklace, both of which I still have somewhere in my room.

In addition, I was given a spotlight dance. Since I didn't have a date, I borrowed my friend's date instead. To this day, I do not remember the song that was being played, what the boy I was dancing with looked like, or even what I had been wearing. None of that was important to me.

What was important was the feeling—the feeling that I was not ordinary or average or boring. For one day, one hour, one moment, I was extraordinary. I was special, radiant, charming, and everything that I wished I could be. Very few people ever get moments like that, and I was just lucky to have experienced it.

The fact that I was Homecoming Queen is not something that I remember every day... quite the contrary. I usually only remember it in passing moments, when people start to reflect upon their high school experiences. Just like them, I too am caught by surprise that it actually happened.

But, then again, that was kind of the point, wasn't it? I, of all people, who was athletically challenged, unpopular, shy, and quiet, was Homecoming Queen. And maybe, as I stood there on that stage, there was a bright-eyed freshman, staring out at me, who was completely blown away. Maybe she was so inspired that three years later, she tried the same exact thing—and won.

~Janelle Coleman

Reprinted by permission of Off the Mark and
Mark Parisi. ©2004 Mark Parisi.

64

A Work In Progress

It is only possible to live happily-ever-after
on a day-to-day basis.
~Margaret Bonnano

As Thanksgiving weekend approached, I looked in the mirror and sighed, not at all happy with what I saw—another holiday, another food fest, and another easy five pounds. Holidays were the perfect occasion for me to go unnoticed, welcoming a fourth serving of delicious sweet potato casserole and a second piece of scrumptious apple pie.

Every Thanksgiving was the same. Intoxicated by the early morning smells wafting from the oven and the colorful presentation on the dining room table, I would stare at the abundance of food. A culmination of ethnic foods, ranging from antipasto, shrimp prepared in a variety of ways, manicotti, baked ziti, pasta with broccoli, and beef brisket, before even reaching the traditional turkey with tempting side dishes. A little while later, our "Viennese table" was filled with Italian pastries, puddings, cakes and an assortment of mouthwatering pies topped with ice cream or whipped cream, Espresso, and regular coffee too; the soul foods I had become accustomed to for sixteen years of my life. Once my relatives arrived, I could barely contain myself as I hurried through the light greetings in "How are you doing?" mode, anticipating the beginning of our feast.

I was a 170-pound teenager, with a self-esteem that weighed me in at what felt more like 300 pounds. Going out with my friends was a nightmare. Wanting to join in the fun, I found myself digging into the bag of chips and ordering that massive fudge brownie sundae "to share" while finishing more than half of it. I remember the countless nights of hating who I was and continually asking God, "Why couldn't I just be thin?" This was not who I was meant to be. I had gotten to the point where I could not stand myself. High school years were supposed to be carefree — the age of fun times, no responsibilities, no worries — but unlike all of my other friends, I could not enjoy any part of it. Always surrounded by what I considered perfect bodies, everyone looked better, skinnier, and happier. I wondered what their lives were like... how easy it must be. What could they possibly have to worry about?

With Thanksgiving around the corner, I did not know how I would face my relatives with a smile while I was utterly disgusted with myself. Sometimes, though, hitting rock bottom is just what it takes. At that precise moment, I resolved that I could not go on for even one more day without changing my lifestyle. This time I was determined not to take the shortcut and try to lose ten pounds in three days, or search for any more quick fixes.... Instead, I decided to take the long way around the track. So, unlike those who would normally plan to start a diet the Monday after a holiday, I was determined to face the enemy, challenge my number one fear... that unspoken giant who followed ominously wherever I went, looming over me like my own personal rain cloud: my weight. I made up my mind; I would no longer let the scale dictate my emotions or allow myself to go up and down like the needle, hovering between happiness and disappointment. This was it!

A week before Thanksgiving Day, a famous cliché finally hit home: "Eat to live... don't live to eat." My new lifestyle was born — a combination of all that I had learned about eating right, making good food choices, and eating in moderation. After surviving Thanksgiving that year, nothing fazed me. I had no desire to binge, not even a craving for chocolate, which was the biggest threat to my new mentality. My sister even jokes that I am her inspiration, because at Christmas I did not even lick the icing from my finger while cutting the cake and passing it out.

As the pounds came off, I shed the layers of self-hatred too. I tore the veil that prevented me from being my best self, the girl who always lived inside me. I've learned that a weight issue is something that cannot be resolved in one day. Most importantly,

I have learned there is no silver bullet, no foolproof method, no mystery pill, or magic solution to solve any of my problems. I realized that everyone has challenges in life. Those girls in school might not have to worry about their weight, but they have their own situations. I am so happy that, after putting myself to the test, I finally see positive results. I've actually accomplished something once thought to be so unattainable, so impossible, and so out of reach. I am also very fortunate to have such incredible support from family and friends, guidance from many sources, and strong faith in God to get me through life's challenges.

Even after losing forty pounds, I sometimes battle to maintain it. Recently, I have been struggling again, but it is okay. I know what I need to do to get back on track. People tell me all the time that I look great, often wanting to know my secret. What do I tell them? I'm just a work in progress.

~Valerie Lisa Weiss

65

Giving Up the Goods

Forever is composed of nows.
~Emily Dickinson

"N o."

"Yes."

"No."

"You know I'm right. That's why you won't look at me!"

She had me there. I raised my eyes and glowered at my favorite teacher. She grinned—she loved to wind me up, and she loved to be right.

"I'm not ready," I tried again.

"Ashley." It was the teacher-voice, the "let's-be-reasonable" voice, the one that I inevitably ended up obeying. "You are a senior in high school. You're going to be a legal adult in three months. There is absolutely no reason for you to still have clothes you wore in middle school in your closet. Give them away. How can you recover if you've got those tiny sizes there just taunting you? Look, if you can't do it, bring them to school. I pass a Salvation Army every day on my way home from work; I can drop them off if you're not comfortable doing it yourself."

Once again, we were discussing the eating disorder that had controlled my life for the better part of three years. Only recently had I seriously begun to focus on recovery, and I was still feeling pretty resistant about some things.

"You know I'm right," Ms. Shea said again. "That's all I'm saying."

And with an aggravatingly self-satisfied smile on her face, she walked out of the room, leaving me sputtering behind her.

I was still sulking later that night. Shea and I were very close for teacher and student, and I knew she had my best interests at heart, but giving away my clothes? Never. I prided myself on never having to buy new jeans out of necessity, because my old ones always fit. However, as I slowly began to eat normally and gain the curves at age eighteen that I should have had at fifteen, those old zippers were increasingly hard to zip all the way. I could still wear the old clothes, but now they felt uncomfortably snug, a frustrating fact that had driven me to confide my fears in my teacher earlier that day.

Still, Shea's words rang in my head. Of course she was right. My old clothes would just tempt me. All right... maybe I would try to thin my closet just a little. Reluctantly, I slid my closet door open, folded my arms, and stared at my clothes.

There was that little Hawaiian-patterned skirt I had worn in ninth grade the day we got our yearbooks. I was also wearing it the first time I met my then-boyfriend. And the cute shirt my friend bought me from Paris the summer after eighth grade; I thought I was so cool because I had an "exotic" shirt. And how could I forget my red sparkly tank top from the Limited Too? Purchased nearly five years ago, it was my first spaghetti strap shirt. I had been ebullient that I bought it with my very own babysitting money.

A pile of clothing grew slowly beside me. As I lifted each article, I paused a moment, thinking of all its associated memories before neatly folding it and adding it to the pile. It was almost cathartic after a while. It was as if I was giving away the old me—the sick me—with that one bag of small clothes. As I turned off my light and fell into bed, a sense of peace washed over me, and I slept better than I had in months.

The relief was short-lived, though. By morning, I was cursing my impulsiveness the night before as I walked into school. The familiar chorus of doubts ran through my mind. This wasn't necessary. I had enough willpower to recover even if my old clothes were present. Besides, on the off chance I dropped a few pounds....

I bumped into Ms. Shea as I passed the office, scowling to myself. Her face registered no surprise at my brooding expression and bag of clothes.

"Are these goodies for me?" she asked. I paused, but then, resolute in my decision, held out the bag.

"Yes. Can you make them disappear?"

A small smile broke through, belying my teacher's unconcerned air.

"They're as good as gone," she said, taking the bag from me. Feeling exhausted, though I had yet to even go to homeroom, I turned to walk away.

"Hey Ash?" The smile lingered on Ms. Shea's face, and when she spoke, her voice was compassionate.

"If it were easy, you wouldn't be having trouble in the first place. This is hard, but you know you made the right choice. Sometimes, to get rid of the bad, you've gotta sacrifice a little bit of the good. But I think you'll see in the long run that the little bit you have to give up is nothing compared to everything you'll gain in return."

I think of those words every day as I continue to break the old boundaries I set for myself years ago. Eating disorders are tricky; they can ruin your life and take it far beyond your own control while they give you the illusion that you are, indeed, in control. Giving up that illusion is one of the hardest hurdles I have had to jump, because it was so comforting. But I know now it was a false comfort. What I have now—growing pride in myself, and comfort with my body—is true, and I know it's worth more than any bag of clothes will ever be.

~Ashley Mie Yang

Speak Now
or Forever Hold Your Peace

There are very few monsters who warrant the fear we have of them.
~André Gide

The most important lesson I learned in high school had nothing to do with calculus or American history. I didn't even learn it during the school year. The lesson came at graduation, minutes before I left Miramonte High forever.

I was incredibly shy back then, content to hang around with my small group of friends and to concentrate on my courses. I was quickly labeled a "brain." I breezed through my classes, doing so well that by the end of senior year I had a perfect GPA and enough college credits to forgo an entire quarter of coursework.

But my immaculate record soon became a threat to my well-being. In early June of senior year, the vice-principal called me into his office. He asked me to give a valedictory speech at graduation. I gaped at him, my heart thumping. This was the reward for my hard work? I'd rather have a root canal. I mumbled something noncommittally and fled the office, chastising myself for staying away from physics, a subject sure to have broken up my perfect record.

I stewed over the decision, finally agreeing to a compromise. I wasn't the only valedictorian—I would share the honor with five other students. I agreed to introduce my friend Judy, who would then give her own, full-length speech. Still, the prospect was overwhelming, a Herculean feat I wasn't sure I could pull off.

I'd managed to get through school with precious little public speaking. I'd done my best to bypass any class that required an oral report. Although I spoke up occasionally in class—especially English—I disliked reading aloud and participating in lengthy discussions. How in the world would I give a speech to hundreds of people and not humiliate myself?

Graduation day soon arrived and, as expected, I was a wreck. I'd been practicing my speech for days, and I had it memorized. But I had never been so terrified in my life. The first half hour of the ceremony passed in a blur, and then my moment came. My name was announced. I managed to reach the podium without falling down. I faced my classmates, scared enough of all of them without considering the multitude of parents and siblings in the bleachers behind me. But within seconds, I was done and heading back to my seat.

I still have the audiotape of that speech. My voice wavered a little, but mostly it was clear and strong. I'm proud of that tape. I accomplished something I'd never dreamed of—I spoke in front of hundreds of people. Although I didn't realize it at the time, the successful completion of that speech gave me the confidence to participate in class at college, to give verbal reports, and to eventually break free of my shyness.

I never would have chosen to give a speech at graduation—or ever. But I'm glad I did. I no longer hesitate when I'm faced with the prospect of doing something I dread. I know it may very well turn out to be one of my shining moments.

~Carol E. Ayer

Election Day

Perseverance is the hard work you do
after you get tired of doing the hard work you already did.
~Newt Gingrich

The large room smelled distinctly of sweat, even though gym classes had been suspended for the day. Looking around at the mats on the walls, the lines drawn on the floor, and the basketball hoops hanging from the ceiling, I felt unnatural in my dressy clothes. When my name was called, I walked to the front of the room, cursing my choice of footwear as I tried not to wince in pain. I wanted to make an impression on my class, but tripping on the way to the podium was not exactly the effect I was going for.

It was the day of the sophomore class elections, something I had been anticipating for weeks. This would not be like last year; I did not want to lose again. I had campaigned more, made more posters, written a better speech. I had been through a whole year of high school, met more people, and made more friends. By working hard on Class Council activities all year, I had proved my worth even without the officer title. Maybe, just maybe, I could pull this off.

I made my way to the center of the room safely, but dreaded the next second when I would have to face the members of my huge class. I heard the crack of the microphone and was relieved to hear, "Good morning," echo in the horrible acoustics of the gym. Introducing myself with a smile and listing my credentials, I hoped nobody could tell that my calm exterior did not match how I felt inside. My speech continued, and the two-minute time limit I had labored over the previous night seemed to stretch on for hours. Thankfully, a voice continued coming out of my mouth, and the minutes passed. Finishing with my slogan, "You'll get more from Moore," I almost cringed, realizing it might be more corny than clever.

I made my way back to my chair, trying to remember how to sit gracefully in a skirt. My hands were shaking so much I had trouble holding on to my speech. I barely noticed my advisor announce the name of my opponent, who was now strolling up to read his own speech. I tried to listen, to compare, to predict my chances, but I had too many other thoughts flying through my head.

I looked at the faces in the bleachers opposite me. My friends gave encouraging thumbs-ups and smiles when they caught my eye. Just as I had suspected, however, the rest of my classmates were filing their nails, doing next period's homework, whispering to each other, and generally not listening to our speeches, glad to have gotten out of class for a period. I was sure some of them cared more about what we were wearing than what we had said. Still, I knew these were the people who would determine the outcome of the race. As each of the next candidates read their speeches, I debated my chances in my head. Were the AirHeads candies I handed out better received than the Twizzlers of my opponent? Would it come down to that?

The assembly ended, and I was forced to go back to class along with everyone else. How unfair—who could think about conjugating Spanish verbs at a time like this? The "good lucks" went by in a blur, and all I could think about was the voting that would take place during lunch. Did people actually care who would do the best job in office? Would it be a popularity contest? Would my supporters even remember to vote?

I remembered my loss the previous year. I was devastated for an entire weekend, but did miraculously get over it. This time, I would not get my hopes up. I would accept the fact that I might lose, and if I did, it would not be the end of the world. If they failed to read my name, I certainly would not cry. As I waited in last period, staring at the clock, waiting to be called down to hear the results, one thought crossed my mind. I knew most of what I told myself was true, but as for the crying... yeah, right.

Finally, it was last period, time for me to head down to the office to hear the results before they were announced to the school. I found a seat and fidgeted with my skirt, my books, my pen—anything to keep my hands busy. The advisor arrived and began her requisite speech about how she hoped we would all continue to work hard, win or lose, but I did not want to hear it. Though negative thoughts kept swirling around in my head, I tried not to be too hard on myself. Maybe I was over-thinking this; maybe I really could win. As the advisor started to read the list, I gripped my plastic chair, anticipating the final item.

When I heard the name of my opponent, all I wanted to do was get out of the room. As I felt my eyes tear up, I was upset more at myself than at what had happened. I was convinced I would be prepared this time, that by expecting the worst I could avoid disappointment. Instead, I had entertained the thought of victory in my head, and now that hope was shattered.

Hearing the news on the intercom was not a good feeling, but I was thankful I would not need to repeat it myself. My friends came to my rescue, cheering me up and proclaiming the injustice of it all. Even people I barely knew stopped me in the hallway to tell me they had voted for me. I was able to appreciate their remarks this time around, and became less focused on what I had done wrong. I did cry, but it took a lot less to dry my tears this time—that must have meant something.

I was ready to relinquish my goal to be a class officer and denounce the elections as a waste of time, but my friends convinced me to run again the next year. I changed my strategy, beginning my speech with, "Good morning, Class. I'm sure you've heard a lot of 'I' and 'me' today, so I'm going to focus on you." By making promises and describing detailed plans that would truly help the class, I tried to become a candidate I would vote for myself. I was flabbergasted when I won, but also satisfied that I had achieved success in a campaign I could be proud of. The next election was an even bigger reward; after a year of service to the class, I ran unopposed.

~Allison Moore

Reprinted by permission of Off the Mark and Mark Parisi. ©2008 Mark Parisi.

It's the Journey,
Not the Destination

Follow your passion, and success will follow you.
~Arthur Buddhold

The first day of senior year was absolutely heartbreaking. I should have been thrilled. I had one year left in the high school where I was chomping at the bit to break out. I was a senior, ruling the school and rocking the privileges afforded to me—better parking, private lounge, the ability to leave school during free periods.

But by third period, the world flipped upside down and broke in half. We were told that Mrs. Doyle, our AP English teacher, had cancer. Everyone was shocked she had come back to teach. We would be her last class, her final students. When she walked into the classroom, it was like a physical blow. She was frail, emaciated, weak and lifeless.

I had been told by various sources that she probably wouldn't survive the year. It didn't seem right that she was spending her precious time with us, in this antiquated classroom, talking about books and poems.

When I first met Mrs. Doyle, I didn't like her. It wasn't that I hated her; I just didn't like her. She was the advisor for the debate team that a friend and I had started, and we expected to have full control of the club. It was going to be our way to stand out and get into college while also having an amazing time.

But Mrs. Doyle had other ideas. She had run a debate team before and she was a speech coach and drama teacher, so she had serious knowledge on how to get a point across effectively.

We didn't really want to hear what she had to say at the time. My friend quit the debate team and it was up to me to not only withstand Mrs. Doyle, but to flourish in spite of her and hold my team together in the meantime.

She turned out to be brilliant and more tenacious than anyone I had ever met. She knew what she had to teach and she wouldn't give up until she taught it to me, regardless of my attitude, which was generally as feisty as hers. She spent hours with us after school, teaching us how to be better speakers, how to form strong arguments, how to listen and respond without letting adrenaline get the best of us. She taught us tactics and courtesy, and how to debate with respect.

I remember the first debate my partner and I won. We were negatives, which meant we had to shoot holes in the arguments of the opposing team. Our friends on our team were positives—they came prepared with an exhaustive case, research, and facts. All we needed was the ability to think on our feet and take whatever came our way, because we didn't know what the opposition would present.

The debate was against a set of boys who were cocky and arrogant, and they were arguing that marijuana should be legalized. A slightly ridiculous premise, but they made an amazing case with extensive data, facts, statistics, and other things that I would have been overwhelmed by.

Mrs. Doyle had told us that any statistic could be flipped and examined in another way to yield the opposite result—it was all about framing. I hadn't understood it at the time, but now I jumped on it, rephrasing and twisting their facts and statistics until the judges weren't even sure what the case was based on. We blew the ground out from under them. It suddenly occurred to me that Mrs. Doyle might know what she was talking about.

By the end of the year, I had a grudging respect for her that, over the next three years, grew deeper and more genuine. She told me I had a gift, and she helped me cultivate it. She convinced me to enter into the American Legion Oratorical competition, helped me write an awesome speech, and then comforted me when I totally blew it (I forgot a few articles of the Bill of Rights, which was kind of problematic). I became the best speaker in my league largely because of the lessons she taught me.

But debating was never my true love. It was useful—my family is full of lawyers—and it was fun. But since age eight, I had been writing, and no one really knew about it.

And then Mrs. Doyle showed up in AP English, and we both discovered a side of each other we hadn't known about before. On the first day, her voice was strong and sure and full of passion, despite her weak body, as she read "Ithaka" by Cavafy, a poem about being formed by the journeys we take, not the destination.

She never faltered as she met my gaze and told the class that we should aspire to be people on whom nothing is wasted.

I'll never forget the way she spoke about Dante. I could have listened to her talk forever—when she spoke about books, plays, and Dante in particular, she lit up. Suddenly, she wasn't sick, she wasn't weak—she was invigorated, strong, impassioned. Closing my eyes, she was young and vibrant and enthused. Even cancer was no match for her love of English.

And when she read my first paper, she pulled me aside and she asked me if I liked to write. I told her yes, I loved it more than anything. She handed me my paper back and told me that I was an incredible writer, and no matter what I chose to do in life, I owed it to myself to keep writing. I would find out later that she bragged about my writing to other teachers, even to her family.

She died that year, before I had the chance to prove her right, before I had the chance to fully understand and thank her for believing in me. It's all I ever needed, and the greatest compliment I ever received. Every day since, I've tried to concentrate on the journey, not the destination. I've kept writing. I've tried—and will always try—to be a person on whom nothing is wasted.

It took me a long time to understand why she came back to teach. With my life increasingly consumed by my writing, I begin to understand. Passion is what makes life move forward. You can't help it, and you shouldn't ever deny it, because it gives others the permission, the encouragement to do the same. She gave us her passion, and in turn, demanded that we live our passion for the rest of our lives.

~AC Gaughen

The Audition

There is no failure except in no longer trying.
~Elbert Hubbard

It was my big brother who really wanted me to try out for the musical.

"It's fun," he insisted. "You should do it. You don't really have to be able to sing; you just have to be able to smile and act like you know what you're doing."

Well, I could do both of those things, but that didn't make trying out in front of fifty people any less intimidating.

I picked a song and practiced constantly when no one was home. I sang in my car, I sang in the shower. But when the day came, and I was in the auditorium after school, I thought my heart would stop beating. There, on the stage, was the ever-intimidating choir director—the one who had never liked me and thought my brother John, king of the theater kids, was a screwball. Everyone cooed at me, calling me Johnny's little sister, giving me words of encouragement. They all sang with such ease, so relaxed and calm. I clutched my sheet music and sat in an auditorium chair, watching people audition until there were only a few of us left.

Then, I stood up and walked out.

John caught up with me and grabbed me by the shoulders. I had tears already coming out of my eyes.

"I can't do this," I announced. "I don't sing."

"Stay right here," John told me. "Don't move a muscle. I'll be right back and if you leave, I swear to God, I'll kill you in your sleep."

I sat there and sniffled, leaning against the hallway wall, until he came back a minute later with Alexis Ray.

Alexis Ray may have been one of my brother's best friends. But she was also popular, gorgeous, and one hell of a singer. If all of those things didn't make her intimidating, there was the fact that she was drop dead honest, with a hint of attitude that made me gulp nervously whenever I saw her.

"Sing for her," John told me.

I shook my head. "No. No way."

But he looked at me, dead calm. "Look. If you suck, she'll tell you. But if you don't audition today, you're going to regret it on opening night, or next week, or probably even an hour from now. Everyone up there is nervous. But you can do this. Now, practice. Pretend Alexis is Mrs. Scholtz." Our eyes met, the exact same shade of bright blue, and electricity jolted through me.

I nodded, slowly. Then I opened my mouth and started to sing.

She was completely focused on me the whole time, her eyes never wavering from mine. When I was done, my heart was beating a mile a minute, and my skin felt all tingly, as if I'd just been seen naked or caught in some other embarrassing scenario.

Alexis slowly nodded. "You," she announced, "are good. And you're auditioning. So get your butt back in there."

I wanted to back out, but now it was too late. John was shoving me out the door, back into the auditorium, and onto the stage just as the choir director was asking if there were any more people going to try out.

I looked back, absolutely terrified, but my brother caught my eye and winked.

And suddenly, I wasn't as afraid.

I sang my song, loud and proud, staring directly at John the whole time. He was grinning and totally paying attention. I swayed a little bit, did a hand motion or two. I smiled and performed, sending my song out to every corner of the auditorium, filling in the spaces and not holding back.

When I was done, everyone cheered extra loud. Mostly because I was Johnny's little sister, but that didn't really matter. All that mattered was that my brother was whistling, standing, and whooping louder than anyone else.

The next day, when I checked the cast list for the musical, my name was not on it.

John drove me to Taco Bell, buying me a Crunchwrap Supreme and small Baja Blast. His mouth set in a thin line, as he firmly announced, "Mrs. Scholtz is a bitch."

When we got home, I ran into my room and sobbed, curling up in a ball. I watched DVDs of Degrassi and took the entire ice cream carton down to my bedroom with me. But after two hours of that, I emerged, took a shower, and sang along to the radio as loud as I possibly could.

Our siblings teach us a lot of things. They are the friends that are given to us, the ones that we don't get to choose. Some brothers or sisters teach us how to multiply, how to tie our shoes, and how to get to the next level on Mario Kart. But my brother taught me a priceless lesson that day, something that had nothing to do with singing or performing.

There are going to be things you're afraid of and times when you don't think you're ever going to be able to do them. You're going to be tapping your toes and biting your nails, wondering if you've got the guts, if you're good enough, if this is worth it. There is always going to be something that you want to do, but are terrified to even attempt.

The most important thing isn't whether or not you end up doing it well, or totally sucking. The important thing is that you do it anyway.

~Claire Courchane

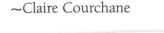

Chapter 9

Teens Talk

HIGH SCHOOL

Tough Stuff

When life's problems seem overwhelming,
look around and see what other people are coping with.
You may consider yourself fortunate.

~Ann Landers

Losing David

*The legacy of heroes is the memory of a great name
and the inheritance of a great example.*
~Benjamin Disraeli

David and I were friends the moment we met. I had a big crush on him. Everyone in the youth group knew it, including David.

I did everything I could to be around him. Getting my friends to help me sit next to him at banquets, playing in the same miniature golf group as David, and somehow ending up close to one another at the skating rink when they called for "couples skate."

I was only fifteen years old, but I felt in my heart that David and I were meant to be together. I couldn't wait until the next meeting at church or the next youth activity to see him again.

He was great with little kids. Sometimes, I'd watch him play with them up and down the halls before church started on Sunday evenings. He tried to be cool, but he was also a nice guy. I liked that about him. I couldn't think of anything I didn't like.

So it made sense that every time I went to church, the first person I looked for was David.

"I haven't seen him," my best friend Karla told me one Sunday night.

"He's not here yet," Michael said when I asked. "I don't know why he isn't here." He seemed surprised. Michael was David's best pal at church.

Even more surprising was that his parents and brothers were there.

David didn't show up for choir practice. I kept one eye on the music and one eye on the sanctuary door. He wasn't there for the youth meeting, and he wasn't there as the first hymn started for Sunday night services.

We were halfway through the song when I heard a commotion at the back of the room. I turned and saw one of the men talking with David's parents. Suddenly, the whole family was leaving. A moment later, the youth pastor walked up to the podium and whispered into the pastor's ear.

He stopped the music. I gripped the pew in front of me.

"We've had some very sad news. David Nelson drowned in a swimming accident this afternoon. Let's pray for the Nelson family."

I sat down hard, rocking back and forth. It wasn't true. It couldn't be true. What a mean joke to play on everyone.

But I'd seen the look on Mrs. Nelson's face. It was true. David had died.

The next few days were a whirl of pain and questions. I read the newspaper account of how David and a friend had gone swimming in a gravel pit. David had started sinking, panicked, and grabbed at his friend. His friend tried to help, but he couldn't.

I hated this friend. I had heard David and Michael talk about him. He was a high school dropout. He didn't go to church. If David had gone to church as usual, this wouldn't have happened. Why had he let this guy talk him into missing church and going to swim in an unsafe area?

Ugly thoughts filled my head. Why couldn't it have been the other boy, Terry? It wasn't fair. David was barely sixteen. He had his whole life ahead of him, his whole life to serve God and help other people. It shouldn't have happened to him. Why?

At the funeral, I learned some answers.

Terry had admired David. David had encouraged him to go back to school. I learned that after the accident, Terry went back to school. He even started talking about church and God. He had been influenced greatly by David's life. It wasn't easy losing a friend. Whatever the reason, David's death had resulted in Terry doing what David had begged him to do—finish his education and find a relationship with God.

I never saw Terry again after the funeral, since he didn't attend our church. And soon after, the Nelsons left to find another church. There were too many memories at our church.

The pain was there a long time. So were the anger and the questions.

But I know that David loved people and that he cared about his friend Terry. I hoped that whatever Terry did when he finished school, it would be an honor to David's memory.

~Kathryn Lay

Lia

You are your own judge.
The verdict is up to you.
~Astrid Alauda

I have a friend. Her name is Lia. Nobody has ever seen her or met her, though if they did they might say we look so identical, we are the same person. I keep her to myself so that nobody has to endure her wrath if she is uncomfortable or angry. And when it comes to "advice," she'll be the first to assist me and guide me to "the right choice." She came into my life in the third grade, when I was the biggest and fattest. We were the same size, so I immediately started to follow her.

As kids, we didn't think too much about diet or exercise, but she would still always be around bugging me about my size without any ideas on what to do to fix it. Nutritionists came in to talk to our class in the fourth grade about healthy eating and exercising habits.

They say kids absorb that kind of information at a young age, so it should be instilled then. Lia absorbed the information immediately. No snacks before bed, she would tell me. And I listened. Suck in your tummy so you look skinnier. And I sucked. Enough with the chocolate chip cookies for breakfast. And I stopped.

Summer brings along pool parties and bathing suits. At the end of fifth grade, our classmate threw a pool party to celebrate the end of the year. I would look in the mirror and notice my expanding stomach. Ew. I can't let the other kids see me in a bathing suit like this, I thought. So Lia saw my mom's magazine claiming a way to lose six inches in seven days. She did the math and told me I could condense it so that my tummy would be toned for the party. I think I did about an hour of crunches daily. And those thighs, Lia said, they're fat, too. I started to ride my bike. Exercising until Lia told me to stop, I didn't feel too different, but Lia was convinced I couldn't be seen fat. I went to the party with my stomach the same size. I figured the magazine had lied.

In sixth grade, we hit our heaviest at 120 pounds. Lia, dissatisfied, began to heckle me all the time. She listened intently in the required nutrition portion of our health class. Sugar, fat and oil, Lia remembered. Sugar. Fat. Oil. Weight Gain.

• • •

Now puberty has finally ended and I begin to lose weight. Lia notices my transformation and she loses weight too. She likes it and the attention we get. "You've really thinned out!" "You're beautiful!" she tells me. Was I that hideous before? Lia thinks so.

If we continue to lose weight, imagine the attention we'll get! Lia says. Lia is such a genius. I can't imagine a better friend. Calories — I can count them, and apparently if I eat only a few I'll stay skinny. What a solution. Five fruits and vegetables a day is the answer to a healthy you, Lia claims. Okay, I can do that. Bananas and raisins for breakfast. Two slices of bread, turkey, five crackers, and thirteen graham sticks for lunch. Smaller sizes at supper. No breakfast on the weekend. The less I eat the more I lose, right?

This is fairly easy. I can see the results. I feel better about myself and Lia likes it a lot too. Okay, now how much do I weigh? Lia will take care of that. Whenever I'm alone in the house, I go up to my parents' scale and weigh myself. 110 lbs. I've lost! Lia is so excited for me and I love it when she's happy. I want this to happen quicker, so that I'm 105 by Christmas! I can do it! Time to eliminate milk. I don't want to drink my few precious calories!

The parents are noticing my lessened meal size, especially when

I refuse pizza at the Wonder Bar, our Friday night tradition. Uh oh. I tell them I'll do better and agree to a nutritionist. I can bluff my way through with Lia's help. She'll tell me what to say. After all, it's worked for the past seven years.

Nutritionist appointment goes well. Lia basically talks for me. We act oblivious to all, and "agree" to make the required changes. And incorporate exercise because it helps maintain your weight. Good information!

I take up running. I can't believe people enjoy this. Lia seems to like it. She tells me it's good for me and will make me skinny. Just the motivation I need. Breakfast is three-quarters of a cup of bran flakes that I measure quickly before Dad can catch me, berries, and one glass of milk. Lunch is down to two slices of light bread, a tea-spoon of peanut butter, fourteen carrot sticks, and two stalks of cel-ery. Sometimes I'll have my friend's Nutri-Grain bar, but only rarely, because Lia screams at me and tells me I look fat because of the extra calories. Oops. Dinner is the smallest chicken breast on the plate and lots of veggies. And forget about dessert — Lia says it's bad.

Going out to dinner is a breeze with the help of Lia. I stop order-ing my usuals and claim, "I can't eat that. I get heartburn," when in reality I don't even know what that feels like. "I had a huge lunch. I'll just get salad, no dressing, cheese, or croutons." I order tall glasses of water that will fill me up, but will go right through me so I'll still feel hungry. Lia and I love the hunger pain. It's the pain of success....

I'm starting to feel weaker. My legs hurt when I'm only walking. I just want to sit down. Don't make me get up. Lia makes me get up. BURN THE CALORIES, she screams. And I listen.

Lia, just leave me alone, okay? She's getting on my nerves. She won't shut up about the calories. She's still fat and thinks I am, too. Even my normal diet of barely anything makes her mad. What do you want me to do, Lia? Starve?

I steal the scale again. 100 pounds. I want to hug Lia. I've never been more excited or felt more powerful.

Lia, I'm serious this time. Please just be quiet. I can't focus on my schoolwork because you're counting calories too loud. I can't sleep because you're counting too loud. I can't do anything because you're COUNTING TOO LOUD!

Lia, I look better in this shirt, right? Lia, stop calling me fat. No, Lia, you're right—I am fat. I have to lose more.

People are giving me concerned looks. "Eat this." "I don't want it." It sounds more like a command when I'm offered a piece of food. Lia won't allow it. You're not hungry, she says, you're not hungry....

• • •

Lia and I are no longer friends. We separated only just recently after months of counseling together. I learned a lot about her. She is a part of me that is evil and conniving, and her name isn't really Lia. It's Anorexia.

~Jillian Genco

Be Strong

Although it's difficult today to see beyond the sorrow,
May looking back in memory help comfort you tomorrow.
~Author Unknown

He had gorgeous, deep brown eyes, and when he looked at you, he seemed innocent, even though he put on a tough guy exterior. I began having conversations with him, trying to get to know him, and slowly we became inseparable. Eventually, we ended up going out.

His name was Sam and he was sixteen years old, the oldest of six children. He and his twin brother, Dan, ran the household while their mom was at work. He was in the school marching band, and he could complete the most difficult math problems in his head without a calculator. He was like a dictionary—he could give me the meaning of any word I didn't understand. He never said anything negative about anyone... except himself.

The more I got to know Sam, the more I realized something was wrong. He would say things like "I'm no good at this," or he would say things about our relationship, claiming I didn't care about him.

One day, I noticed scars on his left wrist. I asked him what they were from and he said he used to cut himself. For some reason, he was not on medication or seeing a psychiatrist, so I tried to act as one for him. Whenever he had a problem, I would help him with it. Sam opened up to me like no one ever had. He told me how he felt about school, friends, and family. He told me everything, especially his feelings.

After about four months, he told me something he had never told anyone before. He had tried to kill himself twice, once by drowning and another time by taking some pills. I was absolutely shocked. I asked him if he had told his mom, or his twin. He said no. I have no idea why he confided in me, but I felt uncomfortable. Soon, I was trying to push myself away from him because of fear. I couldn't be there for him all the time, and he started to bottle up his emotions again.

Soon, I realized he was making threats that seemed serious. His mom would come in and say, "Sam, clean your room," and he would respond with "If you make me do this stuff I'll kill myself!" His mom never said anything about it and never took the threats seriously. One evening, he told me that he had strong feelings for me and that I was the best thing that had ever happened to him—that he would die without me. I thought it was just a way of expressing they way he felt about me, cute and harmless. I was wrong.

One morning, I called Sam around eight o'clock, before school. He said he was okay, but that his brothers had been picking on him all week, calling him names and beating him up. I told him I was sorry and that I would call him as soon as I got home from school.

I walked in the door that afternoon and immediately the phone rang—it was Sam. He told me that he loved me, and I was a little freaked out. I told him I would call him back. Sam kept calling until I answered again. I was uncomfortable, so I suggested we take a break. But Sam started right away with the negative things again: "You hate me, don't you?" and "I was never good enough for you... God, I hate myself!" That's when I snapped at him. I told him to shut up, that this was the reason we were falling apart—I didn't need his negativity and I couldn't be there to solve all his problems. He hung up on me.

I tried to call him back several times, but I received no answer. Around eleven o'clock that night, the phone finally rang again. I looked at the caller ID: Sam. Finally. When I answered, I said, "It's about time! I've been trying to call you for the past three hours." But the voice that I heard on the other end wasn't Sam's. It was a group of detectives who asked me questions about my relationship with Sam and when I had last talked to him.

I called Dan to find out where Sam was. There was silence, and then he told me. Sam was upset after I hung up. He locked himself in the bathroom for two hours, and then his little sister discovered her brother's lifeless body hanging from the ceiling beam by a shoelace.

The next day, I couldn't make it through the first fifteen minutes of school. I was sent home and cried even more when I got there. I told my mother that Sam had tried to kill himself before, and how he had said those things about wanting to try again. She wisely told me that Sam had a death wish, and no matter what I did, nothing could have saved him. She told me that he was happy now and that he had gotten what he wanted. I still felt guilty, but there was nothing I could do to bring him back. I just wished I had said goodbye.

Looking through Sam's things, I discovered quotes and poems about being strong and never giving up. But he did give up—he wasn't as strong as I thought he was. One of the quotes read:

Be strong. Never give in to temptation, love till you can't anymore, and hold every person close to your heart, for you never know who means the most. Keep your head up high and know you're loved.

I started screaming and yelling: "Why would you kid yourself? You lied to me, to your family, to the world!" Then I looked closer at the little slip of paper. At the bottom was Sam's signature, along with the words:

For Kerri

He wasn't being hypocritical. He was telling me to be strong and to keep going no matter what. The quotes weren't for himself—they were for us, the ones he left behind. I finally understood. I was happy, not because of what I found, but because Sam was able to teach me something. I gathered up my courage and decided to try to speak at his funeral.

When I got there, I stood at the podium, his body behind me, tears rolling down my cheeks. I told the crowd how much of a loss this was, but that wherever he was, he was happy. I read the quote I found, and his mom came up to give me a hug and a kiss. I leaned into his coffin and kissed him goodbye. I thanked him, and then we all said goodbye to him, placing flowers on his grave. Everyone came up and shared their favorite memories of Sam. There were close to one hundred kids from his school there who had known him far longer than I had, and they all had great stories full of tears and laughter.

I still talk to Sam's brother now, and I'm close to his family and friends. Every time I look at Dan, I see Sam. I feel special to have known Sam for the brief time that I did. Even though he wasn't strong enough to keep going, he managed to teach everyone to be strong for themselves.

~Kerri Grogan

I Will Remember You

When you are sorrowful look again in your heart,
and you shall see that in truth
you are weeping for that which has been your delight.
~Kahlil Gibran

I didn't know her, but everyone knew who she was. She was warm and quiet, tall and athletic, smart and dedicated, and a superhero to everyone.

What I did know about her were the kind of things that were probably on her college application. I knew she was an excellent student. I knew she was the captain of the crew team, and student head of athletics. I knew that a Multiple Sclerosis organization had honored her for starting her own organization, which had raised thousands of dollars for research. I also knew she'd been accepted to her first choice college, Dartmouth.

I also knew that she had problems with her lungs, and one of them collapsed shortly before her high school graduation. She underwent surgery, but still went to her graduation with a catheter under her white dress. She refused, other people said, to let her friends down. When her name was called, she received a standing ovation.

In the spring, she and other members of the senior student council put on a skit for the entire school, in which they announced their successors. They put her utilitarian, muscular frame into a Japanese sumo wrestler costume, and joked in front of the entire school that she simply had eaten too much to be fit for duty anymore. She had little to say during the skit, and simply stood in the middle, smiling at her friends and at the wisecracking.

As a co-captain of the school's cross-country team, I knew she loved to run, and she would go running with her friends. I didn't know that shortly before graduation, before everything changed, she persuaded one of her close friends to run several miles to a nearby river. They sat down on the wooden dock, dipped their hot, sore feet in the cool water, and gazed into the brilliant sunshine, relishing the lazy days of their senior spring with all the insatiable energy of youth. She and her friend promised each other they would go to the same medical school. They were teenagers, vulnerable and hormonal, but in this moment, they were the epitome of all the lovely sides of adolescence; they embodied the invincibility of two seventeen-year-old girls, fresh-eyed and hopeful.

I can feel what it must have been like for them in the hazy sunshine. To them, every door was wide open. They were going to college, and afterwards, they were going to set out to save the world. They were indestructible.

Less than two months later, she was dead.

Once again, most people only knew of the insignificant things. They knew she had been killed along with her sister and mother during a violent and unprecedented break-in, in the quiet suburb where she lived. They knew that only her father had survived. They read in the newspapers of her achievements, of her co-captaincy of the crew team, her acceptance to Dartmouth, her figure as a compassionate leader on the school campus. They read about her charities and gazed at the picture of her smile, a somewhat shy smile, but also natural and beautiful.

They didn't read about her tender, compassionate heart. They didn't read that her friends were her number one priority, held above grades, colleges, and awards.

They didn't read about the time she had ditched a party to console a friend. The friend, upset at not receiving an invitation to the party, called her, knowing she'd be more sympathetic than anyone else. "We'll do something fun," she promised her friend. The two friends went to the movies instead.

They didn't know what her friend discovered—that she had received the coveted invitation to the party, but she didn't ditch her friend for what must have been a most anticipated party. She ditched the party. She never mentioned it, but simply comforted her friend without a second thought or hesitation. Once again, her friends came first.

Slowly, I grew to see her as a pillar. She supported everyone and everything. She had exerted quiet leadership while attracting little attention. She let other people talk and was a captive audience. She catered to her friends, whether in a sumo suit or ditching a party. She gave and gave.

She had been a beautiful person, through and through, and I wondered how we would ever regain our faith in good after what happened to her. It was the first time anyone I knew who was my age had died—and she had been such an active member in our close-knit school. I don't think anyone could believe she was really gone. But walking through the grim landscape of a cold September day to her memorial, the sky threatening to soak us in our mourning garb, I wasn't sure if anyone was ready to keep on living without her around. Perhaps we were frightened to.

Girls who had already graduated from our school, and had flung themselves into separate corners of the country—the South, Midwest, New England, Canada—rejoined to commemorate her. Girls skipped their college classes and traveled all the way back to their high school. Nearly five hundred people attended the memorial, a sea of black, while her closest friends wore swirls of colors; colors that she loved the most.

Halfway through the memorial, a stream of sunlight slowly per- meated the long windows and cast a gentle, inconspicuous light on a group of girls singing in the center of the church. They had been part of last year's senior a capella group, the most remarkable singing group at the school in fifteen years. Most of them had come back, and their lovely voices hummed and resonated while people broke into sobs. They sang for her, more tenderly than I had ever heard them, so sweetly that I can still hear their soft, trembling voices. The girls sang with their chins uplifted and their cheeks wet. Their eyes were full of love and yearning, and they crooned:

I will remember you
Will you remember me?
Don't let your life pass you by
Weep not for the memories.

And when they went back to their seats and I finished blinking through my tears, I noticed the sunlight — beautiful, radiant sunlight, spilling gently through the towering windows.

There she was again! Gentle, tall, quiet, casting lovely rays on everyone close and far, but without creating a disturbance or diverting attention from others. She was telling us she was all right. That it was okay for us to love and live and yearn for life when she could not. She broke through the cloaked shadows and gloomy clouds, again and again, prevailing, as she had done in life.

I felt relief when I saw the sunshine — she hadn't really left. She was still there in the sky, with her soothing presence, her light shimmering like a promise of hope. We promised her we would remember her; her sunshine sang to us. And our hearts and voices sang back for her.

~Allie Walsh

Don't You Fake It

Take care of your body.
It's the only place you have to live.
~Jim Rohn

There was something wrong. It was in my stomach, beginning in my mind, and working its way through the rest of my body. It was shutting down organs, making me unhealthy, and killing my brain cells. It was something I couldn't resist. A burning fire, a pain exploding through me as each day passed. Slowly, I let myself die.

Anorexia.

My battle with the disorder began when I was thirteen. I wasn't heavy. I didn't consider myself overweight. In fact, the doctor had told me more than once that I was underweight. But peers can be cruel, so the mentality that I was fat progressed until I vowed to skip lunch every day and lose ten pounds.

At first I hated it. In the beginning, my stomach screamed and resisted. I ignored it. I learned to tolerate—and to embrace—the feelings of emptiness, hollow hunger, and burning pain anorexia gave me. It pleased me. Soon, I began to strategize how I would lose more weight. Skipping lunch had become a breeze; why not skip breakfast, too? I was the first one up in the mornings. I wasn't planning to lose enough weight for anyone to notice. Besides, when we had family dinners, I ate enough to make my family think nothing was wrong.

The thrill of losing weight and not getting caught gave me a high I'd never had. Soon, I began losing so much weight that my mother noticed. My dad never paid enough attention to me to notice anything, but my mother was my best friend.

"Honey, this is so strange," she said. "What's going on?"

I shrugged. "I'm getting taller," I pointed out. "I'm probably just losing baby fat."

It was a reasonable enough explanation, and she bought it.

My life went on. Nothing changed until I was a freshman in high school. I'd continued my eating habits all through the year—no breakfast, no lunch, only enough dinner to please everyone. It was a safe balance. Things were bound to become troublesome, though, when all I could see when I passed a mirror was how much weight I needed to lose instead of how small I'd become.

My junior year was the most notable in my battle with anorexia. I began to skip three meals a day—sometimes only eating once every three days; and even then, no more than one plate of food. When my family left me at home and went out to eat so I could study in peace, I would eat one bite of dinner and shove the rest down the garbage disposal. That way, I could say I had eaten... but it did no "harm" to me. I became obsessed with working out. On the rare occasion I did eat, it was usually a banana or apple.

A handful of my friends knew the war raging within me but did nothing. They created their own dramas to cover up mine, and I was happy to let them.

The cycle probably would have continued this way if not for a doctor appointment. Afterwards, Mom and I were both silent because of a single piece of news—I was seventeen years old and ninety pounds.

I rejoiced. I was so small!

Mom was angry.

On the drive home, she grabbed my wrist—she could wrap her fingers around it and they overlapped at the end—and said, "Amy, look at this! I think we need to consider that you might have an eating disorder."

I tried not to laugh. Might?

"Don't be ridiculous," I lied with a roll of my eyes as I pulled my arm away.

She shook her head and we kept silent.

Up until then, I had never called it an eating disorder. I'm not sure what it was to me—it was the way I'd chosen to live, and, according to the doctor, the way I could die. I thought that was so dramatic of them—I would never kill myself.

Nevertheless, it scared me. The idea that I could really be shutting my body down was frightening. I'd always insisted that I was in control of my anorexia... but maybe it was time to admit that it was controlling me.

When we got home, Mom talked to Dad while I went to my room and typed "anorexia" into Google.

What I found fascinated me.

The first website I clicked (http://www.mamashealth.com/anorexia.asp) said anorexia was a disorder in which individuals choose to starve themselves and continued to think they were fat even as they became unnaturally skinny. I sighed. Maybe Mom was right.

Symptoms included refusing to eat in public, anxiety, weakness, and shortness of breath. All were symptoms that I'd been living with for nearly four years.

It also mentioned how, when confronting a family member about it, an anorexic may be in denial, resist help, or even become angry. It made me feel guilty for how I'd treated my mom earlier.

That night I went to her room and broke down entirely. I gave her control over the situation and promised to go along with whatever she wanted for me.

My parents decided to make me see a counselor, and it's helped so much. Through her I'm seeing what I was doing to my body—and I really was killing myself. I was robbing my body of the nutrients it needed to help me stay safe and alive. My skin was dull instead of glistening, my hair mousy instead of shiny. I wasn't making myself prettier by starving myself. I was making myself ugly.

I'm learning safer ways to maintain a healthy weight. I have friends who support me and help me even as I'm struggling.

It's not always easy, but I can see a light at the end of this tunnel and one of these days I'm going to run through it with open arms. The entire thing has been a roller coaster experience of emotions, but at least now I know that recovery is possible. Starving myself isn't the way to be small. Regular exercise and a balanced diet have already helped me so much more than food deprivation could.

If I can do it, you can do it. If you're struggling with an eating disorder, please tell someone. They may be upset, but it's only because they care about you so much. Eventually they'll understand where you're coming from and someday, maybe you'll understand their point of view too.

~Amy Anderson

Crashdown

Someone to tell it to is
one of the fundamental needs of human beings.
~Miles Franklin

"She's like a Disney character," a friend joked one time at our regular cafeteria lunch table. "It's as though she's fallen out of the pages of a fairytale and doesn't have a clue about the real world!" Surrounded by my friends in the security of my small private school, I would giggle and wrinkle my nose. I was always a bubbly, energetic person, the type some people just roll their eyes at, annoyed that anyone could be that perky. A dancer, student council member and International Baccalaureate student, I was on top of the world. At least, that's what it seemed like from the outside.

After two years of commuting from a small town to a private school in the city, my family moved to be closer to dad's office and the school. While it was sad to leave the town I had grown up in, I was thrilled to be living in the same area as my friends and only a fifteen-minute drive from my school, a place where I not only took classes, but spent tons of time after school participating in extracurricular activities and tutoring. My family moved the first week of September while I was away at a camp with my schoolmates as a way to kick off the new school year. I just knew it—junior year was going to be my year.

My world started to crumble when Mom started to feel sick. Two and a half years before, she had been diagnosed with a rare and complicated disease called Systemic Mastocytosis. The disease resulted in her having too many mast cells that had formed a large tumor on her ovaries. After her operation, she had recovered, and while the disease is incurable, it is livable. She continued to be an active member of the community and manage her regular busy-mom schedule. After the move, however, things weren't right. Her doctors ran a number of tests, and because her disease was so rare, her results were sent to the famous Mayo Clinic. We waited and waited, not really knowing what we were waiting for.

A week and a half before Christmas, Mom got the results back. She picked my youngest sister and me up from school. After initial small talk, she began explaining what the doctor had said. "So, it's not cancer, right Mom?" asked Ryleigh rhetorically. When silence hit the air and tears started rolling down her face, we knew. Mom had cancer.

"It's like we're in a movie," Ryleigh whispered, as the two of us collapsed onto her bed. We were in hiding from our other sister, Devyn, who didn't know yet. It was all too strange being around her—both frustrating and refreshing at the same time. Before long, we were sitting formally in our living room, hearing the news officially as well as the details. It was leukemia and had been caught very late, meaning it had spread throughout her body.

I didn't know what to do. Suddenly, the plans I had made that weekend, the conversations I had had that day, the biology test I was supposed to be studying for lost all importance. I went out that night, and when I came home I ran straight to my room, threw on my pajamas, sunk into the covers and sobbed. Mom came in and snuggled me like I was a little girl, saying, "I promise I'm not going anywhere."

The next day was a Saturday, and I composed myself enough to call a classmate I had worked on a school project with and who was supposed to be coming over for dinner that night. I had not planned to tell him why I was canceling, but when he asked me how I was, I started to half laugh, half cry. "Actually, I'm not so good," I told him.

"I just found out my mom has cancer." All of a sudden, he was no longer just someone I went to school with. He was a friend. We met for waffles the next day, talking about cars, film, school, and occasionally the cancer. Sometimes we just sat in a peaceful silence that only true friends can appreciate. I don't remember every detail of that day, but I will always remember the true kindness and friendship he exhibited.

This has not been the year I planned. In many ways, it has been the worst year of my life. I hit some pretty low lows, including developing an eating disorder as an attempt to control my emotions. But the waffle day stands out in my mind as one of the saddest and greatest days of my life. It was the day I created the best support team I could have ever wished for. "It's when you first find out, that's the hardest," my friend had advised me gently. He was in many ways right, and in other ways wrong. There are some days that are harder than others, and other days where the glass is half-full again. Cancer introduces all sorts of scary thoughts: Will my mom be there to see my sisters graduate? Will she be there when I get married? Will she and Dad grow old together? Someone once said that the only certainty in cancer is the uncertainty. While I fight the uncertainties, I know I am not fighting them alone. I have my family, I have my friends, I have teachers who are there for me. Most importantly, I have my mom. And no matter what happens, I will always have her with me.

~Chloe Scott

G-1

He conquers who endures.

~Persius

By the time I turned seventeen, my life had begun to move in a different direction than I ever could have foreseen. At some point, I had become too irresponsible to deal with what I had been handed, and as a consequence I found myself sent home early from boarding school for breaking a major rule my junior year. Facing the initial anger of my parents, I spent my days at home sleeping late into the afternoon and getting high.

One hazy morning, I walked downstairs and found a letter from my school. Faculty had reached a collective decision; I was not invited back for senior year. I was crushed. My parents became concerned and demanded that I fly out in early June to a program called the Aspen Achievement Academy. I refused, not trusting anything they told me. After several weeks of arguing and considerable bribes, I finally gave in to two weeks in the wilderness.

Before the reality of my situation hit me, I found myself staring out the small window of a 747 headed to Las Vegas, endless desert and mountains stretching across the landscape below. Although distraught, I could not help but be somewhat curious about what lay ahead. A long drive to the almost non-existent town of Loa, Utah had me feeling uneasy about what I was getting myself into. With a brief hug goodbye, my mother's rental car disappeared down the dusty road. Five minutes later, I found myself in a secure room, stripped of all my belongings, clothes, and far worse, my freedom. For the next two hours, I sat in the backseat of a locked pickup truck in silence, as we steadily made our way up a rocky mountain path into the wilderness prison.

Taking my first steps into the unforgiving landscape, I was introduced to my group's current site, greeted by silence and a black cloud of insatiable mosquitoes. From sunrise to sunset for three days, I sat in silence in my designated spot. This would only be the beginning of the torture I would endure. Boredom at this level becomes physically painful after a certain period of time. I was temporarily relieved when I was finally initiated into our group, "G-1," on the evening of the third day. Right away it was easy to tell who had been there the longest; a permanent layer of dirt enveloped their bodies, a vacant look inhabited their tired eyes. I was shocked to hear that some had been there for as long as nine weeks. I told myself I would be out in two weeks as my parents had promised.

At first, I welcomed the idea of hiking, as an alternative to my isolation, but as the hours began to pass by, my pack became heavier. I have always considered myself someone who could endure pain, but our daily routine of packing up camp and relocating began to cross this line. As I took on group responsibilities and had to carry food, tarps, water, pots, and pans, my pack suddenly weighed over seventy pounds and the hikes became longer.

Hiking in a group is mostly psychological—no one wants to break down and slow down the group, showing they are the weakest. But everyone is suffering.

There were a strict set of codes in the program, the cruelest being that you never knew where you were, where you were going, what time, or even what day it was while you were hiking. One foot after another, one step at a time, we marched for five, six, ten, fifteen hours—however long it took to reach our destination. Since my shoulders felt like they were being pierced by a long, sharp blade, I often chewed on bark to stop myself from screaming out in pain. I quickly learned the value of conversation during hikes, but at many times, the only thing to do was disappear as far away in my thoughts as possible. Through dense forest, up steep rock falls, the marching never seemed to cease. As my physical limits were pushed, I focused on the mental aspect of the hike. Every heavy step was the last exertion of energy I had. Yet somehow, I had no choice but to keep moving forward, and that is what I forced myself to do.

As the two-week mark approached, I thought I was losing my mind. The only thing I could look forward to was the prospect of sleeping. Sleep was the only escape from this never-ending nightmare, seven hours of wonderful blackness. With almost every task timed by a stopwatch from the moment I woke, I was instantaneously thrown back into a world of unnecessary suffering.

"All ball bundles out, two minutes and thirty seconds to coal pit."

Upon hearing these words echo across our collection of shelters, at sunrise I would throw myself out of my warm bag into the bitterly cold desert air, overcome by an inner fatigue of such fury, that I would often find myself fighting back tears of frustration.

"Belt, check—shoes tied, check—cup clean, check—two full quarts of iodine-dropped water, check." If we were two seconds late on the watch, or someone had forgotten something, pants and shoes were recollected and it was back into our bags. This process was repeated until it was done perfectly.

Once a week, a field therapist would come out to our group for an individual session with each of us. With every visit, the therapist brought a renewed feeling of hope—the hope of word from my parents, of some kind of miracle that would bring us back home. With each visit, it became more and more clear that no such thing would happen. After most sessions, I found myself alone, staring blankly into the horizon. Since day one, almost everyone in the group had talked regularly about escape. For the first time in my life, the idea of risking my life didn't make me hesitate. Over several days, I planned my departure carefully, stealing iodine and extra food from the unsuspecting staff. With enough essentials for a week, I took off with pure adrenaline into the tree line early the next morning. With no map or guide other than the stars and my sense of direction, I tried to make myself invisible as I followed a northern sheep path from the safety of the foothills above. Ten miles later, I gave myself up to a pack of search ATVs and German Shepherds in a nearby valley, and was forced to rejoin the group under heavy supervision.

After the third day back at the campsite, I was finally allowed out of isolation. I accepted that this was my life now. I had not seen any type of modern civilization in over a month. The extreme physical discomfort continued, but I had finally accepted my situation. The modern comforts—food, music, technology, money, and people that I dreamed about seeing constantly—were almost completely forgotten. Most of the original members I respected were gone, replaced by new kids. I now lived day by day for the small things: harvesting new sage for my fire-set, preparing food, waiting for letters from home. One night, a serious storm consumed our small lakeside peak at 11,000 feet. Awakened in the pitch black to the roaring sound of golf-ball-sized hail tearing through the protective pines, the sky began to explode. Lightning like nothing I had ever witnessed before shook the ground, exploding trees into flames nearby. Ears ringing, I cried myself to sleep, writing an ink-stained final letter to my parents between flashes. When I opened my eyes the next morning, I found myself smiling, both surprised and happy to be alive. I knew at that point there was nothing I could not handle.

One week later, it was my time to go. Saying goodbye to G-1, the only world I had known for the last sixty-two days, I turned and slowly walked my final 200 yards to the convoy of trucks parked in the distance. As we pulled away, I looked into the reflection of the window to see an unfamiliar face, staring back with vacant eyes and dark skin. With the passing hours, civilization slowly appeared, and my mind began to start functioning again. I had been able to adapt to the most extreme of situations, pushing past any limits, both emotionally and physically, that I thought I had. Even as memories of pain began to fade, what I had learned about the hidden strength in myself would never be forgotten.

~Adrian McElwee

Pain Long Enough

Turn your wounds into wisdom.
~Oprah Winfrey

Cutting makes the pain go away
Even only for a short time
Just long enough for me to feel normal
For me to stop my crying
For earth to revolve in a normal way
For flowers to bloom again
For the moon to shine like it used to
For me to make a new friend.

My emotions just fly away
On the back of a butterfly
Long enough for that blade to cut just deep enough
For me to reach a new high
For the liquid to run along
My already scarred skin
For things to be back to normal
Back to the way it's been
For the tingling in my fingertips
Because they haven't gotten enough blood.

My parents tried to help
But it just wasn't ever enough.
People act like they're better than me
Just because I love this pain
The sky turns that dark shade of gray
And the clouds cry out rain
That great feeling is over now
But it will be back soon enough
I'm already looking for the next blade
Waiting for the very next cut.

~Samantha Reinke

A Senseless Death

*We can only be said to be alive in those moments when
our hearts are conscious of our treasures.*
~Thornton Wilder

One of the parts of high school that I will never forget—and that also has made a large impact on my life—was the end of my freshman year. Just like any teenage girl, I love my friends. I have known some of them since elementary school, but I also have an extra special group of friends who I have attended church camp with since I was very young. I don't get to see most of them often, but thanks to the Internet we can share our pictures and keep in touch.

As soon as winter passes and the days start getting warmer, we start getting in touch with each other to make our plans for camp. I had one particularly special friend at camp—the sweetest girl I'd ever met, whose smile lit up the room whenever she walked in. She always made it known that she loved me, and that I was something special. I remember one morning at camp I wasn't feeling too well and I was lying on my bunk. She came in and ran over to me, hugged me and said, "Come on, get up, it's going to be alright!" I couldn't help but smile and do what she wanted me to, because she was that sincere.

It was the end of May and camp plans had already started. I remember coming home from school the day after Memorial Day. I logged onto MySpace and found a birthday reminder. I'm sure a big smile came across my face, because it was her, my friend from camp, and I instantly starting thinking about camp. I got up to do a few things, thinking about what I was going to write to her.

I sat back down at my computer and clicked on her picture to take me to her sight. I'll never forget that moment as long as I live. As I scrolled down to leave her a birthday wish, I read what other friends had left just moments earlier. "Happy Birthday Beautiful, RIP... We will always love and miss you." I couldn't believe what I was seeing. Could this be true? My beautiful friend was gone? The comments were left only moments before—was it some sick joke? I ran into the kitchen where my mom was, and told her what I had just read, and I began to cry. I couldn't stop. She tried to comfort me, but there was no comfort. We went back into my room and started clicking on other sites, only to learn that this was true, and she had been killed in a car crash on her fifteenth birthday. She was traveling in the car with four other teenagers—three boys and a girl. They were traveling at a high speed down a curvy road, only a mile from the school. They were headed home to celebrate her birthday.

Even now, I close my eyes and see them driving in my mind. I can hear laughing. I heard they were trying to beat another car to the destination. Then I think of the moment that they lost control, and the way they all felt as the car twisted around trees and down a hill. Both girls were killed, but the boys survived. I wondered if I would ever be able to stop thinking about what it was like to be in that car, looking forward to the birthday celebration. I wondered if I would ever stop thinking about the wonderful fun day she had planned, and the terror she felt as she knew what was happening. I couldn't help but withdraw from my other friends and sink into a depression. The accident was all I could think about. I tried so hard to spend time with my friends and family, but it seemed as though the harder I tried, the more depressed I became. With the love and support of my friends and family, I started to slowly climb out of the despair after about sixth months.

Today, I still don't think I could ever possibly write exactly how I feel about this experience, which completely shattered my heart.

I've been able to find comfort in silly things that make me happy, like going back to our old Xangas and reading her comments that say "I love you" and "I miss you." It makes me happy that she thought of me for a moment. After all this, I don't regret knowing her, no matter how painful it's been to lose her. I feel blessed to have known her for what little time I did.

It's strange how a single death can open your eyes to many things, such as taking friendships and family relationships for granted.

That unexpected tragedy, on a day intended for celebration, changed my life, and the lives of many people I know, forever. If given the chance, I would give my friend one big hug and tell her that I miss her and love her, and that not a day goes by that she doesn't cross someone's mind. She will forever be loved. I just wish I could thank her for teaching me the thing she has. I truly believe that I am a better person because of her, that I love more deeply, and that I appreciate so much more in life than I did before.

~Megan Brooke Conrad

Blood on the Carpet

A true friend reaches for your hand and touches your heart.
~Author Unknown

It was day number one of my first real summer job, and it was April of my senior year. I had, for some reason, decided it would be a good idea to work in the merchandise division—"merch"—at Six Flags Great Adventure, a place infamous in my hometown as the ultimate career destination of the druggies, high school dropouts, and feeble old folks looking for something to occupy their long, lonely days. My only company so far was the other cashier, who stank so strongly of cigarette smoke that I was surprised the sprinklers hadn't gone off. But then again, the sprinklers couldn't possibly make the environment any more miserable than it already was; it was dank and damp and cold, even inside the stupid store.

"Hey, is this your first day?"

I turned. It was one of the higher-ups, an exotic specimen who had wandered away from his natural habitat in the wonderfully warm back room, where the managers pretended to work. He had red hair and a million freckles and a cocky swagger. I was immediately in love. "Yeah," I replied.

He shook his head bemusedly. "I could've sworn I'd seen you before! I'm Kevin."

The rest of the day passed in a blur of tacky superhero merchandise, chilly rain, and red hair. I bid Kevin a flirty farewell and, of course, ran home to look him up on Facebook.

His profile said "In a relationship." I had absolutely no business being upset... but I was. I already really liked this guy—how dare he have a girlfriend? Her name was Crista, she looked like Quasimodo (hunchback and all), and she just seemed like a horrible, horrible, person... not that I was biased or anything.

Over the next few weeks, Kevin and I grew close. He would stroll into my store and, while I took my break, leave a note in my register signed with a heart. He would promise to stop making fun of me if I could answer ridiculously detailed questions about his personal life, like what instrument his younger brother Ian played in the jazz band (the saxophone, but how could I know that?). And on slow days, we would hang out and have long heart-to-hearts. But even through all of this flirtatious tomfoolery, I couldn't get his girlfriend out of my head.

I know I could have just asked him about her, but when's the last time you saw a love-struck teenage girl doing anything that made sense? So, despite our budding friendship, I couldn't help but keep a cautionary distance, mainly because I couldn't figure out what he wanted. Was it only friendship? Or something more?

The next weekend was prom, so I had a bit of a break from Six Flags and Kevin. But my day back was to be a happy one; I was excited to see him, and I was sure he'd be excited to see me too.

But, he wasn't... and he wasn't anywhere to be found. I headed over to his area. His friend looked confused when I asked about my favorite redhead.

"Kevin won't be coming back for a while," he said. "You haven't heard?"

I hadn't, but when I did, I couldn't help but cry.

My freckled friend didn't return for a month. When the day finally arrived, I couldn't help but feel a little nervous.

"Hey there," I said a little bit awkwardly. He turned around, and my heart plummeted to my feet. Something was missing; the light had vanished from his eyes, and there was something old and weary about his face. But then he looked me in the eye and a shadow of his customary spark popped back, and while I didn't feel much better, my heart hovered up somewhere around my knees.

"Hey, you! I hope you took good care of this place while I was gone," he said to me. And while things weren't quite the same, it was still pretty great to have him back, as the hand-drawn stick-figure cartoons and prank calls began again. I finally got up the nerve to get him to my house, though I couldn't escape Crista's looming presence.

It was clear from the second he showed up at my door, though, unshaven and haunted-eyed, that he was ready for the unloading of some heavy emotional baggage. I led him upstairs and we got comfortable at opposite sides of the room.

"My parents and I were at an awards banquet," he said quietly. "I was getting a stupid certificate. I didn't care; I was only going to make my parents happy. They weren't happy though, because my brother had called and said he might fail the eighth grade. When we got home, the house was dark, and we thought that was strange, because Ian always had the TV blaring and every light burning—he was afraid of the dark. I turned on the light in the living room and there he was on the floor. After that, everything happened at once. My mother shouted and my father ran to the kitchen to call 911 and I ran over to give CPR, but I put my hand on the back of his head and everything stopped."

Kevin stopped to take a great shuddering breath.

"It was soft and mushy, and there were sharp edges. I drew my hand away and it was covered in blood and flecks of gray, and there was a piece of bone that pulled off and fell to the carpet. I slowly got up, and everything was going so slowly. My dad's voice was deep and slow and my mom was shrieking but I couldn't hear it. I saw the gun in his hand. He had put a gun in his mouth... my little brother had killed himself."

I let out a muted cry. I knew weeks ago that Ian had passed away.... But I hadn't known that this was how it had happened.

"We didn't know what to do. My parents and I sat around the kitchen table for what felt like hours as the police investigated. We just didn't... know what to do. Then relatives started showing up, and Cris—and friends, and we had to get the carpet replaced. We had to get the carpet replaced because it was covered with my little brother's blood! God, oh God," He shook his head vigorously. "How can I... what am I supposed to... what can I do now?"

I honestly had no idea what to say. But as I saw a tear slowly wind its way down his freckled cheek, I knew what I had to do.

"I don't know," I said, very truthfully. "But I'm always here to listen."

He looked up and his eyes were watery, but he allowed a small smile to cross his face. "Thanks. You're such a good friend."

And a friend was what I needed to be. It didn't matter that I wanted to be something more, more than anything else in the world, or that I wouldn't mind tossing Crista off the top of the Kingda Ka rollercoaster so that I could have this boy all to myself. Right now what he needed was a friend, and so I needed to put aside my own desires and be a friend... just a friend.

And yeah, we did eventually end up becoming more than just friends. But I didn't know that then, and it didn't matter, because I had gained something in myself—something that meant more than a new friend or even a boyfriend.

~Amanda Panitch

Chapter 10

Teens Talk

HIGH SCHOOL

Family Ups and Downs

*Call it a clan, call it a network,
call it a tribe, call it a family:
Whatever you call it, whoever you are,
you need one.*

~Jane Howard

A Fresh Start

Change always comes bearing gifts.
~Price Pritchett

As a teenager, I'm generally expected to hate everything, including — but not limited to — my parents, my siblings, the government, my hometown, and classical music. As a teenager with divorced parents, this stereotypical assumption is strengthened.

But you know what? I'm happy. I'm really happy. Although I've had some tough times recently, I've pulled through. Just like a fever, things had to get worse before they got better.

What I miss the most is breakfast at my old house, with my whole family at the same table. Even if there wasn't any conversation, I would just smile as I read the newspaper or ate my cereal, enjoying the intersection of so many lives, loving the feeling of my family around me. Since then, we've moved, my sister has left for college, and my parents have divorced. Usually it's just one of my parents and me, and if they're at work, I'm by myself.

As fondly as I remember my old house, there was a lot of fighting. My parents were always very honest with my sister and me, to the point where they didn't make an attempt to hide their arguments. Sometimes they even dragged us into whatever the current conflict was. The entire mood of the house was often on edge. I remember one night waking up to shouting downstairs, opening my door, and seeing my older sister sitting at the top of the stairs listening to them, hugging her knees to her chin with tears running down her face. I have a lot of memories like that.

So it was honestly a relief when my parents announced they were getting a divorce. Unfortunately, it seemed like all the crises in my life happened at the same time. My best friend chose that winter to attempt suicide. My grandmother suffered a long illness before dying, and even worse than her death was watching my own mother deal with depression. We were in the middle of moving into two different houses and I was struggling in school. As I said, that winter was horrible.

But it got better. Now that the storm has passed, my parents are really and truly happy, and I feel like I can finally relax. My dad has a girlfriend, and I'm probably supposed to hate her. But she's a really sweet person and my dad is in love with her. It's great to see him so happy, and it's great to have another person in the house.

My mom is happy, too. I get the impression that she's the kind of person who's just happier on her own. She does her gardening, her genealogy, her home-improvement, and she works at the library. She's made herself a little sanctuary and takes care of all the pets my sister left behind from her days working at the animal shelter. She keeps herself busy and she seems content.

My sister is having a blast at college; she's always been the social type. She joined a sorority and has a boyfriend, and is—as always—doing well at school. Which is saying something, since she's at Johns Hopkins. She's a legal adult now, she's started her own life, and she's doing great.

As for me, I'm enjoying the new atmosphere. Both of my parents have settled into their new homes and made new lives. As long as the chemistry is right, I'm happy. I admire both of my parents for taking the plunge and creating new lives for themselves. Now that I'm on the brink of making decisions about college and my own future, I hope that I can someday create the life for myself that I want, even if it takes a few tries and a few fresh starts.

~Amelia Mumford

Finding Karen

What we do flows from who we are.
~Paul Vitale

My future held all the promises of classroom daydreams. I'd be graduating high school early due to exceptional grades, and I'd also been voted to May Court—an honor reserved for the most popular girls.

"I made lasagna," my mother told me after I returned home from school. "Your favorite."

I nodded, noticing that she'd been reminding me of what my favorite slices of life had been. There were times, too, when I'd find her lingering near my bedroom door, appearing uncertain as to whether she should knock or leave. We rarely faced the difficulties most of my friends experienced with their own mothers; yet, something was changing between us.

However, preoccupation with my own world hindered me from thinking much of parent-child relationships. "I'm not hungry now," I said. "I'll eat a sandwich later."

An odd expression crossed her features. "Maybe this evening we can make those chocolate sundaes like we used to?" she asked.

"Can't," I blurted. "I've been invited to a party. Another time, all right?" Not waiting for an answer, I rushed to my bedroom.

Freshening up, I then left the house. While driving to the party, I contemplated my future. My older sister in Florida had invited me to live with her. I could attend a renowned college there, or take time off to deliberate other prospects. An unfinished career puzzle loomed ahead, and although my family offered helpful input, I'd rejected their advice. After all, they still viewed me as the youngest sibling of five and I could do without the familiar stereotypes.

Arriving at the party, I'd noticed my brother's friend waving at me. I smiled—I always liked John, who looked like a gentle giant. Over 6'1", he towered above others, but his wide grin and heart seemed just as large as his physical appearance.

"Hi Karen," he greeted me. "What's your brother Mark up to?"

"Probably the usual."

"I'll miss him when I head to college," he admitted, "but I can't wait to go. I'm checking off the days."

His blue eyes blazed, reminding me of my own enthusiasm for the future.

"I'm studying medical science," he informed, filling me in on the details. Someone yelled to him, and John shrugged. "Well, I gotta go. I hitched a ride with a friend, but knowing him, he'll have three stops planned before I see my porch light." Hurrying away, he turned back. "Tell your brother I'll call him tomorrow. I've got Pirates tickets."

Later that night, I spotted my brother in his room. "John has baseball tickets. He'll call you tomorrow."

Heading to my room, I crawled in bed, noticing a half hour later that my mom had peeked in to make certain I was home. Sighing, I wondered if mothers ever stopped seeing their children as just that—children.

Saturday morning dawned earlier than expected as commotion erupted downstairs. Dressing quickly, I located my family on the front porch.

"What's going on?"

Mark turned towards me, his face unusually pale. "John was in a car accident last night."

"He's okay, though, right?" I'd asked.

"No!" he shouted, pounding his fist on the porch rail. "He's dead! Their SUV flipped over a guardrail, and a tree busted through the windshield, piercing John." He choked on his last words, stopped, and covered his face with his hands. "The driver might've been drunk."

The week that ensued shrouded me in silence. John's death shadowed my every move. Images of his smiling face and his excitement about the future replayed continually in my mind.

One evening, as my father watched a Pittsburgh Pirates game on television, I went outside to sit on the porch steps. John and Mark would never use those baseball tickets, I thought, gazing up at the stars. Nothing made sense any longer. My accomplishments seemed futile and selfish. In a split second, a promising life could be snuffed out.

Alone and uncertain, I lowered my head and cried.

A moment later, someone sat behind me, placing two hands on my shoulders. Catching the unexpected but familiar scent of vanilla perfume, I sighed. Chances were that my mother hadn't stopped wearing her favorite cologne — I'd just stopped noticing.

"Do you want to talk?" she asked, her voice sounding tentative. "Or I could leave you alone."

Her uncertainty as to how to approach me brought renewed grief. New tears surfaced, and I raised my hands to cover hers. "I want you to stay, Mom."

The way that I had distanced myself from her to prove that I was an adult seemed an ironic twist — for it only cemented the fact that I was still young and immature.

"I can't remember a time where I've been so sad," I admitted.

"Oh, there have been many," she reminded me. "Like when your grandmother died. You were only eight at the time, and you two were very close."

"How long did it take before I felt better?"

"Well," she deliberated, "it seemed like forever, until you developed an interest in visiting church at night." Chuckling, she explained. "You'd beg me to take you to St. Paul's so you could sit and think. Throughout your life, up until you were about thirteen, you used to do that whenever something troubled you."

She told other tales of my childhood, and her memories spun

a tender vine throughout my heart. Standing, I kissed the top of her head. "I'll be back, Mom. I have to go find someone."

Hours later, upon returning home, she greeted me at the front door. "I'm glad you're home. I was worried."

"I went for a long drive," I told her. "And I passed by St. Paul's and noticed lights on. I went in and remembered why I'd liked being there. Its peaceful surroundings soothe troubled souls." Pausing, I looked into her eyes. "After I left there, I stopped by other places you'd mentioned tonight. The lake where I caught my first fish, and then the park where I learned to ride a bicycle." Swallowing hard, I confessed, "I've been trying so hard to lose my past — as if it's a requirement for my future — that I failed to understand it's what has shaped me into the person I am."

Sighing, I admitted, "John's death forced me to recognize that there are no guarantees in life." Taking her hand, I squeezed it. "Therefore, I'm choosing to make the most of each day, and I'm starting with you, Mom. I'm sorry for the way I've been acting. I love you."

Her gentle eyes flooded with tears.

"And, Mom," I added. "Thank you for reminding me of who I am, even when I wanted to forget."

She laughed, helping me out of my jacket. "I take it you found who you were looking for, then?"

Nodding, I grinned. "I found me, Mom. I found me."

Clasping my fingers, she pulled me towards the kitchen. "That's the best news I've heard in a long time. Now we can get started on making those special chocolate sundaes like we used to...."

Keeping in stride with her, I heartily agreed.

~Karen Majoris-Garrison

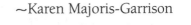

82

Helping My Brother Get Clean

Help your brother's boat across,
and your own will reach the shore.
~Hindu Proverb

The night before the SATs, I found myself wrought with worry. I felt on edge, as though I might burst into tears at any moment, and I was tired but completely unable to sleep. Yet none of these emotions were related to the impending exam. As usual, my mindset seemed to revolve around the state of my older brother, Andrew.

My parents and I had picked Andrew up the night before from his apartment in Boston, where he was attending the University of Massachusetts. I was giddy with excitement. Andrew was two and a half years older than me, and in my mind, infinitely cooler. He had always been funny and charming, and even won the yearbook superlative for most outgoing in eighth grade. I was so pleased whenever I had the opportunity to show him off to my friends or introduce him to others as my brother. Everyone adored him, but no one more than me. Intermixed with my excitement, however, was a growing feeling of stress over Andrew's well-being. His behavior recently had been odd. I hadn't seen much of him while he was at college, but he had posted depressing song lyrics on his profile online, and had spent most of the brief time he was home for Thanksgiving napping or otherwise holed up in his room. Still, I was thrilled to be bringing him home again.

I ran to greet Andrew as he stepped out of his apartment. He smelled of cigarettes as I embraced him and his face looked unshaven and tired. Nothing about this was particularly unusual or concerning. His eyes, however, usually so bright and alive, now seemed somehow empty. This change scared me so much that I found I could not think about it directly without my own eyes swelling with tears.

When we arrived home, I sought distraction in my favorite TV show and invited Andrew to join me. He began to drift off to sleep as soon as we sat down, and as he did so he muttered things to me about how he was in a bad place, and had started something he didn't know how to stop. I hoped that he was half dreaming and didn't know what he was saying.

The next two nights I barely slept. Putting together everything I knew about my brother and what he had told me, it was nearly impossible to reason that something wasn't terribly wrong. Unwilling to confront whatever it could possibly be, I found myself in an internal battle, perpetually suppressing the worry that rose up in me despite my attempts to keep it at bay.

I awoke the morning of the SATs to a pre-test breakfast prepared by my parents. I couldn't focus on the food, and instead immediately noticed that the table was only set for three. "Where's Andrew?" I asked, not bothering to hide the panic in my voice.

"He had to get back to his apartment this morning," they answered. "We drove him in early because he had work to do."

The day before my parents seemed to share my concern and suddenly they acted as though my worries were unreasonable. Couldn't they tell he needed help right now? I was angry that I seemed to be alone in my acute awareness of a problem. "I think something's really wrong with him," I pleaded.

"He'll be fine. We'll check in with him soon," they said, in an attempt to reassure me. I was far from reassured, but I used the SATs as my latest distraction, and tried to convince myself that my College Board scores were somehow more important than my brother.

The test went fine enough, but I returned from it to find my parents sitting solemnly in the family room. My heart dropped immediately. "What is it?" I asked, panicked.

"You were right about Andrew," my Dad answered. "Something is wrong. We didn't want to tell you right before the test." I could hear my heart pounding inside me. I was being forced to confront what I had tried so hard to avoid. "We talked with him about our concerns last night and he confessed to being addicted to heroin."

My dad's final word seemed to echo in my head, but something inside me must have known how seriously Andrew was in trouble, because I didn't feel the slap in the face that ought to have come with this news. Instead, I felt a wave of sadness that seemed to drown out all other emotions, and found myself unable to do anything but cry.

The three years since the day of the SATs have tried the strength of our family in innumerable ways. Andrew came home from college and was checked in and out of rehabs as he struggled to get clean and stay clean. When things were bad, he would steal from my parents and me to fund his habit and lie to all of us. I was easy to manipulate because of how much I looked up to him, and there were times when he took full advantage of this, completely unconcerned with how deeply his behavior hurt me. And when things were good, I would become hopeful that the changes were permanent and let my guard down, only to be repeatedly disappointed.

One time, while driving home, I passed Andrew walking along the side of our road in the rain with a badly abused backpack slung over his shoulder. I pulled over rather recklessly to talk to him, and he angrily announced that he was leaving to stay with a friend. He ignored me when I pleaded with him in the rain, and ended up storming off and not coming home. It was the summer before my freshman year of college, and I was suddenly completely out of touch with the brother who had once been such an important part of my life. It occurred to me then that Andrew might never be able to really understand how his behavior affected me and that I had lost my idol, big brother and best friend all at once.

Anyone who is an expert in the field will tell the family and friends of an addict that addicts are concerned only with getting their drugs, and any hurtful behavior toward others shouldn't be taken personally. I found this advice nearly impossible to accept. How could I not take it personally when my brother, who meant the world to me, lied to me, stole from me, and ultimately abandoned me? I was consistently hurt and surprised when I reached out to him and got no reply. The brother I knew was gone.

Just as things seemed to be at their worst, I got a call from Andrew late one night while I was away at college. My parents had completely cut him off, and he had worn out his welcome at his friend's house, so he was living in the city. Basically homeless and completely broke, he told me that he had been crashing on the floors of his addict friends' apartments with no purpose in life and nothing to look forward to. He announced that he refused to live like this any longer and that he was committed to getting clean. I could tell by his voice over the phone that something in him had changed dramatically. The joy I felt overwhelmed the feeling of hopefulness that had once tormented me. My parents agreed to fund his treatment, and Andrew checked into a detox center the next day.

Now, over a year later, he has never seemed better. Although I am conditioned to expect disappointment, I finally feel like Andrew is happy and stable in his sobriety and is fully engaged in his role as brother and friend again. I am also relieved to understand now that Andrew's new life was never something that I failed to give him: it was always something he had to want for himself.

~E.N.S.

83

Chicken Soup for the Soul

Seeing Double

I may not be different,
but I'm definitely not the same.
~William J. Dybus

I slammed the door to the bedroom I shared with my twin sister, Jill, and dumped my books on the desk. The anger and hurt I had carried through school still boiled inside me. As I threw myself on my bed, hot tears of resentment filled my eyes. It's not fair that Jill was picked and I wasn't!

That morning at school, our principal had announced the names of the girls from our class who had made the daisy chain. "It is my privilege to congratulate the following girls who were selected to carry the daisy chain for this year's graduation ceremony," echoed Mr. Banks' voice from the speaker high on the wall.

When I heard Jill's name mentioned, my ears perked up. Since Jill had made it, surely my name would be next. Everyone knew, even if it was never said, that the girls who carried the daisy chain were chosen by appearance. Since Jill and I were identical twins, it was inevitable that we would both be picked. After all, we looked exactly the same, didn't we? But when the principal finished the list, my name hadn't been mentioned.

I looked around in confusion. Was there some mistake? Had he forgotten me? But the microphone clicked off, and announcements were over. I hadn't been chosen.

Throughout the day people came up and congratulated me for

making the daisy chain. "Good job, Jill," they'd say, patting me on the back.

"I'm not Jill. I'm Jan, and I didn't make it!" I wanted to yell. Instead, I just glared at them.

After a miserable day of classes, I wanted to go straight home and lock myself in my room. But Jill and I were both on the school softball team, and I couldn't miss practice. Though I tried my best, my mind just wasn't on the game. Ground balls whizzed by me unnoticed. I struck out twice. When I finally connected with the ball, I grounded to the shortstop.

"What's the matter, Jan?" my coach asked. "Jill's having a great day today. Why aren't you?"

That was the last straw. I'd already been compared to Jill once today and came up lacking—I didn't need to hear it again.

Lying on my bed that night, thinking back over the day, other times I had been compared to Jill came to mind. Like when I came home from school with a "C" on my math test and Jill had gotten an "A" on hers. If Jill and I are twins, I reasoned, shouldn't I have gotten an "A" too? Our bodies are the same, why not our brains?

Or when Jill scored ten points in a school basketball game and I scored only six. "I always thought you were better at basketball than Jill," my brother said. "Why did she beat you tonight?"

And then there were the dumb games people always played with Jill and me. "Now, which one are you?" they'd ask when they saw us together. "Oh, don't tell me. Let me guess," they'd squeal if we started to explain who was who. Even our friends got tired of hearing this all the time.

Is that what being a twin is all about—endless confusion and comparisons? Is it putting up with nicknames like "Half-and-Half" and "The Twins" till you've heard them so often you start to doubt that you're a whole person? And why were we created this way? God, why did You make us identical twins? Why do you make anyone a twin? These questions rattled around and around in my head.

There was a knock on the door, and my mom came into the room. "Jill told me she's going to be part of the daisy chain this year,"

Mom said as she sat down on the edge of Jill's bed. "She also told me you weren't chosen. How do you feel about that?"

"I don't understand it," I said glumly, as I sat up. "The teachers choose the girls on their looks, and yet Jill was picked and I wasn't. We look exactly the same. How could they choose her and not me?"

"After all the complaining you two do about people treating you as if you're one person, I should think you'd be flattered by this," Mom replied.

Flattered? I looked at my mom in disbelief. Surely I heard her wrong. Flattered for not being chosen?

"You're finally being treated like individuals, and all I hear is that it isn't fair," she continued. "Are you your own person or not? Choosing one of you for something doesn't necessarily mean the other one has to be picked too, just because you're twins."

Mom's words made me uncomfortable—a feeling I usually got when she was right about something and I was wrong. Mom reached across the bed and picked up the Bible that lay on my desk. She quickly found the passage she wanted. It was one that she, Jill, and I had read many times before. It was the psalm about God forming my innermost parts and knitting me together inside my mom. It served as a reminder that I am wonderfully made by God's own hands (Psalm 139:13-15).

Mom set the Bible down in front of me and quietly left the room.

As a minister's daughter, I had always been taught to go to the Lord with my problems. "With God you will find comfort and peace," my father always told me. "There you will find your answers."

I reread the passage slowly while I traced the words with my fingers. "There is only one Jan Dunham," I read. "She was created whole and perfect in her mother's womb—a unique human being who will make her own contributions to the world. Though there is another whose beauty reflects hers, they are not the same. They are separate. They are individuals."

I closed my Bible, reassured once more by God's word. I was

worthy and unique in His sight. Though the world might confuse Jill and me, I knew the Lord never would.

~Jan Dunham as told to Teresa Cleary

84

Chicken Soup for the Soul

Sticks and Stones

Sometimes being a brother is even better than being a superhero.

~Marc Brown

"Sticks and stones may break my bones, but words can never hurt me." We've all used this expression at one time or another. But do you know what happens when the cliché isn't true? I do. I live with someone who was hurt—no, devastated—by words. Words that sliced deep into her brain and to this day have not left. My sister became an anorexic because of a sentence that is merely nine letters long: "You are fat."

In truth, Jennifer was never fat. At most, she was not even ten pounds overweight. Yet on the school bus one day, a peer called my sister fat. The perfectionist in her instantly responded; Jennifer decided to become thinner. Only it didn't stop at thinner. Thinner quickly became thinnest, and the nightmare of living with "the best dieter ever" began.

Jennifer dropped twenty pounds in two months. Her periods stopped. Her hair fell out. Her ribcage and shoulder blades became strikingly defined. I tried to be supportive and understanding of how attaining a common teenage goal (to be thin) had spun so wildly out of control. Her skin turned blue. She grew lanugo hair. Her hands were perpetually icy. She admitted she had a problem; she was resistant to correcting it.

I deeply love my sister. She's my best friend. Many times over the years, I've said that she's the best gift my parents ever gave me. I meant it. As Jennifer continued to lose weight, I found myself resenting her. She would claim to be doing everything she could to gain; in reality, she was doing just the opposite. She'd hide her food in a napkin, dump it down a drain, or drop it in her pocket. She was so zealous in her quest to lose weight that she even stopped wearing flavored lip gloss. (She assumed it must contain calories.) I couldn't understand this behavior: How could someone not want to eat? How could someone deliberately jeopardize his or her health this way?

Jennifer missed the closeness we'd shared prior to her illness. (I did too.) She would silently hand me notes that said, "Do you want to play a game?" or "Please forgive me. I promise I'll get better because I know you want me to. I'll eat right from now on." The next week her weight would be down another pound or two. I started ignoring her—and her notes. She was literally killing herself, and she wanted me to treat her as if nothing was wrong. As someone who values life, I couldn't.

One day, Jennifer handed me a note and walked off, a perfected routine by then. Unlike her prior notes, this one struck me as sincere. For some reason I believed her words—that this time she really would try to get better. I decided that if Jennifer would change, then so would I. I offered to play board games with her, kept her company, gave her advice, and attempted to be her best friend again. Slowly she gained—not just weight, but also a healthier outlook on life and my unconditional support.

Though I would give anything for Jennifer never to have become an anorexic, I've learned a lot from the experience. I've learned how to interact with and be a source of strength and comfort for someone whose problems don't mirror my own—and may actually be beyond my full comprehension. I also now try to keep negative comments about others to myself. Words, like sticks and stones, can be lethal. Thankfully, in my sister's case, they weren't.

~David Clay

85

Chicken Soup for the Soul

Letters from My Brother's Cell

A sister is a forever friend.
~Author Unknown

Once athletic, once so sharp
He walked the halls with pride.
Popular and always loved,
The doors were opened wide.

Football, track and wrestling,
Captain of them all.
But little did he know that soon,
His perfect world would fall.

One small puff just wouldn't hurt,
He chose to try some pot.
But soon the urge to try some more
Began to flood his thoughts.

Losing weight, eyes always glazed,
Bad grades he couldn't hide.
Different friends I didn't know
Were walking by his side.

He quit all sports, began to lie,
And stole my family's cash.
His every thought was focused on
Replenishing his stash.

Kicked out of school, into rehab,
Our love for him grew tough.
His drug-addicted lifestyle
Had started with one puff.

In and out of prison now,
He struggles with each day.
Bad decisions years ago
Have put him there to stay.

He writes to me, and my heart breaks,
His life's a living hell.
And all the words I hear from him
Come from my brother's cell.

~Cheryl M. Kremer

86

Chicken Soup for the Soul

The Unseen Hand

I can no other answer make, but, thanks, and thanks.
~William Shakespeare

I had just sat down to a table full of Thanksgiving food — turkey, mashed potatoes, corn — all the usual dishes, when I heard my name called to report to the administration office. It was my first year of high school, and it was customary for the administration to put on a special luncheon for our small high school of fewer than 250 students.

Nearing the office, I flushed when I saw my mother. Frantically reviewing the day's events, I couldn't come up with a single broken rule that would merit a summons worthy of interrupting such an event and requiring the involvement of a parent.

As I got closer, I could see her reddened, tear-streaked face. A look of concern showed on the school secretary's face. "Eric, go and get your things. We need to go." The words hung thick in the air. I started to protest, asking if there wasn't some way to leave after the lunch. "Eric, now! We need to go right now!" The urgency in mom's voice had kicked up significantly — and my usual teenage rebelliousness faded immediately.

I really had looked forward to the holiday lunch. My father had developed a serious heart condition and had been admitted to the hospital a few weeks earlier. I wanted to be around friendly faces — my childhood comrades — in a setting outside the classroom.

As the car sped away from school, I learned that dad's condition was not good — he had needed an immediate operation, and it hadn't gone well. In medical terms, he had died on the operating table, but some unseen hand had changed this fate, determining that his time had not yet come. His condition had stabilized enough that he could be moved. He had been transported to a different hospital, one known for its exceptional cardiovascular unit. He was in intensive care, and there was no way to know how much time he had left.

We learned late in the day that he would need another operation to attach a pacemaker to his heart. Unfortunately, we also learned this would not be a permanent fix. He had his heart attack more than seven years ago, and the damaged scar tissue remained a problem. He was still very much at risk for serious complications.

Tests and observations and planning occupied the weeks leading up to Christmas. Mom and I accepted the fact that we would be celebrating Christmas at the hospital. As we brought in colored packages, nurses greeted us with an understanding smile. Few people want to celebrate the holidays with their loved ones in a hospital ward, but the few who do, know that a hospital Christmas is better than a Christmas without your loved one.

For once, I could honestly say that I could think of no other Christmas wish, gift, or seasonal blessing that didn't involve having my dad around for many Christmases to come. Video games, electronics, even money for a car that I wasn't old enough to drive just didn't seem important. We had our Christmas in a hospital, and being able to be together made it one of the best.

Dad stayed in the hospital for a few more weeks, and his pacemaker operation went well... but that isn't the end of the story. A pacemaker solved only part of the problem. The scar tissue still posed a significant threat to his life, and without that part fixed, the pacemaker would not buy much time.

The solution was provided by a heart specialist in Oklahoma who had pioneered an experimental technique to repair scar tissue left after heart attacks. The procedure was an expensive one, but somehow the insurance company approved it. Unfortunately, my family still couldn't afford the portion that insurance wouldn't cover, not to mention the significant travel costs involved in going to Oklahoma. Perhaps this is where the real miracle took place.

I had always been fascinated with local politics. As someone too young to vote, I spent time carrying around registration forms to convince and register those who could. A campaign organizer with whom I'd become friends used her talents to organize a local fundraising event at a restaurant managed by a family friend. As my dad's story spread throughout the community, he was interviewed and featured on the evening news!

The fundraising night came and went, and when all the receipts were tallied, there was enough money to cover the remainder of the surgery's cost and for my parents to travel together to support one another as the day of the surgery approached. In the meantime, two complete strangers heard about dad's story and opened their home to my parents to stay with them, rather than having to pay for a hotel.

I've reflected on these events for several years. I've finished high school, completed college and graduate school, and begun a career; and I am convinced that it would not have been the same without the influence, love, and support from both of my parents.

I am also convinced that I witnessed an unseen hand working through the lives of many people, from doctors and nurses to family friends and complete strangers, to give my dad another chance at life. The experience has inspired me and even today I am in awe of the generosity of strangers.

~Eric Egger

Thanks Giving

I feel a very unusual sensation —
if it is not indigestion, I think it must be gratitude.
~Benjamin Disraeli

I shivered with cold and excitement as I scuffed through the yellow maple leaves that blanketed my backyard. The next day was Thanksgiving, my favorite holiday, and I was looking forward to seeing my whole family. Even though my three older sisters were married now, I was sure we'd all get together to eat turkey, relax, reminisce, and watch home movies.

I walked into the house expecting to smell pumpkin pie baking and willing to help my mom get ready for our company. I was surprised to find there wasn't any sign of holiday preparations.

What was going on? Mom must have been planning to start baking after dinner.

At the dinner table, I found I couldn't have been more wrong. "Listen, everyone, I have something to tell you about tomorrow," my dad announced.

Four pairs of eyes looked at him expectantly.

"Your older sisters all have other plans this year for Thanksgiving...."

"But it's a tradition to come here," I interrupted.

"Teresa, you have to realize that once you're married, you have two sets of parents to spend the holidays with. Your sisters can't always be here," my mom explained.

"Anyway," Dad said, "I've decided to give your mom a much-deserved break this year. I'm taking everyone to dinner at the Harvest Cafeteria tomorrow."

Dad's announcement was met with stony silence.

"You're kidding, aren't you?" I was the first to speak.

My dad shook his head.

He was immediately greeted with a chorus of: "But, Dad, that's a terrible idea!" "But, Dad, I don't want to go out to eat!" "But Dad, a cafeteria?"

"Dad," I said, presenting what seemed to me to be the perfect argument, "the pilgrims would never have celebrated Thanksgiving anywhere but at home."

"Teresa," my dad replied, "after nearly starving, the pilgrims were happy just to have food. I don't think it mattered to them if that food was served in their homes or at a restaurant down the street."

I could tell it was no use arguing. As the sound of his proclamation died away, so did my dreams of a homespun Thanksgiving holiday complete with turkey and all the trimmings.

As I lay in bed that night, I wanted to cry, but the tears wouldn't come. "Maybe it's silly to be so upset," I said talking to God through the canopy of my bed, "but how would you like it if someone ruined Your favorite holiday?"

When I awoke the next morning, there was no smell of turkey roasting in the oven. Instead I was greeted by the smell of coffee and burned toast. I burrowed back under the covers. There was no reason to get up.

The day dragged by. At five o'clock, we headed for Harvest Cafeteria. "You could have picked a better place to eat," I grumbled under my breath.

"Enough," my dad warned. "Just enjoy your evening."

Enjoy my evening. Right!

I wasn't surprised that the restaurant wasn't crowded. Normal people have Thanksgiving dinner at home, I wanted to say as I slid my tray down the metal runners, but I remembered my dad's warning and kept silent.

"Turkey or ham?" the lady behind the counter asked.

"Turkey," I mumbled. I chose very little, then followed my family to a table by the window.

As Dad said the blessing, I looked out the window. Instead of sitting at home looking at a backyard full of brilliantly colored leaves, I'm looking at an old black-topped parking lot. This isn't what Thanksgiving is all about.

Throughout the meal, my parents made attempts to lighten my mood. Finally, they gave up and let me sulk.

By the time dinner was finished, none of us seemed to have the holiday spirit. There was no lingering for another piece of pie or a second cup of coffee. We put on our coats and headed home.

Once there, Dad started outside to get firewood. When he saw me heading for my room, he called me back. "I want us to spend some time together as a family." My brother, Marty, was pulling some DVDs of our family's home movies out of the cabinet.

"Do we have to watch these?" I asked. I thought it couldn't be any fun without the whole family together.

"We do," Dad replied.

So I sat and watched my family history pass before my eyes. There were scenes from when we were babies, scenes of the whole family at the park, even scenes from Thanksgivings past. I smiled at pictures of my mom pulling the turkey from the oven and my dad carving it. It felt good to see the whole family around the dinner table. That's what Thanksgiving is really all about, I thought.

As the projector continued rolling, I saw another dimension to our family life. I saw how hard my parents worked to care for seven children. I saw the plain meals we ate. I saw the tired, but happy, looks on my parents' faces as they were surrounded by their children.

I remembered my earlier comment about going to dinner at a better restaurant and winced. Maybe Harvest Cafeteria was what we could afford.

I also thought about how hard my mom worked with four kids still at home. Maybe dinner out was a special treat for her—a break from a tradition that meant hours of cooking and preparation.

As I sat in the dark, the tears I'd wanted to cry last night finally flowed. All these things I have to be thankful for, and all I can do is complain.

I got out of my chair and went to sit at my dad's feet. I laid my head against his knee. "Dad, I appreciate you and mom working so hard to take care of our family," I told him.

If my out-of-the-blue comment surprised my dad, he didn't let on. "You're welcome," he said, stroking my hair.

"I'm sorry for spoiling everyone's Thanksgiving," I continued.

"You didn't spoil it, Hon. You just took longer than the rest of us to get used to the idea of celebrating Thanksgiving in a different way."

As the projector whirred on, I relaxed against my dad, content at last. I'd finally found out just what Thanksgiving was all about.

Be joyful always; pray continually; give thanks in all circumstances, for this is God's will for you in Christ Jesus" (1 Thessalonians 5:16-18).

~Teresa Cleary

HIGH SCHOOL

Overcoming Challenges

It is the surmounting of difficulties that makes heroes.

~Kossuth

88

Tasting Forgiveness

Forgiveness does not change the past,
but it does enlarge the future.
~Paul Boese

I first met my stepmother on a sandy beach in Martha's Vineyard when I was sixteen years old. Really, we'd already met — actually many times before — as she'd been my dad's new wife for a few months by then. I just hadn't faced it until I stood next to her, in her bright orange bathing suit and wide-brimmed hat. It was looking at her flat stomach and my adolescent tummy that made it real. This was the stomach my father had chosen over mine. So for the month of August, I ate small pieces of salmon next to tiny trees of broccoli, drank lots of iced tea, and ran on the beach, sweat dappling my brown curls — a poor substitute for buried tears.

Prior to that summer, I'd always loved the Vineyard, where for one month my parents, sister, brother, and I vacationed. We left the busy confusing life of the New York City suburbs, where my father spent his life on the commuter train, my mother at her keyboard, and my older sister and brother in their field hockey, lacrosse, aftershave and lip gloss worlds. I carried a red rubber ball, played kickball for hours, and wondered what it would be like to have one of those families where everyone wasn't so smart and there wasn't any yelling.

On the Vineyard, my family was more like the one I imagined. My father wore sloppy shoes and khakis with buttery stains from corn on the cob. We rented an old home with dusty books on the bookshelves and stacks of poker chips as bookends. I learned to play poker with pennies we found at the bottom of my mother's purse and in my father's sock drawer. My parents played — my mother laughing at my father's jokes, and I'd catch a wisp of love between them. We played family tennis and I was allowed to rotate in, only knowing how to bounce the ball in front of me to serve. No one seemed to care, as competition was left behind, hidden in the towering trees of the suburbs. I was never scared at night, believing bad things didn't happen to children on vacation. And I'd awake to the smell of toasting bagels. It was okay to have sandy feet all the time and I learned to catch ocean waves, the salty thrill of creating your own ride.

But then it all changed — my parents divorced at a time when having a mom's house and a dad's house wasn't what everyone did. My brother and sister were away at college, so my mother, golden retriever, and I watched my father pack his belongings in big brown leather suitcases. I wondered if there was a way to keep it all secret, so my friends would never know. My father rented an apartment in the city that smelled like boiled potatoes with sparse kitchen counters that made it look like no one lived there.

Soon my Dad started wearing new pressed khaki pants and yellow Lacoste shirts. He introduced me to his new friend who had three children of her own. Then we were all standing around her kidney-shaped swimming pool watching them get married. My father kissed another woman as lamb barbecued on a fancy grill. We all blended together like polite cousins. At first, my stepmother was a distant aunt who introduced me to Bloomingdale's and taught me how to make a piecrust — kneading the dough until it was soft. But it wasn't until that first trip to the Vineyard that I realized she was there to stay. I buried my adolescent grief with every spoonful of food I turned away. I tried to learn the back and forth dance from my mom's house to my dad's house, but I tripped a lot.

After visiting my dad, I'd walk into our quiet new home, for just my mom and me. Instead of feeling the pain, I would feel the cold iron of our heavy black scale, sitting in judgment. I would pull my sweater and shirt off together over my head, my underwear tucked in my pants on the floor. I would put my watch on the bathroom counter. Then I'd pee, flush the toilet, and gingerly step onto the black rubber, lining my feet up perfectly. The numbers would spin high and then settle low, matching my slowing heartbeat. One more time, I would step off and on again for good luck. I would breathe and relax, my ritual completed for that afternoon. The soft yellow blanket I carried as a little girl had been replaced by the sound of the scale's heavy metal — tricking me into believing safety and security were wrapped in my thinness.

As a college freshman, I spent my time running through snow-drifts, reading French novels, eating cottage cheese, and chatting with my friends. But one day, the tone of our conversation changed as I sat pushing lettuce around my plate. You know — it doesn't have to be this hard, comforted my friend. I knew she was right, and I made my way to the counseling office, where a woman with sparkly eyes said, "Here, take a seat, do you want to talk?"

I started crying and my healing began. There were so many feelings buried under my baggie sweatshirt. At first I was so ashamed that I needed help — afraid of people thinking I was crazy. But I slowly learned to change my humiliation into humility. My therapist helped me talk about my feelings instead of swallowing them. One day, I put my scale in a brown garbage bag and threw it away in a nearby Dumpster. I learned to find nurturance in my relationships, wrapped by the security of friendships instead of harsh numbers on a scale. I always thought I needed to forgive the grown-ups in my life who had turned my world upside down. But it wasn't them I needed to forgive. Instead, it was me — the young girl with a small, soft stomach, who believed if I really had been good enough, thin enough, strong enough, I could have kept my parents together. It's amazing the lies we tell ourselves. Someday I'll go back to that beach just to be reminded of the salty, yet beautiful taste of forgiveness.

~Priscilla Dann-Courtney

89

Gift Given Back

Do unto others as you would have others do unto you.
~Matthew 7:12

Throughout my life, I watched high school teenagers in awe. I couldn't wait to be one of them. They looked cool lugging heavy backpacks over one shoulder. The sacks were bursting at the seams, packed with a myriad of mysterious books. I always imagined high school with fun courses, clubs, and sports. My first week as a freshman in high school was exactly as I predicted. Classes were awesome, surrounded by friends and enthusiastic teachers. When it was time to pick a sport, the choice was simple. The thought of running on the track team, swooshing past my opponents, excited me enough to sign up. My mother bought me new running shoes and athletic wear. The school issued team shirts—slick apple red tank tops with white lettering. I felt proud to belong.

My first few jaunts around the track felt good. I took it easy with a nice slow pace. A cute boy sprinted by and that made me release my pent up energy and kick it into overdrive. However, each time my feet pounded against the track, sharp pains shot up my legs. I thought maybe I was out of shape and continued on. But the pain became so intense I had to stop. I sat down on the hot pavement with tears streaming down my face. I was scared when I noticed one leg was swollen. It was red and throbbing uncontrollably. I hobbled to the roadside, called my mother, and waited. I was worried sick. Did I sprain my ankle? Was it a stress fracture?

When I recognized Mom's car I tried to stand up, but it hurt so much that I fell down. Mom rushed to me and I sobbed in her arms.

"What happened?" she asked.

"I don't know, but just look at my legs." I put them together so she could see the difference.

"Did you fall?"

"No, Mom," I cried. "I'm in so much pain, I can't stand it."

Mom reached for her cell phone and called our doctor. At the doctor's office, we listened to the loud ticking of the clock. It reminded me how long I had been suffering. The doctor bombarded me with questions as he scribbled in my chart. He occasionally nodded or smiled while he listened. After he examined me, he cleared his throat long and hard. I couldn't imagine what he would say.

"I'd like to run a few tests," he began, wearing an expressionless face. "I suspect you might have a blood disorder."

My mouth went dry while my palms pooled with sweat. Questions whirled through my head all at once. The only question I managed to ask was, "Can I still run?"

The following week I was diagnosed with von Willebrand Disease (vWD), a bleeding disorder. It explained why I had always struggled with frequent nosebleeds. It also became clear why it took so long for my scrapes and bruises to heal. I didn't know I was bleeding in my joints while I ran. That's why my leg became inflamed and was painful. I had to quit track.

I went to a hematology center where I learned how to live with this lifelong disease. Fortunately, I received a medication that helps control the bleeding. There are people with bleeding disorders who need blood transfusions because the drugs don't work for them. I thought about those people when I looked at the shiny Medic Alert bracelet that dangled around my wrist. I knew I was lucky, but I didn't feel it.

"This isn't what I expected high school would be like," I cried to Juliana, my older sister, who listened with a sympathetic ear. "I wanted to be a part of something. That's why it was so important to be on the track team."

Juliana patted my hand. "You can do other things. Why not join a club? Our school has many different organizations. I'll introduce you to the kids in the Hole in the Wall Club." She smiled confidently. "You're going to love it."

I went at Juliana's urging. Upperclassmen boasted about how great it was. They raised money for kids with cancer so they could attend summer camp at the "Double H Ranch," in the Adirondack Mountains. There, kids have an opportunity to escape dreaded hospital visits and doctor's appointments. Thinking of the children's happiness, I joined the club. Juliana was right! It was a perfect opportunity to do something positive with my life. Imagining kids struggling with cancer lessoned the sting of my recent von Willebrand diagnosis.

I liked the other kids in the Hole in the Wall Club and enjoyed brainstorming ideas for fundraising events we could hold to benefit the campers. When the day came to actually go to the camp, I was beyond excited. Our assignment was to ready the facility for the upcoming summer program. We spent four long hours on a rickety yellow school bus as it drove over twisty back roads through the Adirondacks.

Once there, my task was to clean cabins, scrub tables and chairs, and mop floors and walls. I didn't clean that much at home, but I went above and beyond for these kids. They were sickly and needed a clean, safe environment, and I was going to give them that. Even though I was exhausted, I kept working.

I was given the worst possible duty—I had to shovel horse manure! It was a hot day and that was the last thing I wanted to do. It was a smelly job and backbreaking work, but the thought of the smiling kids' faces when they arrived at camp made me plug my nose and shovel away. I knew I could rest on the bus ride home. Before I could climb on that bus, I had to pick up a rake and clear out some shrubs in front of the cabins. I thought about the sick children, their heads bald from chemotherapy, playing in the shade of the trees. I imagined their squeals of laughter and excitement as they scampered across the lawns. Their stay would be wonderful because of the work I did. I was happy to give my time because they deserved it.

When I got home, I wanted a hot shower and the comfort of my bed. But my mom wouldn't hear of it. She was too excited. She was holding a stack of mail and I could tell she wanted to show it all to me. I wasn't interested.

"I heard from the National Hemophilia Foundation today," she said, shaking a large white envelope.

"That's nice," I mumbled.

"There is a conference you could attend."

"That's nice," I said again, this time talking over a cookie I shoved in my mouth.

"And I found a special camp you can attend this summer."

I stopped chewing and listened.

"This camp looks wonderful and they designated a week just for girls with bleeding disorders."

I swallowed hard and took the brochure. I had to smile and fight tears that crept into my eyes. It was the Double H Ranch.

~Andrea C. Canale

From Death
and Destruction

Every blade in the field,
Every leaf in the forest,
Lays down its life in its season,
As beautifully as it was taken up.
~Henry David Thoreau

A lot of people would say that nothing good can come from death and destruction, but I know better. I have endured many things, but I have risen above them all. Starting at an early age, my perfect world was shattered into pieces. But over all, no year has been as wretched as this last one.

Two years ago, I lost one of the most important people in my life. The only man who had always been there for me, the only person I trusted with every single one of my secrets, passed away in a random accident. This person was my grandfather, my world. After his death, I was lost in a downward spiral.

Following my grandpa's passing, I resorted to using drugs, alcohol, and violence as a means to cope. I became heavily addicted to natural adrenaline and Methamphetamine. As a result of my addiction, I became reckless with family and friends. I burned many bridges as a consequence of these actions. I lied, cheated, and stole from everyone I loved and cared about. But that is not how the story ends.

I had an eye-opening experience during that first year after his passing. Following a weeklong Meth binge and a rough month before, I attempted suicide. To this day, the details of what exactly happened are unclear to me. But I was taken into custody, put under a seventy-two-hour hold at Vista del Mar Hospital, and forced to detoxify. I was scared and alone, and justifiably so. I had no one to lean on because I had hurt everyone I loved. The only people who I saw as still having faith in me were my mom and grandmothers. This hospitalization would be the turning point of my life, but at the time I didn't want to hear that.

Seven days and lots of tears later, I was taken to my first rehabilitation program, in Santa Clarita. I had decided that I wasn't going to be just another burnout. So I took charge and chose the path set before me. I took my sobriety one day at a time, and thirty days later I was taken to SunHawk Academy, an inpatient teen rehabilitation facility, where I spent all of last year. I made many valuable friendships as well as many positive choices.

While at SunHawk I experienced a lot of tragedy. Throughout my stay, I got phone calls with news of different relatives passing away. I received six of these phone calls before I got the most devastating one, a call that my grandmother and aunt had passed away that day. I loved both of these women dearly and was absolutely crushed when I heard the news. It was a blessing in disguise. Both were at different hospitals and died from different causes. One died of old age and the other, my aunt, who was in and out of recovery with an addiction to prescription drugs and alcohol, died from one last relapse. Both were in a lot of pain, though. My aunt's death was part of my inspiration to become clean and sober, and it still is.

Four months later, I am writing this. I have been clean for fifteen months and am going strong on the road to recovery. I am getting ready to graduate high school with my class, something I never thought I could do. I am doing things I never thought were possible and loving every minute of my new life. So whoever said nothing good could come from death and tragedy obviously has not met me or heard my story.

~Capri Colella

Those Detestable Braces

*It is often hard to distinguish between the hard knocks in life
and those of opportunity.*
~Frederick Phillips

Dressing for my first day of school at Tulsa Central High, as I dragged my trousers over those detestable steel braces on both my legs, I couldn't help thinking, "Face it, Louis, you're in for a terrible sophomore year." It was my first year in a new school, in a new town and the worst news of all—wearing braces from my ankles to the top of my thighs with hinges at the knees. I wasn't able to do sports, and I couldn't ride my bike or even climb stairs.

Why the braces? Though I'd had painful knees for months, they were dismissed as "growing pains." But during a wrestling match at the gym, my legs crashed off the mat onto the concrete floor. The instant, unbearable pain merited a visit to a doctor. He said I had Osgood-Schlatter disease—a disease that affects the cartilage in the knees. "It's not bad if caught soon enough. Now you'll be in braces for a year or more," the doctor said. "But then you'll be good as new." When I put on the braces, he said, "Don't move in a hurry when you sit down or you could cut your thigh."

The braces got rid of my knee pain, but I hated starting high school this way. Unable to get around well, I was afraid I wouldn't be able to make friends. Certainly dating girls was also out of the question. I slumped down on the bed in despair. But then Mom was calling me, "Come on, son. It's nearly time for school!"

School that day was my worst nightmare. The teacher of my first class was too busy to give me directions to the elevator for my second class until we were all seated in the room. Then, in front of all the students, she called out, "Louis Hill, where are you?" When I raised my hand, she said, "All right. The elevator is in an alcove to your left all the way around the building from here." The whole class looked stunned that I had to take the elevator.

When the bell rang three boys followed me, taunting. "Poor little baby! Has to ride the elevator with the girls!" Worse, when I tried to walk into the crowded elevator, the girls pushed me out, yelling, "You can't ride! Only girls are allowed to ride the elevator!"

"I have to," I said, "I have permission because I wear braces." The girls made room then, but I was so red-faced with embarrassment that I hid in the alcove momentarily and was late getting to the next class, English. Forgetting the doctor's warning, I rushed to sit down on the back row and caught the flesh of my thigh between the brace and the top of the chair. The brace gashed my thigh and trousers and spurted blood down my pants. I went home in despair.

In the days that followed, however, I discovered that the situation wasn't all bad. Without sports or the outdoor fun I loved, I took more interest in my studies, especially math. I also found time to explore the school library. The new friends I made there were the Arctic explorers and the heroes of history, several of whom also had infirmities. Those heroes' differing paths in life were fascinating, especially the two great generals of World War II — Dwight Eisenhower and Douglas MacArthur. My friends who existed in books widened my horizons.

Presently, another good thing happened. The girls who rode the elevator became my friends. A nucleus of them met at games and sat together, laughing, joking, munching popcorn, and rooting for our team. And they invited me to join them, allowing me to take the stadium ramp "with a girl on each arm," as they put it. It was lots of fun. Since some of the girls were pretty, other boys often joined our group, giving me a chance to make more friends.

One day at semester break, I took stock and had to admit to myself that I was having a really good year in spite of—or maybe because of—those detestable braces.

~Louis Hill, Jr.

When My Teachers Stood Up for Me

Labels are for filing. Labels are for clothing.
Labels are not for people.
~Martina Navratilova

On the day I received my first standing ovation, my boyfriend broke up with me. I was a junior in high school in suburban Philadelphia. It began with my participation in a project called the Day of Silence, a program that's becoming more common in high schools across the country. Its goal is to spread awareness of the silence that many GLBT (Gay Lesbian Bisexual and Transgender) students experience when they approach their teachers and administrators about discrimination, harassment, bullying, and other issues related to being gay or otherwise "not normal." I had managed to sign up one hundred students for the project in my conservative suburban school, and many teachers had agreed to wear a ribbon of support for us. While it wasn't 100% well received, we were making a stir and getting people talking. Through our silence, we were beginning to be heard.

I sent my story to the organization in charge of the project, the Gay Lesbian Straight Education Network (GLSEN), and they asked if I would be the Northeast Regional Student Leader for the Day of Silence the next year. I accepted. In the six months of training that I underwent, I learned how to teach, to listen and to change the world one person, one movement at a time. Part of my training was learning how to lead a Teacher Training session, and how to teach someone else to do the same.

While I never got to train another teen, I didn't want to let my newly acquired skills go to waste. Figuring I had nothing left to lose, since I was already accepted to college, I approached my high school principal, a soft-spoken man by the name of Dr. Bob, who had become accustomed to my presence in his office. If I wasn't launching some protest, I was filing a harassment complaint against another student. Whoever said the suburbs were safe for kids, was never considered "different."

Dr. Bob, I had assumed, would give his usual incredulous, "You want what?" Instead, the reaction I received was equal, but opposite: "Sure!" he said, as enthusiastically as anyone had ever seen him. Dr. Bob informed me that the school already had annual teacher sensitivity training, and that this year's session was coming up. The next thing I knew, I was in a meeting with the training session coordinator, who put me on the agenda. And that was that. This was in January. I was told to show up on the next in-service day: Monday, February 14th.

My boyfriend and I had planned to spend Valentine's Day together. Canceling our mutual day was a big decision, and I considered turning down the teacher training—but I didn't. And so I agreed to spend Valentine's Day with every teacher I had ever had.

The instructions I received three days before making my speech were that I should just talk. I could have prepared something, but they preferred I speak off the cuff.

"Our next speaker is Erik Benau," someone announced. "He is a senior at the high school. He has some things he'd like to say." I grabbed the surprisingly heavy microphone. I looked out into the audience of trained and certified teachers. Some of them had bundles of flowers on the table.

"Hi, my name is Erik," I started, and was immediately interrupted by a cell phone ringing; it was answered by a woman somewhere who said, "I'll call you back."

"You know, if my phone goes off when one of you speaks, I get the phone taken away until the end of the day." They laughed. I pressed on, despite my nerves.

"I've lived here my whole life, and I am completely..." it will never be the same, I thought, "...and 100%..." I knew I had nothing to lose and only everything to gain from the next word I was about to say. If the next fifteen minutes could change at least one person, maybe save one life, then I had to drop this verbal bombshell: "...gay."

I thought I heard a pin drop, but it could have been a jaw or two hitting the floor.

"And I don't have any gay role models. I've spent my whole high school life running from people. I go to the city, where there's a neighborhood of people like me, and then I come home and I hear the word 'fag' everywhere, and teachers, who I know heard it, say nothing."

I proceeded to tell them everything that came to mind. How all the bullying I've experienced basically started with, and boiled down to, name-calling and how that shouldn't be allowed. Not in high school, not in middle school, not ever. I described getting my car keyed, being spit on in the hallway, and how, if I weren't a black belt, I would have been beaten up.

I described the loneliness of not having any role models, and the desire to be with people like me. I also talked about the fact that my story was not unique. How through my work across the nation, I had met people who had it as bad or worse than me. And how I was here today, not for me, but for them—for all the kids who come into this world, come to, and come out in these hostile environments. I continued with, "if teachers won't respect a gay kid, then they are in the wrong profession."

I don't know where the time went, and I wish I could tell you with more detail exactly what I said, because I would like to know. Someone touched my arm and whispered that I was out of time. "Great," I thought. "I rambled too much." So I looked out at the audience, which stretched on for miles and miles of tables and flowers and eyes and thoughts and grades and history and detentions and art and encouragement and report cards. I thought, "What have I done?"

"Well, I guess I'm out of time," I said. I put the microphone down and made a beeline to my seat. Then I heard applause, a lot of applause, which surprised me. I don't know if I expected to be booed, or worse. So with a jerk of surprise I looked up from staring at the ground.

It wasn't just polite applause I heard. First, my history teacher from sixth grade stood up, then my gym teacher from last year, then the entire English department, followed by the French department (whom I never had anything to do with), and finally the whole room. It grew from a trickle to a waterfall of claps and smiles and encouragement.

"If it's okay with him, we have a few minutes for questions," said someone into the microphone, and I agreed.

"How can we prevent some of these events from happening again?" a teacher asked.

"Be there, and don't be afraid to step up and tell someone that they are being disrespectful. Be there and listen. Don't be silent." I replied.

That Valentine's night, I got into a stupid argument with my boyfriend and we broke up and I never saw him again. And for some people, breaking up for the first time on Valentine's Day would be the story that lasts for years. But for me, that story is far overshadowed by the sound of my first standing ovation.

~Erik Benau

I Am a Teen Parent

It is said that the present is pregnant with the future.
~Voltaire

My name is Bryonna Garcia, and I am a teen parent.

"Your pregnancy test came back positive." Those words were the words that changed my life. I was only sixteen years old and had to become an adult and a mother all at once. I didn't know what to do at that point. "Should I keep it, or should I have an abortion?" That was the question I asked myself every day. My mother insisted that I get an abortion, but after ten weeks I decided to take responsibility for my actions.

I was already responsible, especially in school. I was a sophomore at the time, taking honors courses, maintaining a GPA of 3.8, an NS-1 in NJROTC, and I was captain of the varsity cheerleading team. My mother feared that if I went through with my pregnancy, I would drop out of high school and ruin my future. She decided to move us to a different town in an attempt to make things better. My new school was the complete opposite of my previous school. I felt out of place, partly because everyone stared at me and whispered things like, "Oh my gosh, we have a pregnant girl at our school!"

My counselor became my best friend in high school. She helped me with everything and became someone for me to talk to. I had a hard time adjusting to my new school and she helped me. She helped me fill out college applications, scholarships and scheduling for my ACT. She also helped me with personal decisions. It was frightening to know that I would soon be a parent. I couldn't be a kid anymore, and I was clearly not ready for parenthood, but my counselor told me that I would do well, because I am a determined person. She told me to think of how my success would benefit my child.

When I gave birth to my beautiful daughter, it was like my whole world started over. The first night we spent together, I apologized to her for considering abortion as an option. I promised her that I would do whatever I had to do to make her life better than what mine had been.

As the months went on, I got an after-school job and a car. I began working overtime and school became a struggle. I had to juggle work, school, and a child all at the same time. But I knew one day it would all pay off.

One day, my counselor called me down to the office. She told me that she had good news. I had gotten into a competitive school, the University of Minnesota at Twin Cities, and I was Pell Grant eligible, which meant that I could be going to school for free. I began to cry. I was the first in my family to be accepted into college.

My daughter is now eighteen months old and still motivates me. In the fall I will be a freshman at U of M Twin Cities. Ultimately, if I had never gotten pregnant, I would be graduating with honors, but then I wouldn't be who I am now. I wouldn't be as strong and determined. I am proud to be a student parent because it shows how responsible I am. Years from now, when my daughter is all grown up, I hope she comes across this story. If she does, she will know how hard I worked and what I have sacrificed for her because she is what I live for. High school was tough, but I got through it. I did something that I thought was impossible.

My words of wisdom to the incoming freshmen are these: "High school is not going to be what you thought it would be. It will be filled with obstacles, surprises, friends, enemies, and life-changing events, but if you stay focused and set goals, you will succeed."

~Bryonna Garcia

New Life, New Beginnings

In three words I can sum up everything I've learned about life.
It goes on.
~Robert Frost

I t was April and flowers were blooming, buds sprouting on the trees in my rural town in upstate New York. My best friend, Jolie, and I were about to embark on one of life's happiest events—high school graduation. We were supposed to be happy, excited, and planning our next phase in life—but I was about to rock a lot of people's worlds with my secret. It was a secret I had kept hidden for six long, painful months, but I couldn't keep it to myself any longer. The time was now, for I knew I couldn't hide it much longer. In fact I was surprised I hid it so long.

Walking into my bedroom, where Jolie was waiting patiently for me to return from the shower, I smiled at how comfortable she was in my home. Lounged out on my bed listening to music through headphones, she had been my best friend since first grade. We'd been through thick and thin together, and now our friendship was about to endure another challenge.

"What are you doing?" Jolie asked confused. "Why didn't you get dressed in the bathroom?"

"I want to ask you something. I need you to be completely honest with me."

"Sure. You know I'll be honest."

Nodding, I knew she was right. Whenever I wanted an honest opinion, Jolie was my go-to girl.

Sitting on the bed next to her, I took a deep breath. "I'm going to show you something, but you have to promise you won't freak out."

"Okay," she said hesitantly.

"Promise?"

"Promise," she said, holding up two "scout's honors" fingers.

I stood and unwrapped the towel covering my body. "Do I look pregnant to you?"

"Oh. My. God! Kendra!"

"Shhh, I don't need my mother in here right now."

"I'm so sorry." The mixed emotions didn't go unnoticed. Fear and disbelief were written all over her face. "You're pregnant?" she asked in a whisper.

"Yes." It was the first time I admitted the truth out loud. Deep down I knew, but couldn't admit it to myself. "I haven't been to a doctor and David is really worried. He thinks it's time to tell our parents and go to a doctor."

"He's right. You look rather big. How have you been hiding it all this time?"

"Baggy clothing." After all these months of denial and fear, our secret was out.

Later that day David and I sat down with my mother and told her about the pregnancy.

"What are you plans for this baby, Kendra?" My mother was way too calm. I expected her to be screaming and yelling at us, telling us how careless we were and how we'd made such a horrible mistake.

"Give it up for adoption," I said plainly.

"What?!" David and Mom asked.

I knew I'd shocked them both with my revelation, but the truth of the matter was that I had decided on adoption the moment I accepted the truth about the pregnancy.

"Look, we're just about to graduate from high school. I want to go to college. If I become a mother, all those things will have to be put on hold."

"That's true," Mom said.

"I love this baby enough to do what's right for it. And the right thing to do is give it a home with parents who are ready and able to care for it properly."

David agreed with me. Our parents helped us look into adoption. When we met the Madisons, David and I knew they were the perfect couple to raise our child.

A few short months later, Taylor Madison was born. She was the spitting image of her father and the cutest little bundle of joy. Passing her to Sarah's waiting arms was hard, but I knew it was the right thing to do.

It's been over twenty-two years since Taylor was born. People who know about her often ask if we regret giving her up for adoption. To that I reply, "Never!"

She was given a life I wasn't ready to give her. She has two parents who love and adore her.

There isn't a day we don't think about her. The Madisons send us pictures and give us updates as to her progress.

David and I eventually married. We had twin boys Marc and Shane seven years ago. Maybe some day we'll meet Taylor, if she wants to, but I already know her in my heart.

~Tina O'Reilly

Finding My Voice

Panic at the thought of doing a thing is a challenge to do it.
~Henry S. Haskins

The bell rang. Students quieted as they settled into their seats. My English teacher stood in the front of the room, smiling and raising a book high.

"This week, we're reading Shakespeare's *Hamlet*," she said as her eyes sparkled.

Cool, I thought. I loved *A Midsummer Night's Dream* and *Romeo and Juliet*.

I should have held off on my excitement.

"The assignment will be for each of you to memorize the soliloquy, 'To Be or Not To Be,' and recite it to the class."

A few kids groaned. Some grinned. I looked down and watched my foot tap nervously as her words played over and over in my mind. Recite a soliloquy. To the class. That meant reading out loud, risking exposure. Panic gripped my heart and squeezed tight.

Some people struggle with stage fright, but I battled something else. As long as I could remember, my enemy was my voice: "To B-B-Be or N-N-Not To B-B-B-Be," I imagined everyone staring while I painfully repeated sounds like a DJ scratching a record. Why did I have to stutter?

My stammer began when I was a preschooler. My mom and grandma encouraged me to speak slowly and thoughtfully. Sometimes, it worked. Sometimes, I spoke fluently without their prompting.

Other times, I tripped over consonants and squinted as if the effort alone would will the words out.

In elementary school, my teacher, Mr. K, whisked me out of class a couple of times a week for speech therapy. We played vocal games. He taught me to elongate sounds, stutter freely, and keep going. He told me to maintain eye contact and believe in myself. Outside of family, few people even noticed I stuttered. My speech improved for a while.

Then, one day, the stuttering came back—more unpredictable and more distressing this time. I could be fluent one moment and struggle through talking with my mom the next. I thought about the howls of laughter stuttering characters could elicit from movie and TV audiences. I didn't want to be a punch line. So I did what I had been taught to do when I wanted to know more about something: I read up on it.

My encyclopedia told me that three million people stuttered including James Earl Jones. Interesting. Wasn't he the voice of Darth Vader? Four times as many guys stuttered than girls. Great. Why did I have to break those odds?

I hadn't chosen to have a stutter. Even thinking my idea made me feel like a coward. But as I sat there, I came up with a solution to my stuttering problem. Hardly anyone knew that I stuttered. What if I kept it secret?

It wouldn't be that hard, I reasoned. Mostly, I was fluent. I could substitute synonyms for words I thought would trip me up. On bad days, I could clam up or pretend I didn't know the answers. It didn't take long for me to become a master at hiding my struggle with speech.

But that choice came at a cost. The thought of being called on could make my heart pound and stomach drop. If I was asked to read, I nervously scanned the passage searching for words that might betray me. Then, there was a time when my trick wouldn't work. I was playing Mary in a church play and had a script to follow. I sat there thinking about the words and knew I would stutter on some of them. I couldn't change my lines. So I ran off the stage and cried.

Recite a soliloquy. To the class.

What if the same thing happened again? Or worse, what if nothing came out at all?

At home, I practiced in the mirror. I transformed myself into Hamlet for my mom and grandma. I took turns saying the speech with one of my friends. We laughed when we forgot words and cheered when we got through it.

But I never revealed my deepest worry. Alone in my room, I pictured the worst. I saw my classmates' horrified looks as my eyes squinted, my hands balled into fists, and I stuttered over every word. I had never been teased because of my speech and that's how I wanted to keep it. I had enough drama coping with acne and figuring out boys. I didn't need people finishing my sentences and looking away when I talked.

Still, something nagged at me. I was tired of hiding, tired of feeling my stomach lurch and twist at the thought of speaking. There had to be another choice.

On the day when we were supposed to recite the monologues, I sat in English with my foot tapping, my mind focused on Hamlet's words. Some of my classmates nailed the speech. Others forgot parts or trembled through it.

When my turn came, I inhaled deeply and stood up. I had more on the line than they knew. I thought about the words I was about to say and made a decision.

"To be" scared, "or not to be."

I walked to the front of the room.

"To be" a prisoner, "or not to be."

I turned around to face my teacher and friends. I can do this, just like I practiced. I can do this, just like I've done before.

"To be" brave, "or not to be." To be bold.

I started to speak. My hands quivered. The words came out shaky at first. Then, I delivered them louder, stronger. I imagined myself saying the speech to my mom, grandma, and Mr. K. I stuttered, but kept going. I stayed focused and stood tall. Before I knew it, my speech was over. I smiled as everyone clapped for me.

They celebrated my reading just as they cheered everyone else's. But I had a special reason to feel good. I faced my fear. I knew I'd have other battles with stuttering, but I won that day.

I finally found my voice.

~Kelly Starling Lyons

Chapter 12

Teens Talk

HIGH
SCHOOL

Moving On

Begin doing what you want to do now.

~Marie Beynon Ray

No Regrets

There is a good reason they call these ceremonies
"commencement exercises."
Graduation is not the end;
it's the beginning.
~Orrin Hatch

My footsteps echoed in the empty halls, my flip-flops sounding absurdly loud as they slapped against my heels with each step. Already I could feel the change in the school, even though classes had only let out a week ago and finals were still going on. It was as if the very walls had exhaled their last breath. Sure, the halls were empty during the school year while we were all in class—but never this quiet. Never this clean and clear of debris. No half-eaten Pop-Tarts dropped near the cafeteria; no empty Vitamin Water bottles lying abandoned near a garbage can. No lockers bulging at the bottom from a carelessly dropped notebook and no papers scattered in the corners, dusty footprints marring their perfectly photocopied words.

The classrooms were equally still. The wide-open doors could have been waiting for entering students, like any other day. Upon closer inspection, though, you could see the subtle changes. The desks aligned in strict, military rows. The boards showing nothing but the marks of the custodians' sponge, the residue of chalk gone from their surfaces.

I'd come back for one last walk around the place that had

practically been my home for the past four years. Five days a week, seven hours a day, ten months a year—not to mention all the Saturday musical rehearsals and club meetings after school.

I felt restless as I wound my way around the echoing building; certain spots seemed to jump out at me. The bathroom on the first floor, where I'd spent many a study hall crying during my stressful sophomore year, was now newly tiled and painted. Somehow it didn't have half the charm of the old, chilly room with its faucets that never ran warm water. The staircase I took every day for the first half of my freshman year, because I wasn't sure how to find the other steps, had been removed, and in its place was a hall leading to more art classrooms. And the old social studies department office, where I had spent so many joyful hours in the company of my mentors and friends, was now the testing center. The renovations had relocated some of my old haunts, but to me, they had not changed.

I found my feet carrying me faster, up to the second and third floors, around the halls as I peered into classrooms that had once been mine. I felt myself looking for closure, for some sign that it was really over, but all I could think of were the memories. Everywhere I looked, they surrounded me. The stage, where I had performed so many times; my locker, the butt of my frustrations, still slightly scuffed along the bottom where I had given it a vicious kick last year; the library, where I pored over my AP European History textbook until I thought it would burst into flames from the fever of my eyes. All empty and organized, lying dormant for two months until another year began... a year when I would not be present.

I looked at my watch: 2:21 P.M., the time that, for seven years, had signaled the end of my day. I realized with a start that, at this time tomorrow, I would be sitting at my own graduation ceremony. I would be wearing, not simply staring at, the cap and gown that had hung behind my door for the past three days, watching my friends cross the stage, and finally, making the long walk myself.

My feet took me to the main floor, and I sat down at the bottom of the central staircase and rubbed my eyes, suddenly tired. What was it that was nagging at the back of my mind? What hadn't I done yet that I wanted to, that I needed to, before I said goodbye?

Nothing.

The answer came unbidden and surprised me, but then I began to think about it.

I had joined choirs and performed in musicals.

I had danced at prom, marched at Homecoming, and cheered until I was hoarse at basketball games.

I had taken the classes I wanted, worked hard, and been rewarded—most of the time. And when I hadn't, I had learned from my mistakes.

I had pursued my dream of teaching by discussing it with my own teachers. I had met incredible mentors that, hopefully, would remain with me for life.

I had conquered my fear of public speaking through Model UN. I had traveled to Washington to participate in a conference, seen the national monuments by night, and spent six amazing days with some of the people I loved most.

I had given all of myself, and received even more back in return.

The tension left my shoulders as I stood up and looked around, realizing that there was nothing left for me to do. There was nothing in this empty building for me to say goodbye to. What had high school been for me? It had been pride, gut-wrenching laughter, and exhausting tears. It had been hugs that said more than words, and classes raucous with enthusiasm. It had been people. True, all of the above had taken place here, but this was really just the shell that had housed the pulsing life I had lived for four years. The people I would see tomorrow; the memories would always be mine.

It was time to go.

~Ashley Mie Yang

Jump the Bush

The leaves of memory seemed to make
A mournful rustling in the dark.
~Henry Wadsworth Longfellow

There was this bush in the old courtyard of my high school. Its green branches stretched only about chest-high on a senior student. It sat at the edge of the gravel walkway between the main building and the library, just a short distance from the school chapel, and it always looked unkempt and disheveled. While the other bushes were neatly pruned and evened out, this bush had holes on every side. The ground beneath it was littered with twigs that had broken off. Many times, people who came to the school wondered why the administration had taken such good care of the other plants and shrubs but had ignored this one.

That's because this is the bush we used to jump.

To this day, I don't know why the students of Boston College High School, myself included, found it thrilling to jump over a little shrubbery. With our collared shirts tucked into our belted khakis, we'd run full speed from the slope of the incline of the parking lot and, upon reaching the bush, leap with all our might up and over, crashing down onto the grass and dirt of the other side. If we were lucky, we'd only catch our legs on the branches. If we were unlucky, we'd fall face first into the heart of the bush, scraping our face and hands on the pointy bristles and emerging to the sounds of laughter and taunts. It was painful. It was stupid. It was humiliating and it was unnecessary. Maybe it just kept our minds off the fact that this was an all-male high school and would stay that way for all of our high school careers.

Jumping the bush was an instant JUG, a fancy word meaning "Justice Under God" invented by Catholic schools that essentially meant you picked up trash after school for forty-five minutes. The beauty of receiving a JUG for jumping the bush meant that the Dean saw you do it. It was an honor, a sort of weird knighting into the kingdom of troublemakers. A lot of times, if the Dean was outside by the bush, we would jump it anyway just to say that we got jugged for it.

Depending on the season, the bush would take on new roles. In the fall it was a launch pad into a pile of freshly raked leaves. The vivid reds and yellows splashed colorfully into the cold, autumn air as groundskeepers yelled at us to clean up the mess we made. Sometimes, repeat offenders would have to come in on Saturday and rake up the bits of fun that had spread throughout the school week. This just meant more time to bush jump.

The winter probably saw the most bushjumpers. A loose pile of freshly shoveled white goodness made for a cushiony landing but a more difficult flight. We would slip and fall on the icy walkways as we sprinted towards the snow-capped shrub, resulting in several trips to the nurse. The bush was also the best cover for a snowball fight. Unfortunately, it couldn't protect us from an angry teacher who'd just been hit in the back of the head.

The spring was the rebirth of the healthy, green bush that we all came to love. It made a great base for a game of Wiffle ball or pickle. We liked using the bush for these types of non-incriminating games. It let us spend time with our beloved bush without the penalty of picking up empty cigarette boxes until 4 P.M.

The summer was a strange time. Even if we managed to find a bush away from large obstacles, the ground was often too hard or too damp. Landing in a swamp or running head-on into oncoming traffic just didn't do it for us. Sometimes we'd drive into Dorchester at night and jump the bush under the dull glow of the courtyard floodlights. It was almost as if the school didn't care if we jumped in the summertime, even though trespassing seemed a far worse crime than leaping over a bush during school hours.

By the time my senior year began, the school began a renovation process that would make our grounds more "modern." One little gymnasium would be turned into a full-time theater, the laboratories would receive a much-needed facelift, and a whole new building would be constructed. While we loved the idea of a renovation for our future classmates, we were shocked to hear the location of the new building: the courtyard.

Our bush's days were sadly numbered.

The school had to inevitably shut down the courtyard area to pedestrians to ensure safety. About a week before this was done, the school made an announcement that the following week all students would have to use the parking lot instead of going through the courtyard. For many, this was the last time to say goodbye to the bush.

To our surprise, a week after the announcement was made and just before the school was to shut down the courtyard, we came to find that where the bush had once sat was nothing more than a tiny stump. The school newspaper reported that the bush had been stolen the night before, taken right off the courtyard grounds. The school closed down the courtyard for construction and our bush was lost and gone forever, or so we thought.

On the last day of class, I noticed a commotion in the parking lot. There were students gathered around a single red pickup truck that had just pulled in. Two seniors whom I recognized stepped out and walked to the back to unload their cargo. We could only stand in stunned silence as they hauled out a giant red gym mat and placed it in front of the car. Then, without a single word, they went back to the truck and removed the bush—browning, droopy, and dilapidated—and placed it in front of the mat. They each took a seat on the hood of the truck and said, simply, "Who's first?"

It was a hot, sunny day in May that the bush came back for one final run. All day, students took one final leap over the bush onto the soft mat in the school parking lot. I don't remember where it was kept or how they managed to haul it away. It didn't matter. For one more day, our school had our bush back and we knew better than to ask questions.

That bush was more than just a bush to us. It was something that we as students of BC High had that no other school did. It was our tradition, our pride and our unity all rolled into one. Anyone, from the youngest freshman to a graduating senior, could find a sense of togetherness in jumping the bush, even if they had been divided throughout high school. That bush brought more people together than any football game, school dance or Christmas Mass ever did. When I asked the seniors who took it and what they planned to do with it, they said it best:

"We've got to let it go, man. We're graduating this year, and so is the bush."

~Mark Murphy

Questions: A Poem in Two Voices

Patience is the ability
to count down before you blast off.
~Author Unknown

Why don't you clean your room?

Why don't you quit nagging me?

Where will you go to college?

Where can I have some privacy?

What will you do for a living?

What will it take to finally be free?

How will you manage without me?

How can you have no faith in me?

When will you start to grow up?

When will you let me grow up?

~Carmela Martino

Beyond the Brochure

Why not go out on a limb?
Isn't that where the fruit is?
~Frank Scully

As I tried to breathe as quietly as possible, with my face squished against cold, metal springs, I thought that this wasn't exactly what I had signed up for when I decided to go to boarding school.

My roommate, Kat, and I were in our room, ditching Chapel to complete some homework due the next class period while we listened to music. I was tapping my foot to the latest Lauryn Hill hit and finishing up my essay when suddenly we heard footsteps—the "God Squad" was in our dorm looking for skippers. We looked at each other, turned off the music and ducked for cover, wedging ourselves between our mattresses and our bed frames and hoping for the best.

When I tell people I was shipped off to boarding school when I was fourteen, they usually gasp in horror and imagine one of two situations. In the first, they assume I was a disobedient little girl whose reign of terror ended when her guilt-stricken parents made the painful decision to send her away for the good of the family. In the second, they envision my mother as a shrewd woman who never wanted children and marked the days off on her calendar until she could finally export her only child to be raised by strangers. The reality could not be farther from those theories.

The idea of going to boarding school sort of took me by surprise.

On the day of my interview at Brooks, a local independent school, my mom crept down the long driveway into the heart of the school and my eyes widened at the sprawling campus. Knowing the school had a higher percentage of boarders than day students, she asked me what I thought about possibly living there. I responded with an enthusiastic nod as I watched sophisticated-looking students in preppy attire stroll into one of the dorms. The lawns were perfectly manicured, the buildings uniformly white and weathered from New England storms, and the trees were abundant and blossoming. I couldn't imagine anyone who wouldn't want to live there. I was won over by the romantic notion of an academic adventure and the possibility of the unknown. I aced my interview.

As an adult, I've come to embrace the notion of destiny—that everyone has a purpose and every choice we make brings us one step closer to that purpose. That day on campus, I opened my mind to a great adventure at age thirteen. By doing that, I opened a door to countless other adventures that followed.

When I got my acceptance package in the mail, I was suddenly torn about moving to Brooks. My bravery on the day of my interview had suddenly disintegrated. All my junior high friends were going to local public and Catholic high schools. Not only would I be going to a different school than they were, I would be moving out of my childhood house. My best friend, Heidi, and I were inseparable; I couldn't imagine starting high school that far from her. More than that, I was scared to live away from my mom. I was an only child in a single-parent household and she had always been my best friend, as well as a great mom. Who would I talk things through with at Brooks?

Somehow I managed to put my fears aside and agreed to attend, but my feelings of dread and insecurity grew all summer after eighth grade. What if I got homesick? I was going to be living in a room with a stranger—what if she didn't like me?

On move-in day my freshman year, my mom and I packed all my belongings into the car and made the trek to my new home. When we arrived on campus, we followed the signs to the gym and filed in behind the other freshmen to get my dorm assignment and information packets. I ended up meeting Kat, my roommate, and her family in the check-in line. As the time came to say goodbye to our parents, I think we were both relieved to see the other tear up. We were about to spend our first night as fourteen-year-old girls living on our own.

The rest of freshman year was a complete culture shock. Classes were far more difficult than I had anticipated; the days were longer, the teachers had high expectations and the homework was endless. Each class seemed filled with academic gymnastics and a race to rise to the challenges presented. Somewhere in the admissions brochure it said that at Brooks, students find they need less sleep than they thought they did. They weren't kidding. Free time became something I could only reminisce about. I was in classes six days a week, and when I wasn't, I was participating in a marathon of mandatory activity: after school sports, formal seated dinners, club meetings, dorm meetings, and advisor meetings.

And there was a whole new lexicon I learned just to get around campus. There was a laundry list of rules to be broken and a much longer list of punishments that could result. Being late for breakfast check-in with the headmaster might lead to work squad—waking up early on Sundays to clean. Repeated offenses meant being "on bounds"—boarding school code for "grounded."

I was really never one for breaking the rules, and for the most part I stayed out of trouble—but there were always exceptions. That fateful day when Kat and I were suddenly prisoners in forgotten corners of our room was one of those exceptions. The dorms had truly become our home. We had bonded with the girls on our floor and shared microwave popcorn, study guides and stories about the boys we had crushes on. I never imagined the God Squad would invade this haven. As I heard the key turn and our door swing open, the invasion was complete.

The searchers were bewildered. "I know they are in here," one member of God Squad said to the other. They had heard our music, our voices, our scramble to hide, and yet we were nowhere to be found. I held my breath and willed myself not to laugh and blow our cover. Kat and I stayed still for what seemed like an eternity, and when I eventually peeked my head out they were gone. We had successfully survived the attack.

The admissions office had told me two things that really sold me on attending boarding school. First was that I'd get the most rigorous high school education imaginable. And it's true—my brain absorbed more knowledge about more areas of study than I thought possible, and for that I will always be grateful. The second was that I'd make lifelong bonds that would always connect me to Brooks School. What I'm truly grateful for are the times we snuck into each other's rooms after "lights out," giggling until our stomachs hurt, the philosophical talks on the lawns about where our lives might lead, and especially hiding from the God Squad in my tiny dorm room. The day I graduated under a white tent on the lawn in front of Gardner, I knew the most important lesson I'd taken to heart was that there is always a reward in choosing an adventure.

~Tia L. Napolitano

Teacher's Pet

Teaching is not a lost art,
but the regard for it is a lost tradition.
~Jacques Barzun

I am so going to get an eye-roll for this, but my favorite people in high school were the teachers. Sure, I had a great group of friends who I still hang out with to this day, but without some of the teachers I met, I wouldn't be who I am.

Throughout my entire life, I have been hanging out with the older kids. As a freshman, I was friends with seniors. The great thing was, I finally felt like I fit in. Chasing the popular kids and worrying about my hair was just never my style. I still don't do anything to that brown mop that lives on my head and I'm more than happy that way.

Hanging out with older kids made sense to me. They got my jokes, they were much less worried about the stuff that my fellow freshmen obsessed about, and there was less pressure. There was only one problem. The friends I spent so much of my time with would go off to college every year. That's the thing about seniors—they've got a shelf life.

When my junior year rolled around, I turned my eye upward again and found teachers. They were much older than seniors and wouldn't be leaving town come next fall. Sure, they weren't really snappy dressers, but neither was I. Their corduroy jackets were charming and their hair looked even worse, most mornings, than mine.

They were also really jazzed to be at school every day, unlike my student counterparts. I was a total nerd. I loved school. I read too much. I crafted my essays like they were fine glass sculptures, perfect and shimmery. I was a girl, so I didn't really get my butt kicked, but I should have. I was 100% brainiac.

Having a mentor is great. It's like having a free therapist who tells you how smart and wonderful you are. Now I've found a boyfriend who does that. In high school, I had teachers. They were just as lonely as I was, slogging through tests and quizzes. Dodging swear words and teenage glares. I collected mentors like trading cards. I had Bumbling English Teacher, Sarcastic Principal, Artsy Photo Teacher and Bored School Nurse up my sleeve.

By senior year, I had even more mentors among the faculty. None of my other friends were handy for answering the kinds of questions that I could ask my teacher friends. With graduation coming closer and closer, I spent more and more time grilling my teachers.

"What's going to happen after I graduate?"

"What should I do with my life?"

"What did you want to be when you grew up?"

"What should I major in?"

They had the best advice. Bored School Nurse told me to use my hypochondriac brainpower on something other than worrying about whether or not I had cancer. I didn't, she assured me, before giving me a slip to skip calculus and hang out some more.

Sarcastic Principal set up a sting operation when she knew I was going to skip class. She sat in the back of my science lab waiting for me to roll in half an hour late, then cackled with glee when I finally arrived. Bumbling English Teacher lent me all the books I wanted. Some of my favorites to this day came from his library—way more vast and impressive than the school's. I wouldn't know about some brilliant authors if it weren't for him.

Grumpy Computer Lab Gal even let me stay as late as I wanted, editing my geeky film projects on the powerful iMacs. Artsy Photo

Teacher put my prints front and center in the photography class display case and Disgruntled Tennis Coach let me make snack runs to the corner store while the rest of the team ran laps.

I'll be the first to say that this did not make me Miss Popular. However, I highly recommend being friends with a teacher or two, or at least treating them like the spiffy, rumpled human beings they are. In a world of snobby, self-obsessed high school kids worrying about their weight and their boyfriends, the teachers were a glorious dose of perspective.

After I followed Bumbling English Teacher's advice and majored in English at college, I thought for a second that I, too, could become a hip teacher at some high school somewhere. Then I remembered all the kids who treated teachers like crap and walked all over them. I only wanted to teach little nerds, like me.

While I cannot do what they do, I respect all the teachers I've had in my life, with very few exceptions. I think there is something new to learn every single day. When I stop learning, I stop growing. Every person in the world has something to teach me — that philosophy has worked out mighty well. Who better to teach me something than a teacher?

I'm starting graduate school soon and just might have to keep up my geeky habit. More than classes, more than students, more than a student ID that gives me discounts at the movies, I'm looking forward to the guys and gals at the head of the class. While I don't think I'll ever be a teacher, I get another chance to be a teacher's pet.

~Mary Kolesnikova

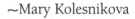

Four Years — Fast

Time is what prevents everything from happening at once.
~John Archibald Wheeler

Who could've imagined there would be such a place?
First day of high school and not a single familiar face
Classrooms, hallways, offices, all strangers to me
Where do I go? What will I do? I just want to be free.

Running around frantically with my schedule in hand
Asking people I've never seen before about the lay of the land.
With their help I found it, the room of my first period class
Hoping this time of terror will eventually come to pass.

Periods turned into days, days into weeks
Weeks into months, internal screams into squeaks
Homecoming dances, first romances
Suddenly, I'm taking chances.

Fall flew away and spring slipped in
Half the year was over; this battle I could win.
Those classrooms and those hallways, the offices as well
Became somewhat familiar, as did the sound of the bell.

The cafeteria was no longer a large, unfriendly foe
I'm sitting with my new friends, together now we go
Pizza and hot dogs, brownies and French fries
Giggles and sandwiches, talking about the many cute guys.

Freshman year is over, summer's calling my name
I survived the first year of high school without going insane.
But two months go by quickly and fall is here again
At least now I'll start the year with people I call friends.

Another year of classes, another year of frets
Another year of teachers, another year of tests.
Years are passing quickly now, faster than I'd like
Suddenly it's senior year and I'm about to take a hike!

Looking back upon these years, there were many lessons learned.
I'm receiving a diploma, but life experience I've earned.
Difficult decisions, hard work, good friends and lots of fun
Yet they say nothing has ended, and that life has just begun.

Friendships that were formed these years are still alive today
Even though each of us has gone our own separate way
But looking at the yearbook I realize four years went by so fast
And that lessons learned in high school are really meant to last.

~Debra T. Scipioni

Chicken Soup for the Soul

Meet Our Contributors!

Nicollette S. Alvarez currently attends high school and lives in Connecticut with her family and two dogs. She enjoys writing and reading and has studied creative writing at Cambridge in England. She aspires to be an author after graduating from college.

Amy Anderson is a senior in high school. She enjoys writing, cooking, golf, ballroom dancing, and volunteering at both her church and local hospital. After high school Amy hopes to study either creative writing or culinary arts.

Carol Ayer is a freelance writer living in Northern California. Her credits include *Woman's World, The Christian Science Monitor, Chicken Soup for the Soul* and *Flashquake*. She has won awards from Artella, The Lucidity Poetry Journal, and Women on Writing.

Monique Ayub is eighteen years old and a senior in high school. She plans to go to college in the fall and work towards becoming a teacher. Monique has been writing since she was about eight years old. She enjoys writing, working with children, and hanging out with friends.

Erik Benau was born and raised in Suburban Philadelphia. He received his Bachelor of Arts at Hampshire College in 2007. He currently works for the University of Pittsburgh, and hopes to work with children professionally someday. Erik enjoys performance, art, and performance art, traveling, cooking, and biking.

Tanya Bermudez graduated from UC Davis with two B.A.s in Economics and International Relations and will graduate in 2010 with her MBA. She works in Sacramento, CA for an educational advocacy firm and is passionate about travel, reading, writing, and being active in the Sacramento community. E-mail her at bermudez.tanya@gmail.com.

Stacie Bishop is currently a sophomore in high school. She's been writing stories for four years and recently started on poetry. She puts her work on Fictionpress.com under the name Shiori Miko.

Nicola Booyse is a South African freelance writer, currently working on her first novel.

Crystal Burgess enjoys expressing herself through creative arts; writing, dancing, making/designing clothes and figure skating. Though she loves her hobbies, Crystal's dream is to become a veterinarian.

Writing is something **Laura Campbell** does to de-stress. She has no professional experience and has never had anything published before. Writing is simply a hobby that really helps her express things that may be on her mind.

Martha Campbell is a graduate of Washington University, St. Louis School of Fine Arts and a former writer/designer for Hallmark cards. She has been a freelance cartoonist and illustrator since leaving Hallmark. She lives in Harrison, Arkansas.

Andrea C. Canale is a junior in high school, maintaining high honor roll for the past three years. She also writes for the school newspaper. She is a percussionist in the school concert and jazz band. She volunteers in her community and hopes to pursue a career in the medical field.

Laura Castro is a junior in high school. She enjoys hanging out with friends and shopping.

Tiffany Caudill recently graduated from high school. In the fall she plans to attend Eastern Kentucky University. Tiffany's friends and family are her life and she would not be who she is today without them.

Jennifer Lynn Clay, eighteen, has been published almost eighty times in national and international magazines and in several books including *Chicken Soup for the Soul A Tribute to Moms, Chicken Soup for the Preteen Soul 2, Chicken Soup for the Girl's Soul, House Blessings*, and *Forever in Love*. She was a State Finalist for Power of the Pen in 2004.

David Foster Clay, twenty-one, is a senior at Vanderbilt University. He is a pre-medical student looking to become a pediatrician. He is happy to report that Jennifer has proven she is stronger than the eating disorder and has been well for the past four years. She is an inspiration to him.

Teresa Cleary has published over 1,800 articles and is the author of *Front Porch Reflections: Devotions for Every Season*. She is currently the publicity writer for her children's school district in southern Ohio.

Janelle D. Coleman is currently finishing up her senior year at New York University where she will receive her B.A. in English and American Literature and her A.A. in Fine Arts. She hopes to one day become a pediatrician and an author of children's literature. Feel free to contact her at janelle.d.coleman@me.com.

Capri Colella graduated high school June 13th, 2008. She is currently attending Oxnard College, studying Addictive Disorders. She is very excited about her future and is still sober. Please e-mail her at stupendous12000@yahoo.com.

Megan Brooke Conrad is almost eighteen years old, family and friends are everything to her. She loves to write. It is her escape and helps her greatly. Megan also loves children and has a deep passion for animals. She plans to pursue a career in education and return to high school as a teacher.

Claire Courchane is seventeen years old. She loves spending time with family and friends. She wrote this story for her family (Mom, Dad, Paul, John, and Ellen) and all of her friends at school (especially Kristi, Jessica, Nikki, and Megan). This is her second story in a *Chicken Soup for the Soul* book.

Amber Curtis is a junior at Western Wayne. She enjoys running and writing. She credits her success to Mr. Rebar and Mr. Usher. She resides with her parents and sister by their grandparents' dairy farm. Please e-mail her at talkativeamber@yahoo.com.

Priscilla Dann-Courtney is a freelance writer and clinical psychologist living in Colorado with her husband and three children. In addition to family and friends, her passions are yoga, running, skiing and baking. Her essays have appeared in newspapers and magazines around the country and read on local public radio.

Marcella Dario Fuentes attends the University of Wisconsin-Madison, where she is a graduate student in bassoon performance. She enjoys playing her bassoon, traveling, reading, and spending time with friends and family. She plans to move back to her native Honduras and play in an orchestra there. Please e-mail her at wereallwright@gmail.com.

Eric Egger received his bachelor of arts at Franklin & Marshall College and earned his MBA in finance and his master of public policy at The College of William & Mary. He currently serves the public sector as a financial management analyst for the U.S. government. Contact Eric at ericegger@yahoo.com.

Bryonna Garcia graduated from high school in 2008. She is attending college and plans to go to medical school. She enjoys dancing, styling hair, working with children, and spending time with her daughter. She plans to become a pediatrician when she finishes school.

AC Gaughen is twenty-three years old, a graduate of the University of St Andrews in Scotland, where she fell madly in love with the UK, and Scotland in particular. Check out her blog at blog.finalword.org, and please contact her via e-mail at acgaughen@gmail.com.

Jillian Genco is a junior in high school. She hopes to study psychology or nutrition in college. Jillian enjoys running, reading and playing with her cat. If you are suffering from an eating disorder, please contact her at jbg125@verizon.net.

Lynn Grasberg is the author of *Bounce Back! The New Play Ethic at Work* and is the behind-the-scenes (ghost) writer and editor for several other books. She is also a humorist, professional speaker and speaking coach, and is currently developing programs on mid-life/menopausal humor. You can reach her at lynn@LynnGrasberg.com.

Kerri E. Grogan is a sixteen year old high school student who has many dreams for herself.

Leah Elliott Hauge is a mother, musician and writer. After high school, she studied Spanish at Arizona State University. Leah now lives in Fargo, North Dakota, with her husband Ray and sons Frederic and Rasmus. She can be reached at senorita_elliott@yahoo.com.

Katie Hankins is a high school student who plans to go to college and major in graphic design or writing. She would like to illustrate and write children's books. Katie enjoys spending time with her friends, drawing, singing, writing, cheerleading, and running. You can e-mail her at cheerkatie717@gmail.com.

Jonny Hawkins is a fulltime cartoonist whose work has appeared in *Phi Delta Kappan, American Educator, Harvard Business Review* and over 400 other publications. His books—*A Joke A Day Keeps the Doctor Away, The Awesome Book of Heavenly Humor* and annual calendars—*Medical, Fishing and Car-Toon-A-Day* calendars are available everywhere.

Natalie Embrey Hikel holds a J.D. from the University of Baltimore. She has a passion for litigation, community service, and creative writing. She dreams of making a living from pursuing all three in tandem. She currently lives in Washington, D.C. with her husband. You can reach Natalie at nhikel@gmail.com.

Louis A. Hill Jr. authored three books and many articles. He earned a Ph.D. in structural engineering, designed bridges and buildings and joined the engineering faculty at Arizona State University. He retired an Emeritus Dean of Engineering from The University of Akron. He is listed in *Who's Who in America*.

Rose Jackson wrote for Donna Partow and five books with Dr. Walt Kallestad, including *Be Your Own Creative Coach*. She shares her slip-ups and victories at retreats and workshops, enjoys camping and dancing, and is a POM (Parent of a Missionary). Read Rose's adventures at www.rospiration.blogspot.com or contact her via e-mail at ecrmjackson@msn.com.

Laurel Jefferson received her Bachelor of Arts, with honors, from the University of Maryland in 2003. She currently works as a paralegal in Maryland while training to run her first marathon. Laurel plans to attend law school and work for the United Nations someday. Please e-mail her at laureljefferson@gmail.com.

Kristie Jones has had short stories and articles published in a number of magazines, journals and an anthology. She has recently completed her YA novel under the mentorship of award winning author Denise Young. She currently works as a Librarian in Cairns, Australia.

Pat Kane, who resides in Joplin, Missouri, with her husband, Walter and their two Yorkies, is a published author who enjoys writing stories and novels for children and inspirational stories of real-life events. She's a member of The Society of Children's Book Writers & Illustrators and The Missouri Writer's Guild.

Anna Kendall received her Master of Arts in Writing from DePaul University in 2007. She works as a freelance writer and editor in Chicago. Anna enjoys writing about her school experiences (and she hopes that other people will be able to identify with—and laugh at—some of her embarrassing school moments).

Author **Roger Dean Kiser's** stories take you into the heart of a child abandoned by his family and abused by the system responsible for his care. Today, Kiser lives in Brunswick, Georgia with his wife Judy where he continues to write and publish most of his work on his Internet website at: http://www.geocities.com/trampolineone.

Kyle Kochersperger is a high school student. A hopeful applicant at Brown, when he is away from the stress of college planning he enjoys traveling, shopping, reading, and of course... dancing. He plans to work in fashion editorials. Please e-mail him at Kyleko123@aol.com.

Mary Kolesnikova is a teen and children's writer based in San Francisco. Visit her website at www.marykolesnikova.com.

Cheryl Kremer, of Lancaster, PA, is married to Jack and has two children, Nikki and Cobi. She works as a teacher's aide for a Christian-based preschool. Her life is filled with the joy of being a wife, mother, and soccer mom. She can be reached at j_kremer@verizon.net.

Kathryn Lay is the author of children's books, *Crown Me!* and *Josh's Halloween Pumpkin*. She loves to speak at schools and conferences and teaches online writing courses. Check out her website at www.kathrynlay.com or e-mail her at rlay15@aol.com.

Jacklyn Lee Lindstrom, a frequent contributor to *Chicken Soup for the Soul*, lives in Spearfish, South Dakota. After surviving teen-age know-it-all years, marriage, child-raising, and empty nesting, she feels at last she knows what she is talking about. Nobody listens, but that hasn't stopped her. She just keeps writing.

Nicole Lee is a junior in high school. She enjoys writing and has future interests in dealing with animals. Her short story was a sophomore English assignment.

Alexi Leigh is a student at the University of Massachusetts, Lowell. She is going to major in English and Journalism. Alexi's two biggest passions are writing and music. For fun, she likes to DJ, go to concerts, and meet bands and then write about it.

Karen Majoris-Garrison is an award-winning author and speaker whose stories appear in *Woman's World, Barbour Publishing, Chicken Soup for the Soul*, and others. She also teaches a support group for writers. Karen credits God and her family as the sources of her inspiration. Visit her website: www.soothingsouls.us, and e-mail her with your comments.

Carmela Martino received her MFA in Writing from Vermont College. Her first book, *Rosa, Sola*, was named to Booklist magazines "Top Ten First Novels for Youth: 2006." Carmela writes from her home outside Chicago, where she also teaches writing workshops for children and adults. To contact her visit www.carmelamartino.com.

Matthew P. Mayo is a novelist and magazine editor living in Montana with his wife, Jennifer, and two dear dogs, Guinness and Nessie. He has published novels, poetry, and short fiction in a variety of genres. Visit him at www.matthewmayo.com.

Aimee McCarron is currently a sophomore at the University of Massachusetts at Lowell. She lives with her family in Burlington,

Massachusetts. Aimee enjoys reading, traveling, watching movies, and baking.

Adrian McElwee is from Brookline, Massachusetts and attends the University of Vermont for film and media studies. He enjoys free-style skiing, advanced media production, traveling, making films and partying. He has traveled to many film festivals across the world with his director/filmmaker father Ross McElwee. Reach Adrian at armcelwe@uvm.edu.

Allison Moore is a senior at Boston University studying journalism. She loves writing and editing, and plans to pursue a career in publishing. You may contact her at amoore09@bu.edu.

William Moore is a sophomore in high school. He enjoys playing football, lacrosse, and piano. He won the Presidential Community Service Award in 8th grade. He was the President of his class in ninth grade, and plans to major in Political Science in college.

Christine Amelia Mumford is a senior in high school. She enjoys walking on the beach with her dog, Chica, and spending time with her family and friends, including her older sister, Anne. Her hobbies include piano, drama, and creative writing.

Mark Murphy is a 2008 graduate of Boston College with a BA in English. He aspires to be a writer and is working on several short stories and a novel, all with a focus on something inherently Japanese. Starting August 2008, he will be an English teacher in Tokyo, Japan.

Tia L. Napolitano graduated Cum Laude from New York University in 2007 with a BA in journalism. She currently lives in New York's East Village where she enjoys her post-college life of working at Thirteen/WNET, writing and exploring the wonder that is Manhattan. She can be reached via e-mail at Tia.Napolitano@gmail.com.

Tina O'Reilly lives with her loving family and three dogs. When not writing, you can find her on the beach dreaming up characters for her romance novels. Please e-mail her at seaswept68@aol.com.

Amanda Panitch is currently an aspiring English major (though that could change any day!) at The George Washington University. She has enjoyed writing ever since she was very young and is ecstatic to be published for the first time. She can be reached at anp@gwmail.gwu.edu.

Mark Parisi's "off the mark" comic, syndicated since 1987, is distributed by United Media. Mark's humor also graces greeting cards, T-shirts, calendars, magazines, newsletters and books. Check out: offthemark.com. Lynn is his wife/business partner. Their daughter, Jen, contributes with inspiration, (as do three cats).

Vinnie Penn is a writer, radio host, and stand-up comedian. He has had his own morning radio show, and is the author of the nonfiction title, *The Guido's Credos*. He remembers his teenage years fondly; some say he never outgrew them. Check him out at www.vinniepenn.net.

Jacqueline Perkins holds an M.A. in Elementary Education from Columbia College in Chicago. She's a teacher, author, and co-owner of Perkins International Academy of Excellence in Abuja, Nigeria. She's married to Bolaji Arigbede and the mother of Adedayo and Oluwawole. Visit perkinsacademy.org and writtendestiny.com.

Julie Pierce is a senior in high school. She is a member of the speech team, National Honor Society and pep-band. She enjoys shopping, going to football games and hopes to pursue a career in psychology. Julie would like to thank her best friend Genevieve for helping her through those embarrassing moments in life.

Stephanie Piro lives in New Hampshire with her husband and three cats. She is one of King Features' "Six Chix" (she is the Saturday chick!). Her single panel, "Fair Game," appears in newspapers and on her website: www.stephaniepiro.com. She also designs gift items for her company Strip T's. Contact her at: stephaniepiro@verizon.net or: 27 River Road, Farmington, NH 03835.

Michael Polanski is an engineering student at Rutgers University in New Brunswick, New Jersey. He is an Eagle Scout who enjoys hiking, camping, rock climbing, and mountain biking. He would like to thank his parents and three beautiful sisters for their love and support. He can be reached at michaelpolanski@mac.com.

Kristi Powers is a mother and has been involved in youth ministry for over twenty-three years. Kristi and her husband Michael have authored the book, *Heart Touchers* and their stories appear in thirty-three books including many in the *Chicken Soup for the Soul* series. Their inspirational e-mail list for teens is at www.Heart4Teens.com. E-mail Kristi at NoodlesP29@aol.com.

Siddart Rangachari is sixteen years of age and studying in high school now, living in Bombay. Siddart enjoys playing and watching football and playing guitar.

Samantha Reinke is a high school student. She is focusing her future on journalism and writing. She lives with her parents and two brothers. Samantha enjoys reading and studying many forms of mythology. Contact her via e-mail at roguelove666@hotmail.com.

Sara Rowe has a B.A. in English Writing and History and is studying for her M.A. in Children's Literature in London. She is a freelance writer who enjoys reading, traveling and spending time with her wacky friends and family. Contact her at via e-mail at s.rowe54@yahoo.com.

Theresa Sanders has four grown children—her greatest joy and accomplishment. She graduated with honors from the University of Maryland, worked for years as a technical writer, and has been published in trade journals. She lives with her husband near St. Louis, and is thrilled to be included in this book.

Thomas Schonhardt is a student at Truman State University, where he is majoring in Public Communications with a minor in Art. He enjoys soccer, fishing, ceramics, and writing. His biggest influence in his writing is his father. Please e-mail him at tms2618@truman.edu.

Debra Scipioni teaches Fourth Grade, Fifth Grade Writing/Grammar, and is a Reading Specialist. She holds certifications in Reading, Elementary, and Special Education. Debra received her Master"s Degree with distinction in 2003. She enjoys reading, writing poetry, and the Yankees. Debra plans to teach college courses for those studying education.

Chloe Scott is seventeen years old, with many hopes and dreams. She would like to dedicate this story to her amazing support network; Lauren, Sage, Ashley, Annie, Gage, Ms. Anson, Ms. Arvidson, Ms. Willard and Angus. Special thanks to Alison, for inspiring her to write, and to her mom.

Jacqueline Seewald has taught writing and has also worked as an academic librarian and educational media specialist. Her short stories, poems, essays, reviews and articles have appeared in numerous publications. Her mystery novel, *The Inferno Collection*, has a sequel, *The Drowning Pool*, contracted for publication February 2009.

Mary Slaby teaches reading and language arts in Northeastern Pennsylvania. She graduated from Penn State University with a degree in Special Education and earned a Ph.D. in Education from Temple University in 2003. When Mary is not reading, writing, or teaching, she enjoys gardening, researching genealogy, and cross stitching. Mary writes under the name Molly Roe.

Belinda Howard Smith is a freelance writer and speaker living in

Austin, Texas. Her formative years were spent in a rural community centered in the heart of the Texas Panhandle—the subject of many of her short stories. She enjoys scrapbooking, reading, Bible study, and teaching. Please e-mail her at belinda@belindahowardsmith.com.

Sarah Jo Smith received a Bachelor of Arts in English Literature and holds a Master of Education from Santa Clara University. She taught middle and high school English, and classic literature through her community's Adult Education Department. She is currently completing her first novel. She lives in Los Gatos, California.

Whitney Smoot was born and raised in Winchester, VA where she is currently attending a community college to become a Juvenile Probation Officer. In her free time she enjoys shopping, spending time with friends and family, and writing. Please e-mail her at whitney1321@yahoo.com.

Pittsburgh native **Kelly Starling Lyons** is the author of picture book, *One Million Men and Me*, and chapter book, *NEATE: Eddie's Ordeal*. She has two forthcoming picture books with G.P. Putnam's Sons. Kelly lives in North Carolina and leads a book club for girls. Visit Kelly at www.kellystarlinglyons.com.

Annie Summers is a Canadian high school student who enjoys reading, drawing, music and drama. Her other interests include scrambling eggs, math and textured scarves. She plans to graduate and go wherever her life takes her.

Michael Tenzer graduated from Columbia College Chicago in 2008 with a Bachelor of Arts degree in Arts Management. He currently is a freelance writer of fiction, non-fiction and essays, as well as music, movie and video game criticism. He can be reached via e-mail at imightbewrong856@hotmail.com.

Terri Tiffany counseled adults for seventeen years before owning a

Christian bookstore. She resides now in Florida with her husband where she writes full-time. Her stories have appeared in Sunday school take-home papers, women's magazines and numerous anthologies. Please visit her at http://terri-treasures.blogspot.com.

Melissa Townsend received her B.A. in Psychology, with honors, from UC Irvine in 2006. She is a freelance writer, editor and karaoke enthusiast. Melissa loves music, the beach, traveling, and helping others. Her lifelong goal is to write humorous advice books and move to Maui. Please e-mail her at mtownsend27@gmail.com.

Cristy Trandahl is a former teacher and, yes, pro-cheerleader (for one month). Today she works as a freelance writer while raising her children. Cristy's stories are published in dozens of nationally distributed anthologies. Check out www.cristytrandahl.com.

Michelle Vanderwist is currently a student at Georgetown University. She loves to draw, paint, play the guitar, work with animals, and stay active. Michelle is a terrible cook but has a hidden talent for hula hooping. E-mail her at mav49@georgetown.edu.

Tasha Vemulkonda is currently in her senior year of high school. She is an active member of her school's student government as well as a devoted writer for the school newspaper. She wants to thank her family and friends for their enthusiasm and support. Tasha plans on pursuing her passion for art and design in college.

Karen L. Waldman, Ph.D., greatly loves her career as a Psychologist. She also enjoys writing, dancing, acting, nature, traveling with her husband Ken, and spending time with their wonderful kids, grandkids, family and friends. Her e-mail is krobens@aol.com.

Valerie Weiss is eighteen years old and shared her story in hopes of encouraging teenagers to have the perseverance and determination to accomplish their goals. She loves to draw, paint, read, and relax on the beach. She attends Rutgers University and plans to pursue a career in law. Valerie can be contacted via e-mail at valgal021@aol.com.

Christy Westbrook completed a BAIS in Early Childhood Education and a Master of Library and Information Science from the University of South Carolina. She lives in Lexington, South Carolina with her husband, Thad, and their two daughters, Abby and Katie.

Renea Winchester is a writer who rescues plants from development in her spare time. Her work received the Wilma Dykeman Appalachian Writers Association Award, and has appeared in *Gardening How-To*, and *A Cup of Comfort* Series. Please e-mail her at Renea.Winchester@yahoo.com.

Karen Woodward managed to survive high school, college, grad school, and the entertainment industry. She's now a freelance writer and web content producer in Los Angeles, CA. She's addicted to e-mail and can be reached at karenwoodward@earthlink.net.

Ashley Mie Yang has been writing for *Chicken Soup for the Soul* since she was fifteen. She is an undergrad at William Smith College and a proud alum of Pittsford Sutherland High School, where she one day hopes to teach social studies. She thanks her teachers for their support.

Meet the Authors
Acknowledgments
Share With Us!

Chicken Soup for the Soul

Who Is
Jack Canfield?

Jack Canfield is the co-creator and editor of the *Chicken Soup for the Soul* series, which *Time* magazine has called "the publishing phenomenon of the decade." Jack is also the co-author of eight other bestselling books including *The Success Principles™: How to Get from Where You Are to Where You Want to Be, Dare to Win, The Aladdin Factor, You've Got to Read This Book,* and *The Power of Focus: How to Hit Your Business and Personal and Financial Targets with Absolute Certainty.*

Jack is the CEO of the Canfield Training Group in Santa Barbara, California, and founder of the Foundation for Self-Esteem in Culver City, California. He has conducted intensive personal and professional development seminars on the principles of success for over a million people in twenty-three countries. Jack is a dynamic keynote speaker and he has spoken to hundreds of thousands of others at more than 1,000 corporations, universities, professional conferences and conventions, and has been seen by millions more on national television shows such as *The Today Show, Fox and Friends, Inside Edition, Hard Copy,* CNN's *Talk Back Live, 20/20, Eye to Eye,* and the *NBC Nightly News* and the *CBS Evening News.*

Jack is the recipient of many awards and honors, including three honorary doctorates and a Guinness World Records Certificate for having seven books from the *Chicken Soup for the Soul* series appearing on the *New York Times* bestseller list on May 24, 1998.

You can reach Jack at:

Jack Canfield
The Canfield Companies
P. O. Box 30880 • Santa Barbara, CA 93130
phone: 805-563-2935 • fax: 805-563-2945
www.jackcanfield.com

Who Is
Mark Victor Hansen?

Mark Victor Hansen is the co-founder of Chicken Soup for the Soul, along with Jack Canfield. He is also a sought-after keynote speaker, bestselling author, and marketing maven. For more than thirty years, Mark's powerful messages of possibility, opportunity, and action have created powerful change in thousands of organizations and millions of individuals worldwide.

Mark's credentials include a lifetime of entrepreneurial success. He is a prolific writer with many bestselling books, such as *The One Minute Millionaire*, *Cracking the Millionaire Code*, *How to Make the Rest of Your Life the Best of Your Life*, *The Power of Focus*, *The Aladdin Factor*, and *Dare to Win*, in addition to the *Chicken Soup for the Soul* series. Mark has had a profound influence in the field of human potential through his library of audios, videos, and articles in the areas of big thinking, sales achievement, wealth building, publishing success, and personal and professional development. Mark is also the founder of the MEGA Seminar Series.

He has appeared on *Oprah*, CNN, and *The Today Show*. He has been quoted in *Time*, *US News & World Report*, *USA Today*, *The New York Times*, and *Entrepreneur* and has given countless radio interviews, assuring our planet's people that "You can easily create the life you deserve."

Mark is the recipient of numerous awards that honor his entrepreneurial spirit, philanthropic heart, and business acumen. He is a lifetime member of the Horatio Alger Association of Distinguished Americans, an organization that honored Mark with the prestigious Horatio Alger Award for his extraordinary life achievements.

You can reach Mark at:

Mark Victor Hansen & Associates, Inc.
P. O. Box 7665 • Newport Beach, CA 92658
phone: 949-764-2640 • fax: 949-722-6912
www.markvictorhansen.com

Who Is
Amy Newmark?

Amy Newmark is the publisher of Chicken Soup for the Soul, after a thirty-year career as a writer, speaker, financial analyst, and business executive in the worlds of finance and telecommunications.

Amy is a graduate of Harvard College, where she majored in Portuguese, minored in French, and traveled extensively. She is also the mother of two children in college and has two grown stepchildren.

After a long career writing books on telecommunications, voluminous financial reports, business plans, and corporate press releases, Chicken Soup for the Soul is a breath of fresh air for Amy. She has fallen in love with Chicken Soup for the Soul and its life-changing books, and is really enjoying putting these books together for Chicken Soup's wonderful readers.

The best way to contact Amy is through our webmaster, who can be reached at:

webmaster@chickensoupforthesoul.com

If you do not have access to the Internet, please contact Amy by mail or by facsimile at:

Chicken Soup for the Soul
P. O. Box 700
Cos Cob, CT 06807-0700
Fax 203-861-7194

Who Is
Madeline Clapps?

Madeline Clapps is an editor for Chicken Soup for the Soul, as well as a co-author of *Chicken Soup for the Soul: Teens Talk High School*. She is incredibly thankful for the opportunities that have been given to her at Chicken Soup for the Soul, and for everything Amy, Bill, and Bob have done for her.

Madeline is currently a student at New York University, where she is on the Dean's List, majoring in Journalism and Vocal Performance with a concentration in Music Theatre. Her passions are writing and singing, but she has also found that editing and book production can be added to that ever-growing list. You can read her stories in other Chicken Soup for the Soul books, including *Chicken Soup for the Soul; Teens Talk Getting In... to College* and the upcoming *Chicken Soup for the Soul: Campus Chronicles*.

Madeline has a very supportive family, and she owes so much to her parents and grandparents. Keep an eye out for Madeline on the stage, in books, and in periodicals in the future, because she has a long list of big goals to achieve.

You can reach her through the Chicken Soup webmaster at:

webmaster@chickensoupforthesoul.com

Chicken Soup for the Soul

Thank You!

We owe huge thanks to all of our contributors. We know that you pour your hearts and souls into the stories and poems that you share with us, and ultimately with each other. We appreciate your willingness to open up your lives to other Chicken Soup readers.

We can only publish a small percentage of the stories that are submitted, but we read every single one and even the ones that do not appear in the book have an influence on us and on the final manuscript.

We owe a very big thank you to Courtney Fogwell, our Greenwich High School intern, who read and graded well over 1,000 stories for this book, and gave us lots of good advice from the perspective of a graduating high school senior. We wish Courtney the best of luck at Penn, where we know she will excel, just as she did here.

We also want to thank D'ette Corona, our Assistant Publisher, who is the heart and soul of the Chicken Soup for the Soul publishing operation, and Barbara LoMonaco, our Webmaster and Chicken Soup for the Soul Editor, for invaluable assistance in maintaining our story database and proofreading this manuscript. We would also like to thank Chicken Soup for the Soul editor Kristiana Glavin for assistance with the final manuscript and proofreading, and Leigh Holmes, who keeps our Connecticut office running smoothly. We also thank our new intern, Nicollette Alvarez, who joined us after her story had already been accepted for publication in this book.

We owe a very special thanks to our Creative Director and book producer, Brian Taylor at Pneuma Books, for his brilliant vision for our covers and interiors. Finally, none of this would be possible without the business and creative leadership of our CEO, Bill Rouhana, and our president, Bob Jacobs.

Chicken Soup for the Soul

Share with Us

We would like to know how these stories affected you and which ones were your favorites. Please e-mail us and let us know.

We also would like to share your stories with future readers. You may be able to help another reader, and become a published author at the same time. Please send us your own stories and poems for our future books. Some of our past contributors have launched writing and speaking careers from the publication of their stories in our books!

Your stories have the best chance of being used if you submit them through our web site, at:

www.chickensoup.com

If you do not have access to the Internet, you may submit your stories by mail or by facsimile. Please do not send us any book manuscripts, unless through a literary agent, as these will be automatically discarded.

Chicken Soup for the Soul
P.O. Box 700
Cos Cob, CT 06807-0700
Fax 203-861-7194